GENDER AND ISRAELI SOCIETY
Women's Time

GENDER AND ISRAELI SOCIETY
Women's Time

Editor

HANNAH NAVEH
Tel Aviv University

VALLENTINE MITCHELL
LONDON • PORTLAND, OR

First Published in 2003 in Great Britain by
VALLENTINE MITCHELL
Crown House, 47 Chase Side
London N14 5BP

and in the United States of America by
VALLENTINE MITCHELL
c/o ISBS, 920 NE 58th Avenue, Suite 300
Portland, Oregon, 97213-3786

Website: www.vmbooks.com

British Library Cataloguing in Publication Data

Gender and Israeli Society: women's time
1. Women – Israel – Social conditions 2. Women in Judaism
3. Women in the Bible
I. Naveh, Hannah
305.4'2'095694

ISBN 0 85303 504 0 (cloth)
ISBN 0 85303 503 2 (paper)

Library of Congress Cataloging-in-Publication Data

Gender and Israeli society : women's time / editor Hannah Naveh.—
1st ed.
p. cm.
Includes bibliographical references and index.
First published as a special issue of: The Journal of Israeli History
(ISSN 0952-3367), Vol. 21, No. 1/2, Spring/Autumn 2002."
ISBN 0-85303-504-0 (cloth) – ISBN 0-85303-503-2 (pbk.)
1. Women in public life–Israel. 2. Jewish
women–Israel–Historiography. 3. Women in politics–Israel. 4. Women
and religion–Israel. 5. Feminist theory. I. Naveh, Hannah. II.
Journal of Israeli History. III. Title.
HQ1391.I75G46 2003
305.42'095694–dc21   2003014722

This group of studies first appeared as a special issue of
The Journal of Israeli History (ISSN 0952-3367),
Vol. 21, No.1/2, Spring/Autumn 2002,
published by Frank Cass

Printed in Great Britain by Antony Rowe Ltd., Chippenham, Wiltshire

Contents

Contributors

HANNAH NAVEH. Professor of Hebrew Literature and Chair of the NCJW Women and Gender Studies Program, Tel Aviv University. Her recent publications include *Min, migdar, politikah* (Sex, Gender, Politics: Women in Israel) (Tel Aviv, 1999) (co-author); and *Nosim ve-nosot: Sipurei masa ba-sifrut ha-ivrit ha-hadashah* (Women and Men Travellers: The Travel Narrative in Hebrew Literature) (Tel Aviv, 2002).

HANNA HERZOG. Associate Professor of Sociology, Tel Aviv University, and editor of *Sotziologiyah Yisre'elit* (Israeli Sociology). Her recent publications include *Realistic Women: Women in Israeli Local Politics* (Jerusalem, 1994); *Gendering Politics: Women in Israel* (Ann Arbor, 1999); and *Min, migdar, politikah* (Sex, Gender, Politics: Women in Israel) (Tel Aviv, 1999) (co-author).

RACHEL ROJANSKI. Lecturer in the Department of Jewish History, University of Haifa. She is the author of *Bein ideologiyah le-etos: Po'alei Tziyon be-Amerikah, 1905–1931* (Between Ideology and Ethos: Poale-Zion in America 1905-1931) (Ben-Gurion Research Center, Sede Boker, forthcoming).

BILLIE MELMAN. Professor of Modern History, Tel Aviv University. She is author of *Women and the Popular Imagination in the Twenties: Flappers and Nymphs* (1988), *Women's Orients — English Women and the Middle East, 1718–1918: Sexuality, Religion and Work* (1992; 1995) and editor of *Borderlines: Genders and Identities in War and Peace, 1870–1930* (1998).

JUDITH TYDOR BAUMEL. Associate Professor of History, Bar-Ilan University. Author of *Double Jeopardy: Gender and the Holocaust* (1999) and associate editor, together with Walter Laqueur, of *The Holocaust Encyclopedia* published by Yale University Press. Her study, *Perfect Heroes: The Parachutist Mission and the Making of Collective Israeli Memory* is forthcoming with the Ben-Gurion Research Center at Sede Boker.

MICHAEL FEIGE. Researcher at the Ben-Gurion Research Center at Sede Boker and Lecturer at Ben-Gurion University. His research focuses on politics of identity, collective memory and social movements. He is the author of *Shtei mapot la-gadah* (One Space, Two Places) (2002).

TSILA (ABRAMOVITZ) RATNER. Lecturer in Modern Hebrew Literature, University College London. She has published works on the poetry of Yair Hurvitz and S. Halkin and more recent publications on women characters in J. Steinberg, Poland in the writing of Eleonora Lev and Yehudit Hendel, and feminist reading in biblical texts.

TOVA COHEN. Professor in the Department of Literature of the Jewish People, and Director of the Fanya Gottesfeld Heller Center for the Study of Women in Judaism, Bar-Ilan University. She has recently published *Ha-ahat ahuvah veha-ahat snu'ah: Bein metzi'ut le-vidyon be-ti'urei ha-ishah be-sifrut ha-haskalah ha-ivrit* (One Beloved and the Other One Hated: Between Reality and Fiction in *Haskalah* Depictions of Women) (Jerusalem, 2002) and is compiling, with Shmuel Feiner, an anthology of Hebrew writing by women in the nineteenth century.

Of Related Interest

Israeli Family and Community: Women's Time
Hannah Naveh (ed.)

Israeli Identity: In Search of a Successor to the Pioneer, Tsabar and Settler
Lilly Weissbrod

Replacing Ourselves: Gender, Place and Memory in the
Modern Jewish Experience
Judith Tydor Baumel and Tova Cohen

New Women's Writing from Israel
Risa Domb (ed.)

Israeli Historical Revisionism: From Left to Right
Anita Shapira and Derek J. Penslar (eds.)

Double Jeopardy: Gender and the Holocaust
Judith Tydor Baumel

Irish Women's History
Diane Urqhart and Alan Hayes (eds.)

Gender, Colonialism and Education: The Politics of Experience
Joyce Goodman and Jane Martin (eds.)

"How can we reveal our place, first as it is bequeathed to us by tradition, and then as we want to transform it?"

Julia Kristeva, "Women's Time"
New Maladies of the Soul

Introduction

Hannah Naveh

The Missing Link

Every narrative presupposes a "policy of time" by which it governs the allocation of narrative space and attention to represented subjects and events. Thus, although the traditional physical concept of time posits time-units as same and equal in actual duration, and therefore deserving of equal space and attention in their representation, narrating time and representing events usually upsets and distorts this concept of equality and sameness and produces a representation which is fraught with difference and discrimination. A policy of differential representation of time for the narration of objectively equal time-units is a result of prioritizing and preferring certain events — along with their active agents — over others. Thus some time segments and some historical agents are highlighted and underscored while others remain insignificant, minor and perhaps even excluded and overlooked.

Thus, recorded time and time laid down to memory (personal and collective) is not homologous to what we imagine as "natural" time. It allots prime time to its favorites and marginal time to its others. History is indeed a mere *histoire*, and like beauty, the distribution of time in it depends on the eyes of the beholder.

It is common knowledge that narrating the stories of human beings, their societies, cultures and histories, has been systematically and consistently governed by the concerns of ruling institutions, be it the kings' scribes or the officially appointed court historians, or be it the body of canonized scholars, whose narratives achieved the status of scriptures and have been disseminated as scientific knowledge and handed down through the education system and cultural apparatus to public consumption. In our culture as we know it, these fortunate masters of history were invariably men who endorsed other men and who made reality appear "linked to the individual and collective history of the masculine subject," in the words of Luce Irigaray.[1] Joan W. Scott, in her seminal *Gender and the Politics of History*, exposed and analyzed this bias and launched a line of feminist historiography.[2] Jewish culture and history have not been exempted from this practice, and it is only in the last few decades that an array of counter-narratives has sprung to re-vision, re-count and subvert the dominant narratives that display them. Counter-narratives expose and challenge the drives and rationale of the selection and composition principles of the hegemonic narratives and suggest their implied policies of inclusion/exclusion. A "class action" on behalf of women has produced some of the most prolific counter-narratives evident in contemporary scholarship, and this volume is a collection of recent work from Israel in the field of women and gender studies pertaining to Jewish and Israeli history and culture.

The paradigm of Jewish historiography is the patriarchal narrative of the Bible, which when condensed into its tightest form, viz. the genealogical lists of fathers and sons, does not have much time for women, nor does it allot them much narrative room. It is basically a story of men — handing to one another the staff of command as in a relay run, in a continual undisrupted patrilineal chain of mastery. The function of women is to assist this project, sometimes by playing an instrumental role in carefully chosen "important" events, but mainly by producing subsequent heirs — viz. sons — to prominent men. Irigaray notes that although our societies are made up half by men and half by women and stem from two genealogies, nevertheless

> patriarchal power is organized by submitting one genealogy [mothers to daughters] to the other [fathers to sons]. Thus, what is now termed the oedipal structure as access to the cultural order is already structured within a single, masculine line of filiation which doesn't symbolize the woman's relationship to her mother.[3]

Women's position vis-à-vis the masters and heroes of history and its narrative ("the story") is therefore contingent and coincidental: they are vehicles (or vessels) bearing the goods — the only goods that matter to the dynastic power and to its recorded history. But in themselves, as proactive agents which may change the course of history and introduce into it events of a different nature, they bear no weight and therefore receive no significant narrative time and space. Any contribution they may have had to the tribal or racial history is virtually erased or subsumed under the names of fathers. Biblical women are not only excluded — normally and normatively — from any share of formal public power, but also even in the privacy of the family (so-called "privacy" — obviously the family too adheres rigorously to the patriarchal order), women's identity and subjectivity are more often than not subsumed by their husbands' or by their fathers' or by their sons'.

Five illustrious and brave women — whose names are recalled only with difficulty and they go down in history usually as "Zelophehad's daughters" (five names we cannot remember although most of us have no problem in rattling off the 12 names of Jacob's sons…) — laid a claim to their father's property after his death (Numbers 26, 27, 36). It was obvious to all that he had no heirs, since he had no sons. The tribal legal gaze was apparently blind to the daughters' position. Moses did indeed allow them to inherit as men, and their success has been heralded by many feminists, but with his sentence Moses also stipulated they must marry into the family of their father, that is, into the tribe, thereby rendering their achievement an act of futile tokenism. Eventually their inheritance was subsumed by men and they were prevented from creating their own dynasty, thus proving that the affiliation men have with each other, even when they are distant blood relatives, overthrows and overrides the primordial first-order kinship of men and their daughters. The daughters' subjects are not weighty enough to sustain the family name and honor and they must succumb to proper men within the family. So the five women's struggle for agentic subjectivity finally resulted in their succumbing in marriage to a family relative, thus harnessing their impressive original assertiveness to their future husbands' status, when what they were actually fighting for was not a larger dowry for their husbands, but for a room of their own and 500 pounds, as Virginia Woolf suggested for the redressing of women's affliction in patriarchal society.[4] So, family politics are subordinated to patriarchal interests: the family is a mirror image of society and its politics are governed by the dominant power.

Nowhere is this policy more evident than in the biblical genealogical lists. These lists, which the Bible abounds in, are basically lists of men, bringing about the birth of each other, as if women had nothing to do with this business of procreation and as if daughters were never born. It would seem that God himself, who governs, overlooks, controls and confirms this version of historiography, is endorsing patriarchy. The historical testimony these lists offer is subject to a strict policy of censorship, which erases all but the significant agents of history. These stock-lists demonstrate the "sameness" of their stock and constitute a paradigmatic relationship between their participants: they must all be the "same" in the sense of being sons to fathers and fathers to sons. The business of history is subsumed by the business of men and "time" is recounted as "men's time." Introduction of any type of "other" as subject into history is thus prevented. "Women are in a position of exclusion," says Luce Irigaray; "Their exclusion is *internal* to an order from which nothing escapes: the order of (man's) discourse."[5] The narrative policy of the Book of Judges bears witness to this concept of the "order from which nothing escapes" and its practice: time is augmented for several illustrious men who saved the Israelites from their foes and oppressors, and their feats are presented dramatically and vividly even when they cover a short span of time (hours, days); and then time is condensed (for 10 years, 20 years, 40 years, 80 years) into one sentence when nothing of value happens, when nothing is worth recording and committing to history. It is obvious that many things must have happened in those so-called "empty years," in that "vacant time" — but it was probably all very mundane and merely instrumental to "real history," viz. the history of men who figure in (or for) the national dynasty. The sound and fury men create when they battle for territorial and dynastic control easily overpowers any commotion women and other others may make in the course of human events. Thus humanity is reduced to "manity" and its history is ordered accordingly.

The opening of Chronicles 1 reads: "Adam, Shet, Enosh, Qenan, Mahalal'el, Yared, Hanoch, Metushelach, Lemech, Noach," etc. — a long line of males, the first ten of which establish the proverbial honorable "Ten," a significant number resonant with royal and majestic design. There is in these lists no mention of mothers, wives, daughters or sisters, although obviously there were some of these around and about. We know of a few of them mainly from the Book of Genesis, where distribution of narrative time obeys a different yet no less strict narrative policy than the one professed in the genealogical lists; and yet they were eventually eradicated from the final documentation of the race history. An instance where this policy is practiced most revealingly is the coda of the Book of Ruth: after conceding to recount a full and well-developed drama of two women — Naomi and Ruth — over a whole "book," albeit only four chapters long, the story of two women who act as very powerful and resourceful agents to change the course of history, the final verses which conclude the book are these:

> Now these are the generations of Peretz: Peretz begot Hetzron, and Hetzron begot Ram, and Ram begot Amminadav, and Amminadav begot Nachshon, and Nachshon begot Salma, and Salma begot Bo'az, and Bo'az begot Oved, and Oved begot Yishai, and Yishai begot David.

This list is the *raison d'être* of the whole book and provides, in the form of an epilogue, the political excuse for valorizing Naomi and Ruth. Here we witness the patriarchal laws of narration and historiography in their full and true color: the drama of women, the action of women, the intervention of women in the public and political sphere, the clever diplomacy of women, the redeeming and redressing quality of women's action — all this sound and fury was for nothing, and collapses into oblivion when the final testimony to the race history is laid down. Or rather, it was for something indeed: for enabling the dynasty of men to proceed towards its goal, to bring about the birth of the jewel in its crown: David. Thus women's time and space is appropriated and abrogated by folding it in neatly into the course of men's and the nation's events.

The "unmentioned" (the erased) of the coda-list of the Book of Ruth includes, to be fair, many men as well as women. Men who did not participate in the direct Davidic line of production also go unmentioned. Yet the striking differentiating category that governs the composition of this list is the gender differential, for women did actively and significantly play a crucial role in the production of David, as is testified in the Book of Ruth. Still, evidently, this was not enough to grant them mention and notice in the final call.

And to go back to Chronicles: the unmentioned are different from the inventory of the "same," again, in that they are not men. Silently, these lists endorse the dominant myth and concept of the inferiority of women by rendering them logically negligible and chronologically invisible (or at best, marginal) for narrated time. The dominant underlying myth in this case is the story of woman having been created through a differentiation from the body of Man — one of the versions Genesis offers — and although this version has been subject to de-patriarchalizing feminist readings, of which Ilana Pardes's *Countertraditions in the Bible* is a brilliant example,[6] its residual consequences are powerfully implied in all our social practices to this day. This is why we can turn a blind eye to the politics of these genealogical lists and depoliticize them in various ways.

So, in its most concise form, the history of Israel is related in terms of a sequential non-broken chain of "same" protagonists, a linear sequence which exhibits no traumatic disruption, which we know did in fact occur, no generational gap, which we know did in fact exist, no missing links and no interference of the "different." If any such intervening events ever happened, they underwent erasure and suppression; they were ironed out of history. Only in the more detailed version of the history of Israel does the narrative make room and time — albeit temporary room and time — for dramatic incidents, which unfold the ironed-out, flattened genealogical list and introduce the problematics of its composition. These are incidents of disturbance, disruption, delay and turbulence for the dynastic continuity. These are incidents in which women figure massively. These are incidents that provide the missing links of history and of narrative time. They also unwittingly disclose and underwrite the politics of the dominant narrative logic, which suffers no missing links.

Taking Time Back

This volume, which is the first of a set of two interconnected volumes, engages in the ongoing revisiting of Jewish and Israeli history by introducing a diversity of missing links. Slavoj Zizek explains:

> What we must be careful not to overlook is how *this retroactive causality, this symbolic "rewriting of the past," is inherently linked to the problematic of the "missing link"*: it is precisely because the chain of linear causality is always broken ... that it attempts to restore the "missing link" by retroactively reorganizing its past, by reconstituting its origins backwards. In other words, the very fact of incessant "rewriting of the past" attests to the presence of a certain gap, to the efficacy of a certain traumatic, foreign kernel that the system is trying to reintegrate "after

the fact." If the passage from "genesis" into "structure" were to be continuous, there would be no inversion of the direction of causality: it is the "missing link" which opens the space for reordering the past.[7]

The "neatness" of the genealogical lists represents a false reality, a constructed reality and a politically ordered reality. In reality, the lineage was not so neat — it was full of punctures, twists and turns of fate and unexpected events. What is represented is the direct line, which cuts through historical mass with posterior precision, to delineate pure uncontaminated and uncontested descent and to obscure missing links. Retroactively, it is only women's final self-subjection to the logic and law of patrilineality that opens up a small enclosure of time and space for them in the historical narrative — a drama in which they enact their disobedience to the governing principle of recorded time. But once tamed and subservient, their drama is incorporated into the long line of events, which celebrate male supremacy and superior designation, and their stories become "normalizing" stories, which serve to glorify the patriarchs and to enforce the stability of their rule.

In this sense, uncovering missing narrative links discloses events that were perceived as revolts against the legal order, inasmuch as they posited a threat to the tight and direct linearity of the genealogical list and to the order of history. Yet it also discloses a diversity of events and experiences, which went unnoticed when the patriarchal and androcentric grid was applied to the study of the past. Many of these events and experiences display women's time. This therefore is the method of "women's time": voicing silences and creating space for untold stories.

But feminist criticism takes a further step past exposing missing narrative links: it goes on to analyze the policy of limited inclusion which patriarchal texts may practice regarding women's time. By inserting women into history, as clearly shown in the many cases of the women of Genesis, it is not necessarily a different woman's interest which is served, since patriarchalism breeds androcentrism even while representing subjects who are not male. Indeed, if anything is served it is the hegemonic interest, in which women may participate by performing designated and valorized female roles (see the concept of *Woman of Valor*, Proverbs 31). Critical inquiry of these roles discerns a basic twofold policy: women's otherness may be heightened by emphasizing their "natural" functions (e.g. reproductive, sexual, biological, socially constructed) or it may be lessened by masculinizing them and enfolding their representation and agency in the dominant story. Both positions produce limited, qualified and restricted women's time.

This volume engages in women's time in these two modes: first is that of recounting stories and histories of women, along with other marginalized groups, categories and classes, and placing them back into history; the second is that of applying a feminist gaze to the dominant order and reason to expose its policies of inclusion/exclusion.

Hanna Herzog's study of the *Yishuv* (pre-state) historiography works in both modes: she exposes the fundamentals of feminist criticism by introducing non-conventional critical parameters to cultural research, and she proves how the production of scientific data when adhering to institutional paradigms is designed to exclude women's significance and achievements in the political sphere. Herzog closely examines the activity of several women's organizations in the period of the *Yishuv*, previously noted for their failure to "make a difference," by applying three new critical dimensions to the basic "raw" data: she challenges the canonized periodization of the years in question, she introduces several aspects of social activity into the political sphere, and finally she adds the dimension of facilitating social change into the study of significant agency. Her conclusion is that historiography, by prioritizing certain parameters over others for judging successful operation in the political sphere, is gender-dependent and discriminatory by its inherent circularity: the terms for excellence of social achievements which it stipulates are attuned to men's activism. Changing the lenses of the study clearly produces fresh evidence regarding the success of women's organizations, which must hitherto be called knowledge, and which must be considered for a sounder history of the *Yishuv*.

Rachel Rojanski also examines the options for success for women within political organizations. Rojanski enters an ongoing debate within the feminist agenda: should women apply their political weight to women's organizations and thus consolidate their power to create significant social change, or should they work from within existing (men's) organizations and political parties and gain access to the public arena with the endorsement of established (male) leaders? Hanna Herzog's paper demonstrated the danger for women's organizations of being historically marginalized by the dominant discourse, and so Rojanski studies the case of Esther Mintz-Aberson, who chose to act in the Poalei Zion party. Poalei Zion in America was a revolutionary party which professed to support equality between the genders. Yet although Mintz-Aberson did gain some leadership position in the party, it was of a restricted nature, and the decline of her career exposes the limits of the liberal-mindedness to which the party was committed. The need to found the affiliated Pioneer Women organization, as well as its reception by the party, demonstrates the relegation of women to the sidelines of public activity and their inability to find equal space and accommodation in the male-dominated Jewish public life. Public life, this study suggests, is androcentric even within a liberalist milieu.

Billie Melman joins in arguing that history and collective memory are gendered and tightly supervised by androcentric interests. Her paper too calls on historians to employ gender as a critical tool and category in the study of the construction of collective memory, and thus she too works in both the mode of women studies and that of feminist criticism. Her study's scope is wide and she considers *Yishuv* historiography as a whole through the gender lens, thus demonstrating the androcentric principles which govern memory and construction of collective identity. She then focuses on the case of Sarah Aaronsohn, whose life story earned her a reputation of heroic conduct much in line with other (few) illustrious historical Jewish heroines. Yet, although Aaronsohn became the site of an alternative memory, competing at times with the hegemonic male-centered myth of Tel Hai, it was accepted after having undergone a process of masculinization. Sarah Aaronsohn's legacy is ultimately appropriated to represent and commemorate a compound myth of a woman who is both a maternal model and a militaristic model. Both aspects of her identity are thus linked to a male-centered view of women's time: romantic and self-sacrificial love together with a desire for motherhood idealize a female subjectivity which is prescribed by patriarchalism; the unusual (and unfeminine) militant and daring nature of a woman may gain her a place in the nation's pantheon but it emphasizes the exclusive gendered highway into it. The construction of Zionist memory and national ethos still resonates with Melman's analysis, and her conclusions are more than pertinent to Judith Tydor Baumel's and Michael Feige's studies in this volume.

Judith Tydor Baumel's point of departure is Melman's principle of gendered collective memory by examining the continuous yet changing representation of women in Israeli military memorials since the establishment of the state. She proposes a typology of various gender motifs, which are prominent in a range of military memorials, and discusses the generational dynamics of their development within the context of commemoration discourse in Israel. Juxtaposing history and memory, Baumel questions whether the representations of women mirror their military or civilian status, thus suggesting the appropriation and subjection of femininity by masculinalism. Baumel exposes tensions and rifts between myth and social and cultural reality, as well as outlining the influences of international and universal commemoration paradigms, which contributed to the gendered narrative emerging from Israeli military monuments. She thus alludes to the broader issue which is of growing interest to historians and to social scientists who employ gender as a critical tool, viz. the connection and slippage between nationalism and militarism on the one hand, and gender stereotypes on the other.

Michael Feige's work joins Melman and Baumel in studying gendered aspects of national commemoration. Feige reflects on changes in the social, political and religious status of religious women in Israel by examining the case of the settlement Rehelim, which was established in 1992 by a group of religious women settlers to commemorate Rachel Druk of Shilo, who was killed in a Palestinian attack. While women were the driving force behind the Rehelim settlement project and presented a reversal of gender roles on several accounts, they nevertheless refused to define their act in feminist terms and insisted on its inclusion in the total scope of the national project, rejecting any affiliation (and sympathy) with other (secular) women's organizations. Feige sees the main reason for this universalist self-definition in the highly institutionalized nature of the narrative of commemoration as it has crystallized in Israel, which deems as subversive any actions of gendered significance. Even the highlighting of women's role within the national project by commemorating a woman under a woman's name (Rachel/Rehelim) is rendered meaningless gender-wise since Rachel is also the name of the biblical national mother figure, and thus she is an ultimate patriarchal woman. This paper raises questions regarding the limitations that religious tradition poses for the development of feminist consciousness among religious women. Within the dialogue of this volume, Feige's study shows that resistance to feminist positions is perpetrated not only by men, but also by women who continue to regard their significance in terms of the patriarchal order and narrative. The women of Rehelim had in fact created "women's time" after a patriarchal fashion, not far removed from the myth of Sarah Aaronsohn: in the "long time" of history the gendered aspect of their project will be totally consumed and subsumed by the national androcentric narrative.

Tsila Abramovitz Ratner addresses religious women from a different aspect: her paper focuses on the representation of women in the contemporary literary works of Israeli women authors who come from a religious background and whose oeuvre centers on depicting religious social and familial life. The recent upsurge in Israel of writing by women of Orthodox background has evoked great public interest and fascination in the secular reading public, for whom the Orthodox world is usually inaccessible especially in matters concerning women, whose political and sexual invisibility nurtures mystification of their otherness. The publication of these works, all coinciding with the rise of women's literature and writing in Israel in general, raises a complex of issues pertaining to women's agency in Orthodox society and to their representational burden. The women represented in these literary works act out and thematize the rift between subjective autonomy and social dictum, more often than not negotiating a personal arrangement for their identity and self-definition. Thus, these women's writing expresses a forged feminism, which is not divisive although it subverts accepted social roles to which they were channeled. This paper, along with Feige's, emphasizes the heterogeneity of the body of Jewish women in Israel: while some may perceive the goal of stepping into the public sphere as the manifestation of women's interests and rights as a class, others, who do the same, regard their actions in compliance with national interests.

The review essay by Tova Cohen, which addresses Iris Parush's recent book, *Reading Women: The Benefit of Marginality in Nineteenth Century Eastern European Jewish Society*, closes this volume. It affords a special opportunity to glimpse at a dialogue between two of the most prominent researchers of women's culture in the *Haskalah* (Enlightenment) period. Parush's concept of the advantages of marginality is the base for Cohen's critique, and it exposes her work on practices of inclusion of *Haskalah* women within an excluding culture. Cohen is the author of pathbreaking studies on the literary policies of women writers, striving to invent a feminine and maternal language within the constraints of the Hebrew language and tradition, and her repartee with Parush is illuminating both in content and in methodology.

*

In the next volume, *Israeli Family and Community: Women's Time*, we go on to explore additional issues. Inasmuch as feminist criticism often turns to the public sphere for detecting discrimination and disentitlement, it has also consistently found the same policies in the "natural" sphere of women's experience, that is, the private sphere — that of the family and the home. Manar Hasan examines the phenomenon of the murder of women in the name of "family honor" within Palestinian society in Israel and exposes the complex set of politics which maintain it; Sylvie Fogiel-Bijaoui turns to the results of the predominant concept of familism in Israeli society, as it is upheld in its main ethno-religious groups: Israeli Jews and Israeli Palestinians (Muslims, Christians and Druze). Amia Lieblich offers a three-stage study of kibbutz women's perception of their role in the creation and maintenance of norms and practices regarding family life and childcare arrangements; Khawla Abu Baker's study provides valuable insight into the question of women's options in the labor/work/career world and shows how attitudes to family, marriage, divorce and other political, social and cultural norms control the freedom of an Arab woman to develop a career, and how she is usually constrained, in cases of relative freedom, to merely "go to work."

Three final studies in the second volume expose various issues of the clash of activism and representations in the public and political sphere with the inherent problem women incur in self-construction. Dafna Lemish studies the portrayal of women in Israeli print and broadcast media to demonstrate the marginality of women in Israeli society. Most significant are those of relegating the female subject to the private sphere, restricting the representation of females to the physical functions of sex and reproduction, and placing women in the realm of emotions, irrationality and uncultivated behavior; Leah Shakdiel offers a radical feminist critique of the activity of the Women of the Wall group (WoW), a group of Orthodox women who seek to give women an active role in public prayer within the limits of Orthodox policies forbidding mixed-sex prayer. She exposes the shortcomings of Israeli liberal discourse to come to terms with the radical subjectivity of WoW and with the challenge it posited for both secular and religious political bodies; Orly Lubin concludes the second volume with an illuminating analysis of a gallery of visual representations of military Palmah women in pre-state Israel and in Israel today. She compounds theories of sexual difference with theories of sexual performativity to expose the egalitarian principle of drafting Jewish women to the Israeli army as a state apparatus designed to include and exclude women from the national project at one and the same time.

It is the editors' hope that these two multidisciplinary volumes of recent work from Israel do indeed create some women's time. As demonstrated here, women's time is based on a procedure of resistance to self-evident truths and knowledge, which are too often constructed within the terms of androcentrism and patriarchy. Women's time decenters dominant narratives and releases gazes, problematics and interests, which have been systematically refused time. The concept of women's time serves also as a model for further investigation of other obliterated narratives, and therefore serves the well-being of all human beings, in Israel and outside.

NOTES

1   Luce Irigaray, *je, tu, nous: Toward a Culture of Difference*, trans. Alison Martin (New York and London, 1993), p. 35.
2   Joan Wallach Scott, *Gender and the Politics of History* (New York, 1988).
3   Irigaray, *je, tu, nous*, p. 16.
4   Virginia Woolf, *A Room of Her Own* (London, 1929).
5   Luce Irigaray, *This Sex Which Is Not One*, trans. Catherine Porter (Ithaca, NY, 1985), p. 88.
6   Ilana Pardes, *Countertraditions in the Bible: A Feminist Approach* (Cambridge, MA, 1992).
7   Slavoj Zizek, *For They Know Not What They Do: Enjoyment as a Political Factor* (London and New York, 1991), p. 203.

Redefining Political Spaces:
A Gender Perspective on the *Yishuv*
Historiography

Hanna Herzog

At the time of the French Revolution, there was a witty revolutionary named Sieyès who also played a major role in the period following the revolution. An astute phrase is attributed to Sieyès. When asked "What did you do during the Terror?" his reply was short and to the point — "I survived." Before the revolution, he had written a greatly admired manifesto, in which he addressed the Third Estate, which at that time had not been liberated "What is it today? Nothing. What could it have been? Everything!" I would like to apply that remark of Curé Sieyès to women. What do women mean to Zionism? I prefer not to say "nothing." What are they capable of, what could they have been? Perhaps everything. And if our propaganda finds the right course of action, we will certainly make it possible.[1]

With these words, Theodor Herzl opened a speech to the Agudat ha-Nashim ha-Tziyoniyot (Zionist Women's Association) in Vienna, on 12 January 1901, going on to discuss the issue of how women could play a role in the Zionist enterprise. The boldness and imagination that informs Herzl's philosophy and vision of the Jewish state seem to have deserted him as he considered women's place in the Zionist revolution. Like many of his generation, he was trapped in traditional molds of thinking regarding women and their role in society. Herzl considered women as proficient in "the way of poetry, art, in a word: beauty." He thought that "if only we could convince women that the sort of Zionism that appears like a new fashion, as it were, contains an inherent beauty that is timeless and is eternally young," then they would do the necessary work "for us," as he phrased it, working as propagandists of the Zionist idea: "They can recount the beauty that was an integral part of Zionism when the idea was born ...", and they can do so as mothers and as educators, "because a woman who is a good Zionist is also a very responsible mother ... the mother must understand that Zionism, if it is great and important, then it is especially great and important for children, who are the citizens of the future...."[2]

This gendered perception of the Zionist enterprise stands in contradiction to the speech Herzl gave in Vienna, some years beforehand, at the founding meeting of the local women's branch, "Zion," when he had demonstrated a liberal gender-blind perception that "[t]he question of women has already been solved in Zionism. Women delegates were present at the Basle Congress, and possessed equal rights."[3]

Herzl's dualism, his universalistic perception of women as opposed to a gendered perception, requires us therefore to ask once again, what is women's place in the Zionist narrative? And the answer, to a considerable extent, is determined by the growing body of knowledge about women in the *Yishuv* (pre-state) period and the first years of statehood.

Shifting Spaces of Gendered Knowledge

Elsewhere I have explored the historical development of "the truth" about women in Israel.[4] The social sciences in Israel have taken a course of development similar to that taken by feminist research in many countries.[5] Five analytical stages typify that development, and we can address them as stages in chronological development. However, characteristics of each stage can still be discerned in various parts of the social sciences, not to mention in social consciousness. Some stages started developing almost in parallel to others. The parallel existence of diverse research questions and methods creates mixtures and overlaps in ways of creating knowledge and tends to blur analytical distinctions.

Even so, I argue in this article that each stage is definable and that we can point out the different ways in which women are perceived in the various research stages. With changing research areas and new questions raised, there are concomitant changes in attitudes towards the status of women, and in the politics that accompany the changing attitudes. To a large extent, the five stages that characterize general research about women are also appropriate for exploring the development of research on women in the *Yishuv* period and during early statehood. A summary of the five stages is given below.

The first stage, mainly composed of studies carried out in the 1950s, was characterized by the absence of women. Sociology and history recounted the Zionist narrative and the building of the new society without mentioning women or women's contribution to the society in-the-making. A world of endeavors dominated by men was identified with the Zionist enterprise. At the second stage, which may be described as "add women and stir," research of the 1960s started to acknowledge women's existence. The variable of "sex" was gradually introduced into research and, as a result, the main thrust of the debate on women dealt with the differences between women and men, or with those areas considered central to women, such as the family. An example for this approach is Yonina Talmon-Garber's research on the family, in particular the kibbutz family in its earliest days.[6] But the inclusion of women in research as researchers as well as subjects of research was not marked by any paradigmatic change or by new research questions. Theory and methodology were phrased in universal language, and men's behavior was the normative criterion. Since women could now be seen in the research field and in research areas, the social sciences were beginning to ask questions about women's condition.

This stage led to the third stage of research, from the 1980s onwards, when discrimination was identified as the pivotal experience in the life experience of women who were attempting to find their place in the public domain. Women were portrayed as a dominated group, and their social experience was defined as "a social problem." Women were compared to other minority groups, while "society" was identified with the dominant groups. The societal problem was recognized by its divergence from what was defined as the dominant norm, those norms that were regarded to be normative and legitimate. Women who entered public life were considered unusual, atypical. Since the male world was accepted as a given, researchers asked why women took up work or entered politics. They examined the difficulties women encountered in their dual roles as mothers and workers outside their homes (men were not asked about their difficulties). Many of the first studies of women in the *Yishuv* period were carried out in the shadow of a mindset which analyzed women's difficulties in terms of male models of nation-building.[7] Indicating discrimination as a pivotal experience gives rise to an image of women as helpless and marginal victims.

A significant theoretical change takes place in the fourth stage, with the transition in the late 1980s from discourse about sex to discourse about gender. The concept of "gender" embodies the insight that the distinction between the sexes is social not biological. The social distinction has been institutionalized and has created a regime of knowledge and social order. That social order is underpinned by a hierarchic dichotomy of power relations between women and men, and the dichotomy is presented as natural, innate and taken for granted.

Conceiving the social order as a gendered one exposes the ideological claim that the existing order is universal or vital, and opens up a different trajectory for researching and understanding social reality. Underlying this alternative trajectory is the claim that definitions of sex, sexuality and gender are cultural definitions that generate arrangements of structure and consciousness that shape self-identity as well as relationships between people. Relationships between and within genders are socially constructed and change over the years and in different social contexts.[8] Not only does the gendered order discriminate, it also enforces and oppresses. Hence research has focused on revealing the mechanisms of oppression and control, and since there are more oppressed women than men in a gendered order, women remained at the focus of research at this stage. What distinguished this fourth phase from others was its focus on women's own perceptions of their social experiences.

The use of women's own terms revealed the richness, diversity, complexity and multiple appearances of their world and gave rise to methodological criticism of research approaches that did not make room for that world. It also shifted attention to spheres of life that had not been previously studied.[9]

The paradigmatic change enabled a debate on the differences between women and the different ways in which the gendered order evolved, eventually leading, from the mid-1990s onwards, to the fifth stage, which was typified by the transition from a discourse on gender to a discourse on genders. The collapse of the myth of equality and the newly formed perception of the gendered order generated a series of sociological-historical studies that tried to investigate women's status in Israeli society in general and the society in-the-making before statehood. Much of the research revalidated the theses of discrimination, control and marginalization. Yet the greatest contribution of these historical studies is not the claim that inequality already existed at the inception of Israeli society, but the new light they shed on the *Yishuv*'s history and on women's roles within it. Women were not just passive partners in the nation-building process but were also active partners who assumed roles in shaping society. Not only did these studies introduce women into history, they also showed that women had a history of their own. History began to be written from the viewpoint of women and from their perception of the nation-building process. Greater emphasis was placed on writing history "bottom up," to include social sites that were not addressed in the dominant narrative.[10]

Focusing research on women and their own experiences reveals a reality in which women are being fettered by a gendered social order, in which they try to find their own paths within it, by surviving, circumventing and challenging. The image of controlled women or women as victims is now replaced by one of autonomous women with different sources of power who are independent, while experiencing changing and widening spaces of their lives and identities. Significant to the inclusion stage is the researcher's search for ways to acquire new knowledge using a multiplicity and variety of methodologies. It effects a critical examination of theories created in the main/male science, and does the same to feminist theories that have become institutionalized. The gendered world was not only a critique of women's relations with men, but it also explored the contexts of class, ethnicity, nationality and sexual preferences. With a growing awareness of the complexity of gendered arrangements, not only did research fields but also diverse representations of women's worlds increase: more women are now included in the academic discourse in general and in the feminist discourse in particular.

This is the research-stage that breaks down the category of "women" that became prominent in previous research phases. Though women live in a world that is chiefly defined by men, women experience that world in different ways and, moreover, they cope with it in different manners. As women are better represented in the feminist discourse, the category of women becomes more diverse and increasingly blurred.[11]

Accordingly, the quotations from Herzl's speech presented at the beginning of this article require a more complex decoding than simply deciding which quotation best describes the situation as it is, and/or which best captures his views on women and the gendered order. The quotations reveal the complexity of Herzl's gendered perception. On the one hand, women are part of the "ethnos," part of us, part of the reanimating people, without any gender distinction. On the other hand, they are "other" in the specific way in which they are perceived and perceive themselves in the Zionist endeavor. That duality can also be found in research on women in the *Yishuv* and early statehood period. Research shattered the myth of equality that survived in canonic history until the late 1970s.[12] At the same time, accumulative research on women in the *Yishuv* period shows that Herzl's aspiration for women — "What could [women] have been? Perhaps everything" — did in fact come true to a great extent, but not only in the narrow field that he marked out for them as mothers and propagandists of the Zionist idea, and not only on the road carved out by men, as canonic historiography has maintained. Women created, worked, built and rebelled in a whole range of fields, in some of which research already exists, while other fields still represent a research vacuum. Additionally, women did not constitute a single category, and a uniform identity of women did not develop: instead we can point out negotiations over different definitions, and the varying choices that women made at the various periods regarding their gendered identity and their societal role.[13]

Accumulative research knowledge about women in the *Yishuv* period allows fresh thinking about their place in the Zionist endeavor, and it allows us to write her-story. But beyond this, it allows us to rewrite *Yishuv* history so that it not only contains the efforts of women but also presents — as a result — a renewed look at the overall period.[14] Rewriting history is without doubt a burdensome task that I do not intend to assume, certainly not in one article. Still, I am daring to suggest a number of dimensions for a re-exploration of social endeavors and their political significance as a result of research on and accumulated knowledge about women in the *Yishuv* period and the first years of the Israeli state.

Reperiodization of the Narrative

Academic discourse, and certainly the public discourse, on the ordering of time and the division by era is part of the social struggle between and within identity groups over the collective's social boundaries and its nature. "Every year can be considered the first year," writes Michael Young in his book on time, "The important step is to frame a number of events in a given time and make them 'ours' — an opening date with special significance must be chosen for this purpose."[15] Exploring changes in periodization and in selecting formative events reveals the changes in defining "our" identity and, no less than this, it discloses the changes in those groups that take an active part in defining the social borders of the collective and its identity. So, the key questions are: who are the framers of the events? And how, and by whom, does the historical story become part of constituting "us" or "ours"?

Until recently, the historiography of Israeli society was grounded on validation deriving from the life-experience of dominant groups.[16] The dominant periodization built the historiographic narrative around the nation-building model. The collective narrative that was constructed and institutionalized was anchored in a perception of a new society built on a foundation of waves of immigration (*aliyah*). This validation is based on the distinction between the "Old *Yishuv*" and the "New *Yishuv*," where the history of the "New *Yishuv*" is being referred to as a continuum of immigrations (*aliyot*) that become part of the nation-building process. The sequence, the time and the historical narrative that transforms the events into "ours" are part of and within the dominant discourse of those who lived at that time and who represented the stream that would become the dominant one.

The narrative of the immigrations is founded on a dual logic of similarity and otherness, congruence and difference: on the one hand, all the immigrants (*olim*) form part of the collective, since all of them took part in the "ingathering of the exiles" and in rebuilding the nation. On the other hand, in this narrative not all the immigration waves enjoy equal significance: they are assessed by the contribution they made to the process, whose end-goal was the establishment of the Zionist state. As the criterion for perceived contribution, the definition that became dominant was the one determined by the Labor movement. In this narrative, it is the Second *Aliyah* and the Third *Aliyah* that laid down the foundations of the social order. The political arrangements that they determined, the values and culture they institutionalized and the motives for their immigration (as they were recounted) were applied to evaluate and judge all previous and ensuing waves of immigration.[17] If women were included in this narrative, it was subject to the periodization ascribed to by the studies dealing with women in the Labor movement, but also by many other studies that accept this periodization as a given.[18]

Growing criticism of the dominant narrative was leveled by the Jewish groups that had been "forgotten" and marginalized, and which attempted to enter the national narrative. Some of those groups whose voices were stifled are the *hugim ezrahiim* (Civic Sector), the political right, the urban middle class, non-Ashkenazi groups, the veteran population who were classified as the "Old Yishuv," the religious public, women and others. The studies engendered by these groups helped to enhance knowledge, to compensate and empower the excluded groups, including women.[19] However, the principal criticism is leveled by those who have been called "the New Historians and Sociologists": they urged a reexamination of the dominant Zionist narrative from the colonialist viewpoint, which created the conflictual encounter between the Jewish-Zionist Yishuv and the local-Palestinian residents.[20] The colonialist viewpoint is also being tried out in other fields, such as the nature of the encounter between the colonial state, the indigenous population and the immigrant population. It asks what sort of collaboration and/or conflict emerged between the colonial state and which Jewish and Arab groups (and among these) — in the Israeli context, for example, the changes during the transition from one colonial rule, that of Ottoman Turkey, to British Mandatory rule, or the contexts and affinities between the Jewish middle class and the British colonial state.[21] Obviously, such criticism gives rise to a different perspective on the historiography of the Yishuv period and the first years of the State of Israel. It is worth noting that much of this writing suffers from gender-blindness.

With the change in the distinct point of view, there is a concomitant change in the narrative's starting point and in the significant milestones selected for constructing it. The crucial milestone in each narrative does not necessarily create an unvarying and/or complementary sequence. Thus a dual research challenge is set — not only telling the story of the different histories and their inclusion in the collective memory, but also identifying the points that enable a meeting, if at all, between them. I wish to make some proposals from a gender perspective.

The periodization based on the waves of *aliyah* told the story of building the new nation with the First *Aliyah*. But the milestone chosen in the dominant historiography, and which became the story of "our" *aliyot*, was the Second *Aliyah*. In the collective memory, this was considered to be "*the*" *aliyah* that laid the foundations for nation-building and determined the course for achieving the Zionist vision in the pioneering spirit of the Labor movement.[22] More often than not, scholars researching the groups marginalized in that historiography have chosen to examine the changes that occurred in the Jewish *Yishuv* in *Eretz Yisrael* before the pioneering *aliyot* — for example, the rediscovery of the First *Aliyah* and Old *Yishuv*, research on the Sephardim, the *Mizrahim* (Jews from Muslim countries), the bourgeoisie and other neglected groups. In the process of exposing the forgotten stories, new starting points of the story are chosen, alternative perceptions of social changes come into view, as well as repressed images of society and nation.

The body of research that has accumulated about women in the *Yishuv* and women's endeavors from the gender perspective allows us to propose a different validation for the phenomenon of revival and the structuring of new social arrangements. Many studies have shown that, in many societies, women serve to signify the sites where the social boundaries of the collective are negotiated and fought. Fostering the "new woman" in the nation-building process was typical of national thinking in the nineteenth century.[23] Women's education, consideration for mothers, and women's public work flourished in different countries in the early nineteenth century, and also in the Jewish *Yishuv* in Palestine, even before the new *aliyot*. In other words, a gender perspective on the nation's renewal might suggest a different periodization, including a choice of a different "beginning," that is, prior to the arrival of the First *Aliyah*. The schools for girls that were opened in Jerusalem in the mid-nineteenth century heralded the start of the process. Margalit Shilo examines young women's education and notes that such schools constituted a means for shaping a new woman and a new society. Gender relations and women's rights to schooling provided arenas where battles were waged over preserving the borders of the old collective, in contrast to attempts at sketching the new borders in processes of change that commenced in the religious sections of *Yishuv*, mainly in Jerusalem. She maintains that objections to educating girls, raised by the Ashkenazi public in Jerusalem, did not stem from the anticipated implications of the schools for girls on the status of women, but from worries that the establishment would lead to the opening of parallel institutions for boys "because from this springs the evil of opening schools." The new schools were perceived as antithetical to traditional Torah education. Indeed, the Agudat Ahim (the Association of Brothers), a philanthropic society founded in 1871 by English Jews, saw it as a national mission to provide Jewish education, in particular for Jews living in Palestine. In the nineteenth century, Shilo points out, educating girls was considered to be the prime means for instituting social change.[24]

The concern for women's health is also one of the landmarks of renewed Jewish settlement in *Eretz Yisrael* as shown by first attempts at institutional care for childbirth and by the battle waged against child mortality by Dr. Albert Cohen, the representative of the Rothschild family who had set up a maternity fund in 1854. In 1913, the first center for mother and baby health was opened by Rose Kaplan and Rachel Landi, two nurses, who came from the United States accompanied by Nathan Strauss, who provided the funding. This endeavor grew into the institutions of mother and child clinics and *Tipat Halav* (literally, "drop of milk") clinics that were founded by Hadassah in collaboration with the Histadrut Nashim Ivriyot (Association of Hebrew Women).[25] It became one of the public welfare institutions operated by and for women. In the first two decades of the twentieth century, the foundations of organized social work were also laid, along with programs for training women to perform nursing work.[26]

The narrative of the rebirth of the nation from a gender perspective takes us back to the end of the nineteenth century, where the locus of social activity is the "women's sphere," and where women are the target of change and its social carriers. It locates changes within the veteran-local population that was excluded from the dominant Zionist narrative.

Redefining Political Landscapes

As well as starting the narrative of national rebirth at different points in time, those milestones also propose a narrative on the origins of the Israeli welfare state and its institutionalization. This gender perspective of the state in-the-making maintains that women's organizations, which were characterized by "broad national liberalism," laid the foundations of Israel's welfare policy.[27] This contradicts the image according to which welfare policy in Israel stems from the socialist ideas put forward by the labor parties that grew into the nation's dominant political force. Writing in 1926, Hannah Tahon points out that "the attitude of the women workers to society, which was determined by denial of the differences between women and men, destroyed their interest in social work for other people in *Eretz Yisrael*." "The interim women," as Tahon describes them, recognized

> in the family the natural cell of the state and related affirmatively to women's elementary role in caring for children and home ... by understanding and acknowledging *the general goal of building the nation* ... [but] these women do not make do with looking after their household, but take on other roles ... many women fulfill their obligations towards the people and the country by working in a particular profession: as teachers, doctors, journalists, and so forth. Others find mental satisfaction in social activities....[28]

Concerns for health and education, particularly of the future generations — the children — is perceived as part of the national mission. Women were diligent in laying the foundations of Hebrew education as teachers in schools and kindergartens and assumed vital roles in inculcating the Hebrew language, which they defined as the reborn nation's mother tongue.[29]

Women who developed the various ideas on welfare were influenced by progressive ideas and belief in the advancement of humanity and its environment. These ideas were anchored in the belief in science, in education as a lever for progress, and in rational, professional and efficient management of aspects of the home, as well as of education, health and welfare. Most of the ideas were imported from Western nations, chiefly from the United States, and symbolized the renewal of the people and its liberation from backwardness. As Tahon argued:

the fact that the majority of work for the good society in *Eretz Yisrael* falls on women's shoulders is made clear by the particular national conditions, which strongly resemble those in American life. In our country, like in America, the man is busy with earning a living and with the family to such a great extent that he has no time to devote to other roles. In both countries, people can dedicate at least some time to political, but not to social, nation-building, Here too, this vacuum is filled by the work of a number of women.

The article then lists the women's associations in various welfare spheres.[30]

Once the foundations for welfare activities were in place, we can indicate the different points in time when the ideas were taken up by different agents in the *Yishuv* and eventually by the state, and when they were incorporated in the formal political arrangements. The *Tipat Halav* clinics for mother and baby, for example, which were founded by the Histadrut Nashim Ivriyot at the turn of the century, were handed over to Hadassah due to economic difficulties in 1923. Hadassah alone was involved in regular work, while the members of the Histadrut Nashim Ivriyot, which would eventually become the Women's International Zionist Organization (WIZO), continued to support it voluntarily. The clinics that provided care for infants and the distribution of milk gradually became part of the *Yishuv* landscape. The importance of the endeavor was acknowledged by the public authorities and they gradually joined the work of municipalities and the *kupot holim* (sick funds). In 1950, with the consolidation of Ben-Gurion's idea of statism, it was decided to turn this public service into a state service. By 1952, all the *Tipot Halav* were handed over in stages to the Ministry of Health.[31] It is worth noting that the Ministry of Health continued operating its services in the format laid down by Hadassah; the service operated in the Ministry's framework until 1995 when, with the introduction of the Law of Compulsory Health Insurance in Israel, it passed into the hands of the Health Medical Organizations.

Another example is the story of the politicization of the social work which was known in the first years of the state as *sherutei ha-sa'ad* and later as *sherutei revahah*. The Histadrut Nashim Ivriyot initiated and planned organized aid to those in need already in the early 1920s. It was the first organization to employ a salaried social worker (a public inspector, in the language of that period), and adopted family treatment that was then a revolutionary perception. It started developing professional work methods, such as keeping statistical records to monitor the patients, in the spirit of the scientific management of the day.[32] The sphere of women's activity was not enthusiastically received by the workers' organizations, whose opinion on aid and charity was far from positive. WIZO worldwide also preferred support in the areas of production and manufacturing. The Histadrut Nashim Ivriyot, as an organization lacking resources, opted for the political way in order to advance its concerns. It founded a political list together with the Hitahdut Nashim Ivriyot le-Shivu'i Zkhuyot (Hebrew Women's Association for Equal Rights) whose goal was to establish a social department in the Va'ad ha-Le'umi (the National Council). Henrietta Szold headed the list. The list took three seats in the 1931 elections for the General Assembly, which was not enough to be represented on the Va'ad ha-Le'umi.

Mapai, which had recently been founded and was seeking to bolster its status as a leading agent in the *Yishuv*, relinquished one of its seats on the Va'ad ha-Le'umi in favor of Henrietta Szold. Social work thus gained some public recognition and support. The guidelines for work that Szold prescribed would funnel the social services in the local authorities during the *Yishuv* period and, after the state's establishment, would form the basis for the Ministry of Welfare.[33]

While the dominant narrative written from the perspective of male endeavors underscored the building of state institutions and economic institutions, the alternative narrative reveals that the education and welfare institutions that emerged within the civil society were mostly carried out and supported by grassroots women's organizations. They were co-opted and institutionalized within the national framework. However, the dominant historiography deleted this chapter from the national historical memory A gender observation of women's activities requires not only recording the areas of women's efforts, but also critically examining their significance. The women's strong emphasis on the world of women, and their work for women and children, can be assessed, on the one hand, in terms of contribution to the collective. Women not only took part in the national project but were pioneers who paved new social roads. At the same time, however, these practices reproduced and supported the dominant gendered division of roles. Apparently, rewriting history from the perspective of women includes women in the collective, but as "others" operating in different social spheres than men; thus women's practices constituted the category of women as a discrete category — one that is engaged with women as an object, and for which women subjects are working. No doubt, until recently, the reproducing elements were the decisive and powerful forces that situated women in society and historiography. However, rewriting history in the current context, where there is a rediscovery of civil society, a revival of grassroots movements and a redefiniton of power as diffuse and fluid, a gender perspective highlights the fact that women had challenged the dominant definition of political power already at the beginning of the Zionist project. Through their social practices they had constituted the then alternative political spaces.

Challenging the Boundaries of the Imagined Community

Exploring formative events and initiatives reveals the shifts in definitions of "our" identity, says Young, as well as changes occurring in the composition of those groups involved in the process of defining identity.[34] The dominant critical historiography, in the spirit of the New Historians, related the story of the state's establishment by charting the boundaries of the Jewish collective and its attitude vis-à-vis the Palestinians, on the one hand, and the British on the other. In this story, the emphasis was on the conflictual relations and struggles on the way to "conquering the land" and achieving national independence.[35] Ronen Shamir proposes examining the relations with the colonial regime not only at the points of divergence but also at the sites of convergence.[36] Similarly, Deborah Bernstein suggests scrutinizing sites of convergence and divergence between Palestinian Arabs and Jews under the British colonial regime in Palestine.[37] By shifting the perspective of analysis new social boundaries are drawn.

Observing the initiatives of women from the middle class and/or what was known as the civic sector brings to light everyday practices that sought to demarcate the social boundaries of the imagined community in a manner that challenged the definition which was rapidly becoming institutionalized. Gerda Arlozoroff-Goldberg, who was at the time a journalist with the *Jüdische Rundschau*, published in *Ha-Ishah* (The Woman) a critique of the women's movement in *Eretz Yisrael*:

> In *Eretz Yisrael* and in the Zionist Histadrut it becomes customary to describe anything belonging to Jews in this country as "Eretz Yisraeli." It is common to talk about *"Eretz Yisraeli"* agriculture or industry — meaning Jewish enterprises; about "Eretz Yisraeli" schools — referring to schools attended by Jews, and we have also become used to speaking about the "Eretz Yisraeli" women's movement, understanding by this the movement of Hebrew women in this country. It is still too early to speak about a movement of *Eretz Yisraeli* women that could encompass and unite in shared labor women from both neighboring peoples — the Jews and the Arabs.[38]

Later, the correspondent complains about the lack of places for meetings between Arab and Jewish women, about the fact that the Hebrew woman is busy with her affairs and knows very little about non-Jewish women. When an encounter occurs, it is "in the sphere of handing over and receiving work. In cities and rural areas alike, we find the Arab woman as a helper with housework, under the Jewish housewife's supervision."[39]

Conceiving the women's movement as a social site for the encounter of women, Arlozoroff-Goldberg criticizes the ethnocentric definition of the social boundaries that emerged in *Eretz Yisrael*/Palestine. She advocates the overcoming of national boundaries that were constructed within the women's movement and offers an inclusive, non-hierarchical, social definition of identity. Another meeting-point that the author identifies are

> The nurseries (*Tipot Halav*) of Hadassah in the cities with mixed populations, mostly Jerusalem, where Jewish nurses treat Arab women too, though this is still a very limited treatment.... even so, they should not be disregarded, because this is actually the only point where a relationship is conducted between the Jewish and the Arab woman that is not a purely business one, but is based on educational objectives.[40]

The service provided at the *Tipat Halav* clinics in Jerusalem was offered in the first few years to Arab and Jewish women. The Arab mothers, Muslim and Christian, generally arrived at the clinic at the suggestion of their Jewish neighbors or were referred to the clinics, since they gave birth at home, by private physicians. From August 1923 onwards, an Arabic-speaking nurse joined the Jewish nurses, and in 1924 a clinic for Arab women was opened near the Damascus Gate in Jerusalem's Old City. In so doing, Arab women were de facto separated from Jewish women. Gerda Arlozoroff-Goldberg writes that:

> It is unconscionable that eventually the Jewish woman will know nothing about the Arab woman ... like a mother's duty to inculcate her children with general knowledge about the country, so it is her duty to enable them to learn the languages of the country; that is, not only the Hebrew language, but also Arabic ... the main thing is to awaken in the Jewish woman the awareness that her world does not come to an end in the Jewish environs and that perhaps it is her duty to fight *shoulder to shoulder with her Arab counterpart* for changes and improvements.[41]

She believes that Arab and Jewish women have shared interests to fight for and regrets that no movement of Arab women has been formed and, in particular, that a joint movement of the two peoples has not been set up. Although she calls for challenging the borders of the collective and the inclusion of Arab women, it is clear that the author identifies Jewish women as representing modernity and Europeanness and she therefore charges the Jewish women with an educational task.

Attempts to chart different social borders that do not overlap the national boundaries is found in the Palestine Association of University Women (PAUW), a branch of the International Federation of University Women. The *Eretz Yisrael* branch was open to English, Arab and Jewish women. Though it was a small, elitist organization, it continued to function even with the deterioration of the Jewish–Arab conflict into a conflict between Jews and the

British. Founded in 1923, it was established by two Englishwomen, who spent every winter in Jerusalem — "to get away from the British cold" — Miss Hanbije, the headmistress of a London girls' school, and Mrs. Bartlett, an inspector of schools in India. At its peak in 1933–34, the PAUW had 150 members from 51 countries, who had graduated from 36 different universities. Only women with degrees awarded by recognized universities were admitted, and they had to pay membership fees. The International Federation, with which it was linked, had the general goal of improving the social and cultural position of women academics and of fostering international friendship. The PAUW stressed the advancement of friendship and understanding between women academics living in the Holy Land who held different professions and different beliefs and came from different countries. The emphasis was on ties between Jewish, Arab and English women.[42]

The PAUW had three branches, in Jerusalem, Tel Aviv and Haifa, though the principal activities took place in Jerusalem and Tel Aviv. The association had a social nature, focusing on monthly meetings where the women attended lectures given by other members or by a guest lecturer who was either local or foreign. The meetings had a very English style. Once a year a "birthday party" was held with great ceremony, attended by members of the academic communities in Palestine and overseas, the High Commissioner, and the Solicitor-General. Sessions were usually conducted in English, the language in which lectures were given, apart from meetings where only Jewish women attended, when Hebrew was the spoken language. For a long time, only one Arab woman, Olga Wahabi, was a member of the organization; she eventually received a senior position in the Jordanian Ministry of Education, but later four Arab physicians joined. Despite the low participation by Arab women, members of the PAUW emphasized the association's general nature. This was reflected in lectures that dealt, inter alia, with various aspects of Middle Eastern culture and Islam, as well as Jewish and Christian culture.

The efforts that the organization instituted attest to a similar trend. In 1935, a list of books was drawn up by the International Federation, "Books of Many Lands"; the Palestine branch sent titles of 52 recommended books that had been printed there, including one in Arabic, one in German, 31 in English and ten in Hebrew. In 1937, the PAUW organized a survey of children's libraries which, inter alia, brought to light the fact that there were few children's books in Arabic. Consequently, the Tel Aviv branch drew up a list of 722 children's books that had been published in Hebrew and were recommended for translation into Arabic. Even though the recommendation did not include reverse translation, from Arabic into Hebrew, one cannot ignore that this enterprise attempted to create a dialogue between the two societies.

Another research study conducted by the PAUW explored "the higher education of Palestinian women and girls in the past hundred years": it also examined the situation in the Jewish and the Arab sections of the population. The organization's report for 1945–48 notes the difficulty of carrying out meetings in view of the worsening relations of the *Yishuv* with the British Mandate and with the Arabs. The report stated that "[un]til that last day, 15 May 1948, the association served its finest purpose, to bridge the ever-widening gulf between Jew, Christian, and Arab: a handshake in those days often meant more to many of us than the social meetings of many years' casual intercourse."[43] The report was published in 1949, after the State of Israel had come into existence. It expressed hopes that peace with the neighboring countries would soon arrive and pointed out that, in the first elections held in the young state (on 25 January 1949), Arab women cast their votes and enjoyed full electoral rights, like Jewish women.

In an interview I conducted in February 1987 with Hilda Boires, who for many years was the secretary of the PAUW, she explained that:

> [w]omen academics were a minority in the *Yishuv* of *Eretz Yisrael*, just as men with an academic education were a minority. They [the women] were marginal in terms of the general population, and in relation to women, in particular. Their prestige did not accrue to them from the Jewish *Yishuv* (although they were objects of envy) but from the international contacts that they created and nurtured. Due to the English, snobbish character of the association, few women from Eastern Europe were members. It was criticized by the Working Mothers' Association because its members were neither workers nor politicians. At any rate, the opinions they held were not those of Mapai-Mapam, they were not part of the left.

Still, from this marginal position, they espoused a different statement about the social boundaries and nature of the imagined community in which they wanted to live.

With regards to boundaries within the Jewish community, women expressed different opinions. Gerda Arlozoroff-Goldberg, who wanted to challenge the boundaries that were being drawn between Arabs and Jews, critically examined the attitudes towards the *Mizrahim*:

> Women's work and the women's movement are constrained by the boundaries of the Jewish settlement to a specific circle of women, who are mostly either of European or American origin. In most cases, Jewish women from Oriental (*Mizrahi*) countries are now the object of organized activity by women ... for the moment, there are no signs of independent activity by Oriental women — no doubt since they *have not made vast efforts* to stimulate and nurture their urge to act accordingly.[44]

The writer laments the hierarchy among women:

> On the one hand are the Jewish women from European countries, who are the active members of women's organizations; alongside them, the Oriental woman, and the women from the old *Yishuv* who are rooted in another culture and in different ways of life ... and finally, completely separate from the Jewish camp, the vast majority of *Eretz Yisraeli* women, are the Arab women. None of the activities and experiments pursued by the women of the Hebrew *Yishuv* relate to them [the Arab women]... .[45]

Some women were among the first who identified emerging and intensifying social boundaries between Jews and Arabs and groups within the Jewish community, which in days to come would cause huge conflicts and struggles. From these early stages women not only discerned the boundaries, they also recognized the arbitrariness, discrimination and injustice embodied in delineation, and therefore called for the subversion of these restrictions.

Various women expressed their disappointment with the divisions that had developed amongst Jewish women — between women from the right, from the left (the workers), and religious women, as well as the division between Ashkenazi and *Mizrahi* women.[46] References to a range of women of different national origins, from the Old *Yishuv* and the New, from different ethnic groups and with different political and class attributions, appear in writing about the need to include them in a single women's movement. However, that writing also makes a clear statement about the nature of the imagined community, which was striving to broaden its boundaries and to include within it as many women as possible. It takes into account the fact that women are not a uniform category, as well as the boundaries of political endeavor that the women wanted to extend through their efforts. These nascent voices were stilled by the emerging social borderline between Jews and Arabs, and the social hierarchy that was institutionalized between *Mizrahim* and Ashkenazim. Only in the past two decades has the call been heard to take issue with the ethnic hierarchy among women and with the social borders separating Arab and Jewish women.[47]

A Reexamination of Women's Place in Yishuv Politics

Research on the subject of women in politics overlaps, to a great extent, with the stages of development of research on women in general. From an almost total absence of women as an object of research, a shift in focus occurred towards an examination of women's marginal place in the political system. In these studies, explanations for such marginality were offered, especially for the women workers' movement, which started out as a radical movement but gradually capitulated in the face of party mechanisms. These mechanisms marginalized women, subordinated them to the rules of the dominant-male discourse and extinguished their unique voice.[48] Subsequently, studies unveiled women's political achievements, such as the struggle for suffrage and the politicization of social work.[49] Finally, there were attempts at rereading politics and expanding the boundaries and meaning of politics by underscoring the special path taken by women as discussed above.

So far, my analysis has focused on the new fields of political initiatives, but there is also room to reexamine the place of women in the formal, institutionalized political landscape, and to offer an evaluation of the political system from a gender perspective.

Israeli democracy is perceived as a political system that from its inception granted voting rights to women. This right, however, was achieved only after a prolonged struggle. In *Yishuv* historiography, the period of the struggle (which was eventually successful) is overlooked. Neither the women who led the fight nor their organizations, who were partners in the political achievement that made the *Yishuv* one of the first democracies to give suffrage to women, were preserved in the pages of history books. It was only in the late 1970s that the struggle was analyzed for the first time by some women researchers. While Sylvie Fogiel-Bijaoui, Ofra Greenberg and myself analyzed the struggle for women's franchise within, and from within, Jewish *Yishuv* society, Hannah Safran was the first to open the discourse on the connection between the local women's organizations that struggled for suffrage and global forces, even though she mainly deals with the impact of American women.[50]

This research approach not only changes the perception of political space in which women functioned, but also locates the *Yishuv*'s political system, in general, in a wider context. We should recall that women's battles for suffrage throughout the world were carried out by a wide range of global actors who formed a global agenda that constituted women as gendered political citizens and created international organizations and a worldwide solidarity of women, which became a driving force for changing women's status. Nitza Berkovitch stresses that the impact of global action is not confined to the international arena but also affects nation-states. The broad cultural and political contexts in which nation-states have operated influenced the various patterns by which women's issues were defined and their status regulated in the nation-states.[51]

Safran's research shows that women's organizations that struggled for equal rights for women in the *Yishuv* saw international women's organizations as reference groups: they were influenced by global discourse and adopted and modified their modus operandi to the Israeli context. Local women's organizations were linked with Jewish women's organizations all over the world, but they aspired to a connection that went beyond the constraints of the Jewish collective. The Histadrut Nashim Ivriyot, a local organization, was the first *Yishuv* organization that successfully joined any sort of international organization, though it was not the only one. The organization of university women, as I show above, suggested definitions of global political space as part of their social action by women and for women, and the Labor movement women also forged ties with socialist organizations.[52]

The suffrage struggle around the world generated women's organizations as well as women's parties.[53] However, establishing a women's political party that included women from the entire political spectrum and competing in general elections was an unusual phenomenon. Sarah Azaryahu, one of the leaders of the Hebrew Women's Association for Equal Rights list, addresses this unique feature of the struggle in her memoirs and compares the Hebrew organization with equivalents in Britain and the United States.[54] At the same time the Hebrew Women's Association for Equal Rights relied in its struggle on the support of various international forces such as the International Alliance of Women for Suffrage and Equal Citizenship, international congresses and conferences of women, and prominent women activists.[55] Azaryahu's comparison of the local organization with other women's organizations, and the reliance on the support of international organizations — like the powerful need of women's organizations to join the international women's organizations and obtain international recognition — show that the women who fought for voting rights had both a national-local and a global political orientation.

The historiography narrated from the point of view of the dominant groups highlighted the Eastern European influence in shaping the cultural and political patterns, because most of the dominant groups' leaders were raised in Eastern Europe and the source of their imagery was Europe. They imported political and social models inspired mainly by the socialist movements.[56] American influences were marginalized, perhaps because America was identified as a capitalist society. Yet an examination of women's undertakings and their place in the global context brings into focus a different picture. The historical narrative from a gender perspective uncovers the influence exerted by cultural origins and political images from America and Britain. It also examines the role played by women immigrants from the USA, who took part in initiating and shaping political activity and patterns of organization as well as the setting of an alternative social welfare agenda. Progressive ideas, cloaked in scientific, rational and democratic discourse, permeated various administrative and cultural areas of *Yishuv* life. This was the case in the managerial discourse dominated by men as well as in the new projects initiated by women, such as the "professional" social work, the establishment of a nursing school and the development of a discourse on hygiene.[57]

One cannot speak of a one-way influence, but more of an encounter between global and local forces that did not always accord with each other. Women's struggle did not simply "import" and "adopt" ideas and patterns of action. A crucial influence was exerted by special local conditions in forming patterns of struggle for women's equality. The fight for equality was part of negotiations both over the identity of the Jewish society and over the rules of the game of the *Yishuv* democracy that emerged at that era.[58] Women endorsed the pattern that was starting to take shape: setting up a political list. Dan Horowitz and Moshe Lissak argue that political organizing in the *Yishuv* was voluntary and its authority prevailed only over those groups that subjected themselves to its rules.[59] The proportional electoral method, which became institutionalized in Israel, stems from the pre-1948 political system, where — in the absence of sovereignty — proportional representation functioned both as a tool for participation and as a means for granting legitimacy to the *Yishuv*'s institutions. Researchers of Israeli democracy are deeply divided as to the characterization of Israel democracy, but all of them agree on the centrality of the parties in the political arena of the *Yishuv* and, eventually, of the state.[60] When women organized themselves in a political list that stood for elections, they turned into active agents of establishing Israeli democracy.

The politicization of the women's struggle over "women's" issues, which was channeled to the formal arena and reflected in the founding of a political party, occurred in all four elections held during the *Yishuv* period and in the elections to the first Knesset. Women's lists introduced women's issues to the public agenda, and in the first Knesset they also launched the Law of Equal Rights for Women.[61] The Women's Party introduced the draft bill to the state's political agenda, and the law was ratified in the Knesset, although without the support of the woman who had set it in motion — Rachel Kagan, the representative of the Women's Party — because the amendments it underwent during the Knesset debate changed its spirit and did not meet the expectations of its instigators.[62]

Paradoxically, the establishment of the state and its transformation into the center of Jewish organizations ended the politicization of women's issues. In 1951, WIZO — which was a major driving force in the women's parties during the *Yishuv* years — announced that it was abandoning the political scene. In the same year, it was decided to transfer the organization's international center from London to Israel, and as result a resolution was passed that WIZO's national branch would abandon any political activity and would not run in elections, either national or local. The principal rationale for abandoning the political arena cited a preference for the shared Zionist interest and the desire to avoid party-political disagreements between women.[63] The stifling of the women's voice for the sake of what was identified as a broader interest was the mechanism that had already neutralized women workers in the late 1920s and prevented them from becoming an autonomous political power.[64] It served as an exceedingly powerful mechanism for blocking many more attempts at independent organizing by women from the 1950s onward.[65]

Redefinition of Power and Politics

The construction of the *Yishuv*'s political system has been described by political sociologists mainly as a process of centralizing power and political organizations. There are two competing versions regarding the nature of this process. Lissak and Horowitz have defined the process of building up the political system as one that integrates political elites: ideological designation spurs them on towards collaboration in the national center as a focus of authority and as an alternate regulator. In contrast, Yonathan Shapiro characterized the nation-building process as one motivated by a national-building elite which built a centralized political system with a dominant party at its center.[66] Without venturing into an in-depth debate on the differences between these approaches, there is room to highlight the similarity between them. The two competing theses examine the dominant centers of power and narrate the story of winners in politics. The emphasis is on political organizations; on an analysis of the struggles for control of the major power resources and their expressions in party arrangements, and in the staffing of key positions in power foci; and on the politics conducted by elites. The emphasis is also on the forces that act "top down" and shape the system of values, authority and the political arrangements. As a result, the most researched area is politics at the national level, elite forces and forces that achieved dominance, the Labor movement most of all.

Political power, political importance, as well as prestige and influence, are measured in light of the organizational forms institutionalized by those identified as being central to that construction process. As a result, women, the right wing and the middle class were excluded, those economic forces that were directly independent of the centers of political power and local politics.[67] The classical political sociology, which focuses on the institutional system, relations between elites, and ideological perspectives, tends to emphasize what goes on in the public arena and almost completely ignores quotidian life, the private sphere and many groups who are not part of the elite.[68] This perspective on politics and power reflects the traditional grasp of power, which emphasizes the exercise of power by government and organizations and, above all, reflects a male image of power and politics.

As a result of the dominance of this approach, the research and analysis of civil society have been shunted to the sidelines of sociological-historical analysis. The past two decades have witnessed a rediscovery of civil society and its mission in shaping the political space — opposing or collaborating with the state. A gender observation of *Yishuv* society elicits that the *Yishuv* period was crammed with civil endeavors that did not originate in the leading political bodies, but in philanthropic and voluntary organizations. Very often those organizations were based on local coalitions and were supported by similar global forces. They proposed an alternative agenda as well as alternative patterns for social action to those that, in the event, became institutionalized and dominant.

As early as the 1970s Kay Boals suggested a reconceptualization of the nature and scope of politics. She defined "as political any human relationship, at any level from the intrapsychic to the international, provided it can be shaped and altered by human decision and action."[69] Politics resides in all human relationships, and to politicize means not only to bring individuals or issues within the arena of conventional electoral and governmental politics, but rather "to bring to conscious awareness the political nature of existing social arrangements."[70] Hence, not only is power found in all social relations, but it must be identified in various loci of activity; moreover, there is an ongoing struggle over the boundaries of the political scene.[71] This redefinition of power draws our attention to the different roots of power and mechanisms (such as social capital, resources related to the private-personal world), to the exercising of power and decision making and influence, not just in the male-dominated economic-political-military sphere, but also in broader activities that shape everyday practices in a range of areas. And finally, exercising power, according to that redefinition, is neither limited to the hierarchies controlled by men, nor to competition and conflict. Rather, we must examine numerous sites and practices where social reality is explored, and which share the constitution of social agenda. The redefinition of politics extends the boundaries of the concept to include social actors and social spheres that play a part in it and, at any rate, women who are the chief actors in certain fields.

Exploring women's activities and initiatives during the *Yishuv* period involves not only writing *her*story but also confronting the political perception. Reexamining politics from a gender perspective proposes an alternative take: instead of describing the political process as centralizing and taking control of power foci, the gender perspective enables us to view it as a patchwork process. And during that process, in various arenas and at different levels of human relations, the *Yishuv* society came into being. Power also grows from the bottom up, and at different sites. The metaphor of the patchwork quilt is not only meant to indicate the multiplicity of groups and organizations that took part in this process. It is also intended to dissolve the hierarchies of power and prestige that became institutionalized and created a hierarchy of importance and contribution of the different social efforts. In this way, not only are women's activities in the field of welfare included in *Yishuv* historiography, but they are also defined as a pivotal political contribution.

In any case, this generalization also challenges the hierarchies that sprang from attitudes that succeeded in establishing dominant groups, and from the power that appropriated for itself the definitions of what was political, what was pioneering and what was a contribution to building the *Yishuv*. The generalization, the co-opting and the inculcating of women's work show that social change is not necessarily conceptualized in terms of large organizations that obtain formal representation and enforce themselves and their agenda. Without overlooking the fact that this was a key aspect of *Yishuv* politics, research on women reveals that there were other ways of exerting power: a plethora of groups engaged in everyday activities where the aggregate of social practices and voices is transformed into a power that generates change. This is not an explicit, but a slow-moving, in-depth, pervasive change.

NOTES

1 Theodor Herzl, *Ne'umim ve-maamarim tziyoniim* (Zionist Writings) (Jerusalem, 1976), Vol. 1, p. 96.
2 Ibid., pp. 98, 99.
3 Herzl, *Ne'umim ve-maamarim tziyoniim*, Vol. 2, p. 364.
4 Hanna Herzog, "Yeda, ko'ah u-folitikah feministit" (Knowledge, Power and Feminist Politics), in idem (ed.), *Hevrah be-marah* (Society in Reflection) (Tel Aviv, 2000), pp. 269–93.
5 Margrit Eichler, "And the Work Never Ends: Feminist Contributions," *Canadian Review of Sociology and Anthropology*, Vol. 22, No. 5 (1985), pp. 619–44; Joan W. Scott, "Women's History and the Rewriting of History," in Charles Farnham (ed.), *The Impact of Feminist Research in the Academy* (Bloomington, IN, 1987), and "Gender: A Useful Category of Historical Analysis," in Elizabeth Weed (ed.), *Coming to Terms: Feminism, Theory, Politics* (New York and London, 1989), pp. 81–100.
6 Yonina Talmon-Garber, "Social Change and Family Structure," *International Social Science Review*, Vol. 14, No. 3 (1962), pp. 468–87; idem, "Sex-Role Differentiation in Equalitarian Society," in Thomas E. Lasswell, John H. Burma and Sidney H. Aronson (eds.), *Life in Society: Introductory Reading in Sociology* (Chicago, 1965), pp. 144–55.
7 For example, Deborah S. Bernstein (ed.), *Pioneers and Homemakers: Jewish Women in Prestate Israeli Society* (Albany, NY, 1992), p. 92.
8 See, for example, Cynthia Fuchs Epstein, *Deceptive Distinctions: Sex, Gender, and the Social Order* (New Haven, 1988); and Judith Lorber, *Paradoxes of Gender* (New York and London, 1994).
9 Bernstein (ed.), *Pioneers and Homemakers*; Margalit Shilo, Ruth Kark, and Galit Hasan-Rokem (eds.), *Ha-ivriyot ha-hadashot: Nashim ba-yishuv uva-tziyonut be-re'i ha-migdar* (Jewish Women in the Yishuv and Zionism) (Jerusalem, 2001) (hereafter *Ha-ivriyot ha-hadashot*).
10 Yossi Ben-Artzi, "Ha'im shinu heker nashim u-migdar et yahasenu le-havanat ha-historiyah shel ha-aliyah veha-hityashvut?" (Have Gender Studies Changed Our Attitude towards the Historiography of the Aliyah and Settlement Process?), in Shilo, Kark, and Hasan, *Ha-ivriyot ha-hadashot*, pp. 26–44; Deborah S. Bernstein, "Heker nashim ba-historiografiyah ha-yisre'elit: Nekudot motza, kavanot hadashot ve-kavanot sheba-derekh" (The Study of Women in Israeli Historiography: Starting Points, New Directions, and Emerging Insights), in ibid., pp. 7–25; Billie Melman, "Min ha-shulayim el ha-historiyah shel ha-yishuv: Migdar ve-eretz yisre'eliyut (1890–1920)" (From the Periphery to the Center of *Yishuv* History: Gender and Nationalism in Eretz Israel [1890–1920]), *Zion*, Vol. 62, No. 3 (1997), pp. 243–78.
11 See the essays in Shilo, Kark, and Hasan, *Ha-ivriyot ha-hadashot*.
12 Deborah S. Bernstein, *The Struggle for Equality: Urban Women Workers in Prestate Israeli Society* (New York, 1987).
13 See Melman, "Min ha-shulayim."
14 Ibid.; and Hanna Herzog, "The Fringes of the Margin: Women's Organizations in the Civic Sector at the Time of the Yishuv," in Bernstein (ed.), *Pioneers and Homemakers*, pp. 283–304.
15 Michael Young, *The Metronomic Society: Natural Rhythms and Human Timetables* (London, 1988), p. 197.

16 See Bernstein, "Heker nashim"; and Hanna Herzog, "Kol shanah yekholah lehihashev ka-shanah ha-rishonah: hesderei zman ve-zehut ba-viku'ah al shnot ha-hamishim" (Any Year Can Be Taken as the Beginning: Periodization and Identity in the Debate of the 1950s), *Teoriyah u-Vikoret*, No. 17 (2000), pp. 209–16.

17 This explains the late start of research on the First *Aliyah* and the Fourth *Aliyah* and, in particular, the marginal status of immigration in the 1950s, both in *Yishuv* historiography and in the social hierarchy.

18 Deborah S. Bernstein, "The Women's Workers Movement in Pre-State Israel," *Signs*, Vol. 12, No. 3 (1987), pp. 454–70; Yael Azmon, *Eshnav le-hayehen shel nashim be-hevrot yehudiyot: Kovetz mehkarim bein-tehumi* (A View into the Lives of Women in Jewish Societies: Collected Essays) (Jerusalem, 1995); and Ben-Artzi, "Ha'im shinu heker nashim…?"

19 Ibid., pp. 32–3.

20 Deborah S. Bernstein, *Constructing Boundaries: Jewish and Arab Workers in Mandatory Palestine* (Albany, NY, 2000); Ilan Pappé, "Ha-historiyah ha-hadashah shel ha-tziyonut: Imut akademi ve-tzibori" (The New History of Zionism: The Academic and Public Confrontation), *Kivvunim*, No. 8 (1995), pp. 39–48; and Gershon Shafir, *Land, Labor, and the Origins of the Israeli–Palestinian Conflict, 1882–1914* (Cambridge, 1989).

21 Ronen Shamir, *The Colonies of Law: Colonialism, Zionism and Law in Early Mandate Palestine* (Cambridge, 2000).

22 Shmuel N. Eisenstadt, *Ha-hevrah ha-yisre'elit: Reka, hitpatehut u-va'ayot* (Israeli Society: Background, Development, Problems) (Jerusalem, 1967); Dan Horowitz and Moshe Lissak, *Origins of the Israeli Polity* (Chicago, 1978); and Yonathan Shapiro, *Ha-demokratiyah ha-yisre'elit* (Israeli Democracy) (Ramat Gan, 1977).

23 Nitza Berkovitch, *From Motherhood to Citizenship: Women's Rights and International Organizations* (Baltimore and London, 1999); Margalit Shilo "Hinukh naarot ke-emtza'i le-itzuv ishah hadashah ve-hevrah hadashah: Ha-mikreh shel beit ha-sefer Evelina de Rothschild, 1854–1914" (The Cross-Cultural Message: The Case of Evelina de Rothschild School for Girls), in Shilo, Kark, and Hasan, *Ha-ivriyot ha-hadashot*, pp. 229–47.

24 Ibid., pp. 232, 234.

25 See Shifra Shvarts and Zipora Shory-Rubin, "Histadrut nashim le-maan imahot ve-yeladim be-Eretz Yisrael: Po'alan shel 'Hadassah', 'Histadrut Nashim Ivriyot' ve-'Wizo' le-hakamat tahanot la-em vela-yeled ('tipot halav'), 1913–1948" (On Behalf of Mothers and Children in Eretz-Israel: The Efforts of Hadassah, The Federation of Hebrew Women, and WIZO to Establish Maternal and Infant Welfare Centers, 1913–1948), in Shilo, Kark, and Hasan, *Ha-ivriyot ha-hadashot*, pp. 248–69; Ofra Greenberg and Hanna Herzog, *Irgun nashim volontari be-hevrah mithavah: Trumatah shel Wizo la-hevrah ha-yisre'elit* (A Voluntary Women's Organization in a Society in the Making: WIZO'S Contribution to Israeli Society) (Tel Aviv, 1978); and Herzog, "The Fringes of the Margin."

26 Nira Bartal, "Yisud beit sefer le-ahayot be-Yerushalayim al yadei ha-mishlahat ha-refu'it shel tziyonei Amerikah bi-shnat 1918: Hemshekh o mahapekhah?" (Establishment of a Nursing school in Jerusalem by the American Zionist Medical Unit, 1918: Continuation or Revolution?), in Shilo, Kark, and Hasan, *Ha-ivriyot ha-hadashot*, pp. 270–91.

27 Hannah H Tahon, "Ha-ishah be-tzibor eretz-yisre'eli" (The Woman in the *Eretz-Yisrael* Public), *Ha-Ishah*, Vol. 1, No. 1 (1926), pp. 5–10.

28 Ibid., p. 7 (emphasis in the original).

29 Rachel Elboim-Dror, *Ha-hinukh ha-ivri be-Eretz-Yisrael* (Hebrew Education in *Eretz Yisrael*) (Jerusalem, 1986); and Aharon Bar Adon, "Ha-imahot ha-meyasdot u-mnat helkan be-tehiyat ha-ivrit ve-hithavutah" (The Founding Mothers and Their Role in the Making and Revival of the Hebrew Language), *Lashon ve-Ivrit*, No. 3 (1990), pp. 5–27.

30 Tahon, "Ha-ishah be-tzibor eretz-yisre'eli," p. 8. The organizations that are mentioned are: "Ezrat Yoldot — support for poor women and their newborn infants; Ezrat Nashim — assists a sanatorium for the mentally ill; Histadrut ha-Nashim ha-Mizrahiot looks after immigrant women from the Mizrahi Party; Histadrut ha-Tze'irot — apart from educating its women members, also offers hot meals to hungry schoolchildren. The numerous associations in the towns and the moshavot extend frequent help to the sick, to pregnant women, and to the

infants of poor families."
31 Greenberg and Herzog, *Irgun nashim volontari*, pp. 25–30.
32 See Yehouda Shenhav, *Manufacturing Rationality* (Oxford, 1999).
33 See Herzog, "The Fringes of the Margin."
34 Young, *The Metronomic Society*, p. 197.
35 See Horowitz and Lissak, *Origins of the Israeli Polity*; and Shafir, *Land, Labor*.
36 Shamir, *The Colonies of Law*. In his analysis of the failure of the attempt to constitute a Zionist, community-based system of law in Palestine, he claims that that it was not the colonial regime that marginalized the Hebrew Law of Peace, but rather forces from within the Zionist community that aligned themselves with the law of the state.
37 Bernstein, *Constructing Boundaries*.
38 Gerda Arlozoroff-Goldberg, "He'arot le-tnu'at nashim eretz-yisre'elit" (Notes on an *Eretz Yisrael* Women's Movement)," *Ha-Ishah*, Vol. 3, No. 2 (1929), pp. 6–7.
39 Ibid., p. 7.
40 Ibid., p. 8.
41 Ibid., pp. 9–10 (emphasis in the original).
42 S. B. Mohl, *History of the Israel (Palestine) Association of University Women* (Jerusalem, 1950).
43 *Report of the Palestine Association of University Women 1945–1948* (Jerusalem, 1949).
44 Arlozoroff-Goldberg, "He'arot," p. 6 (emphasis in the original).
45 Ibid., pp. 8–9.
46 See, for example, Rachel Cohen, "Ha-ra'eyon ha-merkazi be-yetzirat Histadrut Nashim Ivriyot be-Eretz Yisrael" (The Leading Idea in Creating Histadrut Nashim Ivriyot in *Eretz Yisrael*), *Ha-Ishah*, Vol. 2, No. 5 (1928), pp. 13–15; Tahon, "Ha-ishah be-tzibor eretz-yisre'eli"; and idem, "Ha-ishah ve-ahdut ha-am" (The Woman and the Unity of the Nation), *Ha-Ishah*, Vol. 1, No. 6 (1927), pp. 6–9.
47 Henriette Dahan-Kalev, "Nashim Mizrahiyot: Zehut ve-historiyah" (Oriental Women: Identity and Herstory), in Shilo, Kark, and Hasan, *Ha-ivriyot ha-hadashot*, pp. 45–60.
48 See Sylvie Fogiel-Bijaoui, "The Struggle for Women's Suffrage in Israel: 1917–1926," in Bernstein (ed.), *Pioneers and Homemakers*, pp. 275–302; Dafna Izraeli, "The Zionist Women's Movement in Palestine, 1911–1927: A Sociological Analysis," *Signs*, Vol. 7, No. 1 (1981), pp. 87–114; and Bat Sheva Margalit Stern, "'Knafayim yesh ve-la'uf ein ko'ah': Tnu'at ha-po'alot ha-eretz-yisre'elit bein shlitah 'nashit' le-shlitah 'gavrit'" (Between Female and Male Dominance: The Women Workers' Movement in *Eretz Yisrael*), in Shilo, Kark, and Hasan, *Ha-ivriyot ha-hadashot*, pp. 292–314.
49 Herzog, "The Fringes of the Margin."
50 Sylvie Fogiel-Bijaoui, "The Struggle for Women's Suffrage"; Greenberg and Herzog, *Irgun nashim volontari*; Herzog, "The Fringes of the Margin"; Hannah Safran, "Maavak bein le'umi, nitzahon mekomi: Rosa Welt Strauss ve-hasagat zkhut ha-bhirah le-nashim, 1919–1926" (International Struggle, Local Victory: Rosa Welt Strauss and the Achievement of the Women's Franchise), in Shilo, Kark, and Hasan, *Ha-ivriyot ha-hadashot*, pp. 315–30.
51 Berkovitch, *From Motherhood to Citizenship*.
52 Safran, "Maavak bein le'umi," p. 320.
53 See Berkovitch, *From Motherhood to Citizenship*; Nancy Cott, *The Grounding of Modern Feminism* (New Haven and London, 1987).
54 Sarah Azaryahu, *Hitahdut Nashim Ivriyot le-Shivu'i Zkhuyot be-Eretz Yisrael: Prakim le-toldot ha-ishah ba-aretz* (The Hebrew Women's Association for Equal Rights in *Eretz Yisrael*: Chapters for a History of the Woman in the Land of Israel) (Haifa, 1977), p. 18.
55 Safran, "Maavak bein le'umi," pp. 85–93.
56 See, for example, Anita Shapira, *Berl, the Biography of a Socialist Zionist: Berl Katznelson, 1887–1944* (Cambridge, 1984).
57 Michal Frenkel, "Ha-historiyah ha-ne'elmah shel ha-yad ha-nireit: Misudo shel sdeh ha-nihul be-Yisrael" (The Invisible History of the Visible Hand: The Institutionalization of Israel's Field of Management) (Ph.D diss., Tel Aviv University, 2000); Hanna Herzog, "The Fringes of the Margin"; Bartal, "Yisud beit sefer"; Dafna Hirsh, "'Banu henah lehavi et ha-maarav': Ha-si'ah ha-higyeni be-Eretz Yisrael bi-tkufat ha-mandat ha-briti" ("We Came Here to Bring

the West: The Discourse on Hygiene in *Eretz Yisrael* during the British Mandate), *Zmanim*, No. 78 (2002), pp. 107–20.

58 See Hagai Boas "Ha-status quo: Tarbut, politikah ve-hevrah be-yahasei dat u-medinah be-Yisrael" (The Status Quo: Culture, Politics and Society in Religion and State Relations in Israel" (M.A. diss., Tel Aviv University, 2001); Menachem Friedman, *Hevrah ve-dat: Ha-ortodoksiyah ha-lo tziyonit be-Eretz Yisrael, 1918–1936* (Society and Religion: the Non-Zionist Orthodoxy in *Eretz Yisrael, 1918–1936*) (Jerusalem, 1977).

59 Horowitz and Lissak, *Origins of the Israeli Polity.*

60 For differing views, see for example, ibid., and Shapiro, *Ha-demokratiyah ha-yisre'elit.*

61 See Nitza Berkovitch, "Eshet hayil mi yimtza? Nashim ve-ezrahut be-Yisrael" (Women of Valor: Women and Citizenship in Israel), *Sotziologiyah Yisre'elit*, Vol. 2, No. 1 (1999), pp. 277–318; Pnina Lahav, "'Ksheha-pali'at rak mekalkel': Ha-diyun ba-knesset al hok shivu'i zkhuyot ha-ishah" ("When the Palliative Simply Impairs": The Debate in the Knesset on the Law for Women's Rights), *Zmanim*, No. 46–47 (1993), pp. 149–59.

62 Lahav, "'Ksheha-pali'at rak mekalkel'," p. 159.

63 Hanna Herzog, *Gendering Politics: Women in Israel* (Ann Arbor, 1999), pp. 159–60.

64 Izraeli, "The Zionist Women's Movement"; Margalit Stern, "Knafayim yesh."

65 Hanna Herzog, "Nashim be-folitikah u-folitikah shel nashim" (Women in Politics, and Politics of Women), in Dafna N. Izraeli et al., *Min, migdar, politikah* (Sex, Gender, Politics: Women in Israel) (Tel Aviv, 1999), pp. 307–55.

66 Horowitz and Lissak, *Origins of the Israeli Polity*; Shapiro, *Ha-demokratiyah ha-yisre'elit.*

67 See Herzog, "The Fringes of the Margin"; Shamir, *The Colonies of Law.*

68 Deborah S. Bernstein, "Mah she ro'im mi-sham lo ro'im mi-kan: Hebetim ve-tovanot ba-historiografiyah ha-yisre'elit" (Seen from Above and from Below), *Sotziologiyah Yisre'elit*, Vol. 2, No. 1 (1999), pp. 23–50.

69 Kay Boals, "Political Science," *Signs*, Vol. 1, No. 1 (1975), p. 172.

70 Ibid., p. 173.

71 Herzog, *Gendering Politics*; Carole Pateman, *The Sexual Contract* (Stanford, 1988), and idem, *The Disorder of Women: Democracy, Feminism and Political Theory* (Cambridge, 1989).

At the Center or on the Fringes of the Public Arena: Esther Mintz-Aberson and the Status of Women in American Poalei Zion, 1905–35*

Rachel Rojanski

The Poalei Zion Party of America was founded in December 1905 on an ideological Zionist-Socialist platform imported into America from the Russian Pale of Settlement. Although Poalei Zion in America formulated its own distinctive ideologies, it still maintained close ties with its sister parties elsewhere and regarded itself as a revolutionary party. However, while in other revolutionary Jewish parties, Zionist and non-Zionist alike, either in America or elsewhere, women were prominent and perhaps even influential, a study of the history of Poalei Zion in America, from the pre-party stages of organization in 1903 until the early 1930s, reveals almost no female participation.[1]

Indeed, the group that served as the nucleus for the early organization of Poalei Zion in America in 1903 included two women. The sources merely mention their names, and even those are incomplete: Sarah Kotin, and Miss Glazer.[2] In those early years, two other women were active in Poalei Zion of America: Bella Pevzner and Shoshana Bukhmil. Pevzner, who had been active in Jewish self-defense and Poalei Zion groups in Grodno (Belorussia), came to America after her university studies in Paris, and in December 1905 joined the 22-member group that re-established Poalei Zion in America.[3] For a brief period, she was engaged in propaganda for the movement's work, but within a short time left it.[4] Bukhmil, who had a Ph.D. in philosophy from a Swiss university,[5] came to America in mid-1908 as a Poalei Zion member in Palestine on behalf of an organization engaged in settlement in Palestine, called Shilo (an acronym for *Shuvah Yisrael le-eretz ha-avot* [Israel Return to the Land of the Forefathers]). By May 1909, she had already left America.[6] Golda Mabovitch, who later became Golda Meir, also participated in Poalei Zion of America, but only as a member of the Milwaukee branch of the party, while still a young woman.[7] The one exception was Esther Mintz-Aberson who was the only woman apart from Bella Pevzner in the group that re-established Poalei Zion in America in December 1905.[8] But unlike Pevzner, Mintz-Aberson soon became a key figure, also serving for a short time as the party's acting secretary.

Esther Mintz-Aberson was an exceptional figure among the members of Poalei Zion in its early days. She stood out from the moment she entered the political arena, through the incisiveness of her arguments, the determination with which she fought for her views, and her superb command of Hebrew, which singled her out from the others who knew only Yiddish. She also played an important role in the ongoing ideological debates during the formative years of the party in America and in the stormy political controversies that rocked it. Yet, even before the end of the First World War, she had left the political scene. Although from the mid-1930s until her death she continued to be a devoted and active member of the Pioneer Women's branch where she lived, she never returned to the broader public arena. Her contemporaries believed that Mintz-Aberson had left the political scene because of her husband's illness and his premature death, following which she had to earn the family's livelihood.[9] However, she had already vanished from public life even before her husband fell ill.

Despite her many talents and achievements, Esther Mintz-Aberson disappeared not only from the active political life of the party, but also from its historiography.[10] Moreover, after her, not a single woman reached the top ranks of Poalei Zion in America. These facts strongly suggest that Esther Mintz-Aberson's political fate was not an outcome of her particular personal circumstances, but rather reflected the status of women in Poalei Zion in America, and perhaps also in the society of Jewish immigrants from Eastern Europe in general.

However, Paula Hyman, in discussing the place of women in this society, argues that the immigrant community "repeatedly expressed its support of women's activism."[11] As an example, she cites the kosher meat boycott imposed by women in New York in 1902, which earned the support of the Jewish immigrants in America, as well as the strike by Jewish women workers in the clothing industry in 1909. "This communal acceptance of women as active subjects, rather than as passive objects, of history," Hyman concludes, "recognized and promoted the status of women as partners in negotiating the public role of Jews in American society."[12]

There were indeed women who gained achievements in Jewish public life in America. Joyce Antler, in her extensive study on Jewish women in America, cites a long list of women who attained important positions in various spheres, including some who were active in revolutionary movements — in the labor movement and the Zionist movement.[13] But both Antler, in the chapters of her book dealing with the first decades of the twentieth century, and Hyman describe women who were active within a female public: organizing women, leading women, or working for women's causes vis-à-vis the male public or alongside it. Esther Mintz was an exception because she tried, and even succeeded for a short time, to attain an official position of influence and leadership within the male establishment. For this reason, her short public chapter is a matter of some interest.

Theoretically, Poalei Zion in America supported equality between the genders, an attitude that was natural for a revolutionary party. This message was also conveyed in the section devoted to women in its daily newspaper *Di tsayt*, which expressed support for women's equality.[14] Nonetheless, in this article, I will attempt to show, via Esther Mintz-Aberson's personal story, that in actual practice the party's attitude — of both its male and female members — towards women's status was far more complex.

First, I will portray Esther Mintz-Aberson's public-political profile and the unique role she played in the Poalei Zion Party in America. Second, I will argue, on the basis of these facts, that Esther left the political scene not for personal reasons, but rather as a result of the party's attitude towards women's place in public life. Third, I will support this claim with a discussion of the formation and development of the two women's organizations affiliated with Poalei Zion — the Farband Women and Pioneer Women — and in particular how they were received by the party.

In 1929, Golda Meir visited America, and upon her return described the situation of the members of Pioneer Women, as follows:

> I asked myself what led these women … to set themselves apart and form their own federation? … These women only discovered themselves and their latent strengths within the league [Pioneer Women], and the men in the party cannot be accused of having interfered with them. But these women themselves did not have confidence in their own abilities.[15]

Here I will try to refute this view and to offer a counter-argument. I would assert that Pioneer Women (first called *Pyonerin*) was the only option available to these women. The need to found it at that time as well as the process of its establishment and its reception by Poalei Zion, reflected, as did the case of Esther Mintz-Aberson, the relegation of women to the sidelines of public activity, as well as their inability to find their place in public life in any other manner.[16]

Leaders of Pioneer Women, women who were educated in America, understood the situation and consciously adopted the model that already prevailed in America — activity through a women's organization, which would create a reserve of leaders and educate women to engage in public life. Esther Mintz, who had been schooled outside the United States, tried to become active within the mainstream of public life, but it turned out that this was not possible in the long run. In this article, I argue that, paradoxically, while women's awareness of their status in society led them to shun the center of public life, it was precisely their organizing on the fringes that paved the way for their eventual integration into the main, male-dominated sphere of public life. Women who, like Mintz-Aberson, lacked such awareness and attempted to enter public life directly were destined to be ousted from it.

From Baranowitz to New York

Esther Mintz was born on 17 March 1881 in Baranowitz in the Minsk district, the eldest of ten children.[17] She learned Hebrew in a *heder*-type school located in her parents' home. During her youth, she left home to pursue her studies in Warsaw.[18] In the summer of 1904, she left Russia and on 17 August 1904 arrived in New York.[19] There is no information about her connections with the Jewish labor movement that was active in Warsaw from the end of the nineteenth century, or with the Zionist movement there. We also do not know where she studied in Warsaw, nor the exact date when she joined Poalei Zion in New York. It is known, however, that she was active in the initial stages of the party.[20]

The first group of Poalei Zion in America was founded in New York in March 1903, and during the following couple of years additional Poalei Zion groups were established in different parts of America.[21] Fom 29 April to 30 May 1905 a convention took place in Philadelphia with 22 representatives attending from New York, Philadelphia, Boston and Baltimore. Although Esther Mintz's name does not appear on the list of representatives in our possession, it is only a partial list, and in any case, as noted above, it is known that she was active in the party before its official founding.

Although the convention devoted most of its deliberations to the issues of Zionism and socialism, its participants focused most of their energy on a question that had been uppermost on the agenda of the Zionist movement since the Sixth Zionist Congress: Zion (Palestine) or (any) territory.[22] The discussion on this question was lengthy and heated. An overwhelming majority supported the idea of a territory, namely, the establishment of a Jewish state in a territory other than Palestine, while only a small minority (about 18 percent) were in favor of founding the Jewish state in Palestine.[23] In order to avert a split, a compromise resolution was adopted, which allowed the members and the local societies freedom of choice between the two views.[24] Nevertheless, early in the summer of 1905, a new group of Poalei Zion was organized, which attempted to set up a new Society in support of Palestine.[25] This Society was the nucleus for a renewed organization, which served as the basis for the Jewish Socialist Labor Party Poalei Zion in America, and among its founders, the name of Esther Mintz stood out.[26] After the Seventh Zionist Congress (27 July – 2 August 1905), which ended with the absolute victory of those favoring Palestine, a process of a split between the two views began. And on 23–26 December 1905 a convention of the Poalei Zion societies supporting Palestine took place in Baltimore (Maryland). In the historiography of Poalei Zion, this convention is noted as the founding convention of the party, and Esther Mintz was one of the 22 participants.[27]

Zionism, Hebrew and Palestine

The only surviving document from the first Poalei Zion convention is a copy of the party program without any mention of the name of its author.[28] We know that one of those attending the conference — A. S. Waldstein — played a major role in its formulation, but later memoirs describe it as a collective composition by several authors.[29] It is reasonable to assume, in light of her prominence in ideological thinking in the coming years, that Esther Mintz played an active role in the discussions that preceded the formulation of the program, but this is merely a hypothesis.

This first ideological platform of Poalei Zion was characterized by a vague, not clearly defined socialist ideology, which left room for every socialist stream, and made no effort to formulate a new, coherent doctrine; and by a Palestine-oriented Zionism, focused on work for *Eretz Yisrael*.[30] Controversies arose in relation to both of these points, but the second was the most important of the two, for it formed the basis for the reorganization of the Poalei Zion party in America at the end of 1905. Esther Mintz, who was clearly in favor of the Palestine option, knew Hebrew well and was very interested in activity related to Palestine.

The first expression of Mintz's interest occurred at the second party convention of Poalei Zion in America (Boston, 15–18 December 1906), when she criticized the party weekly *Der idisher kemfer*. She explicitly leveled her criticism at the preponderance of literary writings in the paper, as opposed to theoretical articles that she believed ought to appear in it. She was, in fact, implicitly inveighing against the political views of its editor, Kalman Marmor, which were not consonant with her own. Marmor, she asserted, was one of the supporters of the ideology of the Minsk Poalei Zion group, and hence had no interest in activity in Palestine.[31] Since Poalei Zion of Minsk adhered to the territorialist view, Esther Mintz was obviously directing the barbs of her criticism at what she saw as the insufficient emphasis on the movement's activity in Palestine. She later expressed this view even more strongly on a variety of occasions.

The question of the national language of the Jewish people, which had engaged Poalei Zion of America since its inception, was directly linked to the debate about what was defined as "work for *Eretz Yisrael*" versus what was known as "work for the present," namely, activity in the diaspora.[32] The first debate on this question was also conducted at the second party convention. Esther Mintz, as one might expect, was firmly in favor of Hebrew, but the basis of her argument is an interesting one.

The advocates of Yiddish usually argued that since Hebrew was the language of the distant future (namely the language of Palestine), and not the language of the present, in the diaspora, Yiddish should be preferred.[33] This claim generally served those in favor of "work for the present," so it is interesting that Esther Mintz not only used it as a basis for her own arguments, but actually adopted the terminology taken from the concepts of Simon Dubnow and the Bund, which based Jewish nationalism on Yiddish culture. Explaining her support for Hebrew, she argued that "The Hebrew language belongs to our existence. Our identity is based on our culture. If we want to educate a new generation, this endeavor must be grounded on the foundations of our culture."[34] In other words, "our culture," according to Mintz, was Hebrew, not Yiddish, culture. This was not merely a rhetorical tactic, making sophisticated use of the adversary's own line of argument, but illustrates Esther's mastery of the intricacies of the debate between the rival sides on the issue of language and her understanding of the ideological elements it involved. This is also evinced by the notes she prepared in Hebrew for a lecture she gave on the subject, apparently a short time after the conference on languages held in Czernowitz on 30 August to 3 September 1908.[35] The starting point for her lecture was the resolution taken at that conference that Yiddish was a national language in countries with a compact Jewish population, and she reacted by stating that the decision aroused her "anger and compassion." She asserted that Yiddish was not "the language of the past and the present, and has no place in the future, because the Hebrew language is the national language." To substantiate this claim, she surveyed — in a manner that corresponded to Dubnow's view — the history of Jewish languages, and argued that for generations the Jewish people had had many languages that had been forgotten. Among these was Arabic, which had been the language of both the people and scholars, but which nonetheless had been forgotten. This was all the more true of Yiddish, "which by its very nature is the language of the market and of the masses, but not the language of the people. And the people despise it and leave it whenever they have the opportunity to rid themselves of it."[36]

While these words are both trenchant and outspoken, they are also inaccurate. They overlook the fact that the Czernowitz conference did not decide that Yiddish was *the* national language of the Jewish people, but merely that it was *a* national language, that is, not the sole language. Although this may be merely a case of misinformation or misunderstanding, nonetheless, in light of the severity of other statements recorded in the same document and her method of argumentation in later letters (which will be discussed later) and particularly in view of the resistance her firm stance aroused, it is probable that Esther Mintz's extreme tone was deliberate.

Although Poalei Zion in America declared in 1905 that they regarded Hebrew as the national language of the Jewish people,[37] in December 1906 there was already a majority within the movement that favored Yiddish.[38] Moreover, the support for Yiddish was closely aligned with the view of Poalei

Zion parties elsewhere in the diaspora, which held that only in Palestine should any action be taken to make Hebrew the sole language, while in the diaspora every effort should be made to save the Jewish people from the danger of cultural assimilation, and hence there should be no attempt to change the language they were familiar with.[39] To Esther Mintz, the question of language was a fundamental issue *par excellence* and an indivisible part of her Zionist outlook. But for the purposes of argument, she knew how to separate the two issues.

She expressed her Zionist views, in particular her strong desire to emigrate to Palestine, in a series of letters to Kalman Marmor, who in the meantime had resigned as editor of the *Idisher kemfer* and in 1908 was visiting Palestine. Some of her letters were written in Hebrew in the margins of Yiddish letters written to him by her future husband Dov Ber Aberson, and in these she spoke of her yearning to emigrate to Palestine: "Would you have an offer for me too? Every offer that would lead me to *Eretz Yisrael* I would accept happily. My desire is not only to dream of returning to Zion but actually to do something for our great goal."[40] The detailed reply Marmor sent her, in which he provided her with concrete information about job opportunities in Palestine, indicates that her intentions were indeed serious. He also emphasized that her knowledge of Hebrew would be of great help to her in obtaining a teaching position.[41]

Evidently, Esther Mintz and Dov Ber Aberson did look for a place in which to settle, and considered various possibilities — including some in the American midwest. As far as they were concerned, Palestine was not only the realization of the Zionist dream but also a practical option that they considered but never fulfilled because there were no employment opportunities there for Aberson.

At the Head of the Central Committee

In the writings of party members — both those of a semi-scholarly nature based, at least partially, on documentation, as well as those in the form of personal memoirs — Mintz-Aberson is mentioned as the assistant to the party secretary, Chaim Feinman, for a short period during 1908.[42] However, the sources at my disposal indicate that for a certain period she held the title of party secretary herself.[43] In any event, in 1907–1908 she was a dominant figure in the administrative top echelon of Poalei Zion in America.

From 1907, Poalei Zion in America was on the verge of a crisis, from which it emerged only on the eve of the First World War. Some local societies closed down while others were seriously weakened. The leadership of the party was also torn by friction and dissension. Although as far as we know, Esther Mintz held an official office only in 1908, the party documentation beginning at the end of 1907 shows that she was constantly involved and made her mark on party activities. In December 1907 a circular in her handwriting was distributed to the party members dealing with ways to overcome the organizational difficulties of the party. It asserted that the major focus should be on the activity of the local societies, whose meetings should contribute to the members, providing them with "spiritual nourishment" or some practical benefit. Her suggestion was to prepare lists of lecturers who could attract large audiences and to make use of the party administration to obtain their services. Even when Poalei Zion was at its lowest ebb, Esther Mintz did not forget the strike fund, which she called "our weapon when the time comes."[44] Moreover, the major part of the circular was devoted to the *Idisher kemfer*.

From the publication of its first issue, in March 1906, the weekly *Idisher kemfer* was the pride and joy of Poalei Zion in America, and they invested great efforts to keep it going. Although it presented the positions of the party on various issues on its Jewish as well as its general agenda, the newspaper was not a party mouthpiece. Along with political affairs, it also included articles on literature and philosophy as well as polemics, of a very high standard, written by intellectuals, party members and people from outside the party. The weekly was also regularly discussed at the party conventions. As we have seen, Mintz-Aberson was critical of the weekly, a view that reflected her perception of its function and of the difficulties it faced.

Apart from the criticism she voiced at the second party convention, on other occasions she also criticized the weekly for failing to target both the popular and the more educated reader, and for lacking a clear editorial line. She also made detailed comments about the literary articles that had been published thus far, as well as about the technical editing of the weekly.[45] It is no wonder, then, that the circular she sent to the members soon after the second party convention, reflects a sober view of the weekly's situation and a despairing call to them to take action to ensure its continued existence. "My hands tremble as I write this," she wrote, but we must "muster our strength to save the weekly."[46] In fact, by January 1908, the *Kemfer* had ceased to appear and was published again only for a brief period from March 1910 to May 1911. (The *Kemfer*'s publication was renewed in April 1916 until August 1920, and again from 1932 onwards).

The central place of the paper in the life of Poalei Zion in America, in particular as Esther Mintz saw it, was reflected in another circular she distributed to the members after the party council met in January 1908, this time under the signature: Esther Mintz, Secretary.[47] More than half of the circular, which was longer than usual, was devoted to the question of the *Idisher kemfer* and the discussion that had taken place in regard to the paper. Other than the informative part, which was very detailed, the circular described the dismal feelings of the participants, who realized that the weekly was closing down and — at least for the time being — would have no replacement. Indeed, the situation of Poalei Zion in America in the months in question was extremely adverse. The party vitally needed Esther Mintz's activity, her energy, strength, and most of all, her broad knowledge, and she in turn was aware of the contribution she could make.[48]

In the first half of 1908, Dov Ber Aberson moved to Cleveland, where he had obtained a position as editor of the daily *Di teglekhe yidishe prese*.[49] Esther's public commitment prevented her from even visiting him, and early in June she wrote that she very much wanted to come to him, at least for a visit, but the grave situation of the Central Committee prevented her from doing so.[50] And two months later she wrote: "If I leave now the Central Committee much of our achievements will be ruined"; but, she added: "for the sake of your well-being I am ready to come to you now."[51]

At that time, *Di teglekhe yidishe prese* found itself in financial difficulties, and Aberson once again had to look for a job. Esther tried to find a job for him in New York as editor of a paper that was about to be established, but nothing came of it.[52] From these and other letters, we can see her commitment to her duties in the Central Committee, but at the same time she had a commitment to her spouse. It is interesting to note that she did not see any tension between the two commitments and regarded it as only natural that she should give up her public career for her man's sake. This attitude shows that Esther did not devote any particular attention to the question of women's status and self-fulfillment Even though she was a talented, wise and educated woman, with a comprehensive national world view and political aspirations, she seemed not be concerned with questions regarding the status of women. She maneuvered instinctively between her roles as wife and mother and her political ambitions, without even paying attention to the limited possibilities that Jewish society in America presented to women who wanted to participate in public life. She tried naively to place herself at the center of the public arena and to take some part in its leading ranks. But, as I will show in the following, these efforts were doomed to fail.

Early in 1909, Esther Mintz and Dov Aberson got married. At the end of that year, after a lecture tour for the party on the West coast, Aberson found a job in Chicago and settled there.[53] In 1910, after the birth of her son, Esther Mintz-Aberson joined her husband.

In the Chicago Poalei Zion Society

Although the couple's move to Chicago was dictated by Aberson's need to find employment, it very soon provided them both with opportunities for political activity, Esther in particular.

In October 1909, Poalei Zion in America merged with the Socialist Territorialist Party of America and with the former members of the Sejmist

Party led by Chaim Zhitlowsky. Following the merger, a new party program was formulated, which in the world-view of Poalei Zion no longer gave work for *Eretz Yisrael* absolute priority over work for the present. The merger was implemented after detailed ideological discussions that lasted about a year. In its wake, the great and important project of national-radical schools in Yiddish was established.

As Esther Mintz was among the extremists in the camp of Hebrew supporters, it is not surprising that she was opposed to Poalei Zion's new program in America. On 4 August 1911, a few months after she had joined her husband, a branch of Poalei Zion was founded in Chicago.[54] The new Society had 18 members, and Esther Mintz-Aberson became its secretary.[55] Its first act was to formulate a declaration of principles that decried the new party program and was in fact a kind of independent program of the Chicago branch. The declaration emphasized three principles: (1) that Palestine was the Jewish homeland; (2) that Hebrew was the national language; and (3) that the Society's activities would be conducted according to progressive and socialist principles.[56]

The major points of contention between the platform formulated by the Chicago branch and the party program centered on two fundamental topics. The first was the definition of the Jewish homeland, which the 1909 program defined as Palestine and the neighboring countries — a compromise formulation to placate the territorialists under Nachman Syrkin's leadership. The second was the declaration in the 1909 program that Yiddish was one of the two national languages of the Jewish people — a change necessitated by the inclusion of "work for the present" in the party program. In other words, the Chicago branch's declaration of principles took exception to the elimination of the clear Palestine-oriented line of Poalei Zion's ideological platform.

Mintz-Aberson reported to the Central Committee about the declaration of principles, but without noting who had formulated it. However, it seems reasonable to assume that she was at least a party to its formulation since its contents were consistent with her views, and she not only presented the declaration to the Central Committee in New York, but also justified it in her arguments with the committee, in a series of curt, contentious letters.

The declaration of the Chicago Society angered members of the Central Committee, and Mintz-Aberson's reply (in Yiddish) was somewhat derisive: "Our members were amazed at your naivete. You apparently fail to understand the significance of our principles. Consequently, our society has decided not to judge you harshly." She continued:

> We have decided on three principles which are binding on anyone who wishes to join our society. The Chicago program [the program adopted

by Poalei Zion in October 1909] as well as some additional errors by our party have created confusion within the ranks. Many members have left our camp and others have remained in it only because they are unable to decide which organization to join. *The contradictions between Zionism and territorialism, between Palestine and the diaspora are blurred in their minds, and Palestine has become a meaningless name. We have seen fit to emphasize that Palestine is our homeland, and all others are nothing but colonies.*[57]

She added that in the new Society they had founded there was no place for those who believed that the major effort should be concentrated on work in the diaspora and that Palestine had the same status as that of any other country. The Society was also opposed to those adhering to various types of autonomist-culturist views. In another letter, she clarified these points: "The major focus of our work is Palestine, and all of our work in the diaspora will be carried out in light of the Palestinian point of departure."[58] And most importantly, the Society wanted to avoid becoming a "fifth wheel of the Socialist Party's wagon," and it therefore declared its support for progressive socialist principles.[59]

Although this formulation is quite vague, it obviously challenges the decision taken by Poalei Zion in America in 1905 to refrain from formulating any socialist doctrine of its own. Chicago was home to the center of the Socialist Party of America. The Jewish Socialist Federation was founded there in November 1912, and as an ethnic section of the Socialist Party also established its center there.[60] We can assume, then, that the last clause in the declaration of principles reflected some influence by the Socialist Party.

Esther Mintz-Aberson served as secretary of the new Society, almost continuously, until the end of 1915.[61] During those years, the Society knew many ups and downs, and Mintz-Aberson carried out her activity with great dedication, trying at the same time to exert influence on the national level as well.

On 8–12 October 1911, Poalei Zion of America held its sixth convention in Detroit. One of the convention's main objectives was to strengthen and regulate the organizational apparatus of the party.[62] Esther, who was also a delegate to the convention, submitted proposals to the agenda. In addition to detailed organizational proposals, she incisively analyzed the problem of how the party should disseminate information after the closure of its weekly, *Der idisher kemfer*, in May 1911. She suggested the publication of a monthly bulletin, and submitted financial calculations to persuade the delegates that her idea was practical.[63]

At the beginning of 1912 Esther tried to persuade the Central Committee to expand its activity in Palestine, in particular to take steps to establish an office there that could revitalize Poalei Zion's activity.[64] On 17 December 1915 *Unser lebn* (Our Life), a radical national weekly, began to appear in Chicago. Its publisher was the D. Aberson Company, its editor Dov Aberson and its manager, Esther Aberson. Although the name Poalei Zion did not appear on the paper's masthead, it was the newspaper of the Poalei Zion societies in Chicago.[65] Aberson wrote many articles in the paper, but was unable to make a living out of this work, and the family had to move again.

From the Center of the Public Arena to Its Sidelines

From the end of 1914, Aberson was unemployed and Esther supported the family with the salary she received as a part-time teacher. During 1915, she tried to find work for him in New York,[66] and they returned to that city in 1917. Aberson immediately found his place within the top ranks of Poalei Zion, and at the eleventh party convention (24–29 December 1918) he was elected to the Central Committee.[67] His wife, Esther, on the other hand, was silent. From the time she returned to New York, she totally abandoned the political arena. In the 1920s, she ran a family guest house,[68] but her yearning for public activity never diminished, expressing such desires in letters she wrote at the time.[69]

She joined the Pioneer Women's organization after its foundation and for many long years she was active on the local level as branch secretary.[70] From letters she wrote during the 1920s it is evident that she did not lose interest in public life.[71] We may assume that she avoided participating in the Pioneer Women on a national level, because this kind of activity did not attract her and she yearned to be active within the Poalei Zion Party.

In the mid-1930s, Mintz-Aberson tried to obtain a job as principal in one of the *Yidishe folks shuln* that Poalei Zion founded in 1910. Teaching in such a school, and certainly managing it, would have provided her not only with a livelihood but also with the kind of ideological activity that was well suited to her character and talents. However, she did not succeed in obtaining a position, as there was no vacancy, and the entire school system was in disarray.[72] This was her last attempt at becoming part of any Poalei Zion activity.

The documentary material at my disposal does not relate to Esther's disappearance from the public scene. The articles written in her memory after her death in the party newspapers implied that the problems and burdens of everyday life led her to discontinue her political activity.[73] Esther was indeed faced with a series of vexing personal problems which undoubtedly stood in the way of her public activity. The most grievous was the death of Dov Aberson in 1929, which left her as the family's breadwinner.[74] However, not only had she left the public stage before Aberson's death, but even when he was alive, she had had to support the family with her earnings for long periods. It is difficult to assume that Esther retired of her own free will. Her activities, as we have seen, were intensive and comprehensive even when she had already become a wife and mother. Her enthusiasm and devotion did not weaken, and her ideological drive did not fade. Moreover, as her letters reveal, she had a high esteem for her own contribution and importance to the party. She was also aware of her talents, including her writing ability, which was demonstrated only rarely in published articles.[75]

It is interesting to note that Esther Mintz-Aberson's public career can be divided into two clearly distinct chapters. The first was the very early period of Poalei Zion in America, when it was at its lowest ebb. At the time, the young party had a problem finding a secretary for its Central Committee, and Esther was chosen to fill the position jointly with Chaim Fineman. The second was at a time when Poalei Zion in America was very active, but Esther was then in Chicago. Although Chicago was the center of American socialist organizations, and the Poalei Zion branches in the city were active and at times even militant, it was too far away from the Central Committee in New York and was regarded as a periphery.

Esther Mintz-Aberson succeeded in demonstrating her abilities and her devotion only at the margins of Poalei Zion's activity. When she returned to New York, at a time of prosperity for the party, no leadership position was available for her. This situation was apparently neither accidental nor personal. I would argue that the fact that Esther Mintz-Aberson's career moved along a narrow and restricted path was not of her own choosing. Rather, it reflected the status of women in Jewish public life in America in general and the specific view of Poalei Zion in particular.

To bolster this argument, and to gain a better understanding of Poalei Zion's attitude towards the inclusion of women in public life, it would be desirable to look at the cases of other women. Unfortunately, however, there do not appear to have been any other women who tried to make their way directly into the top ranks of Poalei Zion, either in the branches or in the Central Committee. Although women did aspire to take part in the activity, make their contribution to it and exert their influence, they tried to work indirectly, not within the party apparatus as Esther Mintz had done, but through separate women's organizations, affiliated either organizationally or ideologically with Poalei Zion.

I shall now discuss how these women's organizations were organized, who their leaders were, and in particular, how they were received by Poalei Zion. My major claim is that Poalei Zion's attitude to the women's desire to found national organizations strengthens a premise based on Esther Mintz-Aberson's career, namely, that Poalei Zion believed women belonged to the fringes of public life, not at its center. But dialectically, those same women who did not rebel against this attitude or tried to change it and were active on the fringes of public life, making no attempt to find their place at the center, were the very ones who succeeded in engaging in public activity in the long term, as well as in establishing frameworks that would later become a platform for their integration into the general public arena.

Women's Organizations and Their Reception by Poalei Zion

In 1918, women first attempted to achieve recognition as activists with equal rights in an organization affiliated with Poalei Zion in America. This was in the framework of the Poalei Zion fraternal order, the Idish natsyonaler arbeter farband, founded in 1910 by leaders of Poalei Zion to provide its members with medical insurance and mutual aid, as well as to promote education and culture in the spirit of Poalei Zion.[76] However, only men were admitted into the ranks of the Farband. The question of women's membership in the organization was brought up for discussion only at its fifth convention, held in Rochester on 19–23 June 1918.[77] Although the subject was apparently discussed at length, this issue was not even mentioned in the convention's report printed in the *Idisher Kemfer*, and the resolution adopted at the convention to found special clubs for women was not included in the partial list of resolutions published in it.[78] All the information about the discussion and the resolutions adopted is summed up in the memoirs of the Farband's founders.[79] These memoirs make no mention of who raised the issue of women's status in the organization, but Meir Brown, who headed the Farband for a long period, stresses that the women wished to become members of the Farband branches themselves, and were opposed to the formation of separate branches for them.[80] Nonetheless, from 1918, a number of auxiliary clubs for women were founded, whose activities mainly focused on helping Yiddish schools, providing educational programs for their members and for Jewish women in general, and assisting in the establishment of health facilities in Palestine, including a convalescent home on the Carmel named in memory of Ber Borochov, the ideological leader of Poalei Zion in Russia.[81]

But these women's clubs were short-lived, and by the 1930s, women were welcomed as members into the Farband branches.[82] As a result of this change, women's contribution to the organization was acknowledged, but this did not lead to the recognition of any equality between the sexes. On the contrary, the women's devotion to the organization was regarded as a "feminine" trait,[83] and their acceptance as full members was the result of practical considerations. Meir Brown explains that when the Pioneer Women organization was founded in 1926, many members of the Farband's women's clubs joined it, causing a decline in those clubs and even some concern that the ranks of Farband would dwindle.[84] Moreover, as the women's clubs began to decline, the heads of

Farband realized how important the women's contribution to the organization had been, and they started admitting women into its branches as rank-and-file members, although not in any official positions.[85]

The Pioneer Women organization was, unlike the Farband women's clubs, a platform for public involvement and political leadership, and some of its founders were impressive women. However, the process of its establishment in the 1920s, and in particular its reception by Poalei Zion, substantiate, and even underscore, the picture that has emerged so far concerning Poalei Zion's attitude towards equality between the genders. Unlike the situation in the Farband, membership in Poalei Zion was open to both genders, and there were quite a few women members on the lists of the branches. But nothing is known about women who held positions in these branches, and certainly not on the national level. Thus, although the initiative for the founding of Pioneer Women came from women in Poalei Zion in America, the driving force behind this initiative came from Palestine, where an organization of women workers already existed.

The birth of Pioneer Women in 1924 came about purely by chance. Rachel Yanait, one of the founders of Ha-Shomer and a leader of the women workers' movement in Palestine, had appealed to Sophie Udin, the wife of Pinhas Gingold, one of the heads of Poalei Zion in America, to help her raise $500 to dig a well for a girls' agricultural school in Talpiot near Jerusalem.[86] Udin enlisted the help of some other friends, and in a short time they succeeded in raising the required sum of money. In the wake of this success, the women in this group decided to found an independent women's organization, which would be a part of the Poalei Zion party in America and act under the aegis of Mo'etzet ha-Po'alot, the organization of women workers in *Eretz Yisrael*.[87]

The founding group comprised seven members: Leah Brown, Chaya Ehernreich, Rachel Segal, Luba Horowitz, Eva Berg, Nina Zuckerman and Sophie Udin, all wives of party members, five of them wives of oldtimers in the top ranks of the party — Meir Brown, Hirsch Ehernreich, Shmuel Segal, Baruch Zuckerman and Pinhas Gingold (Udin's husband).[88] In the first stage, the group of seven set up a women's club, *Froyen klub far Erets Yisroel* (Women's Club for Palestine), which was active in New York, under the leadership of Sophie Udin.[89] But within a few months, at the fifteenth convention of the Poalei Zion Party (New York, 27–31 December 1924), Udin raised the question of the establishment of a national women's organization, affiliated to Poalei Zion in America.[90]

The convention's report states that the issue evoked a "lengthy and interesting debate." The participants were divided in their opinions. Those in favor argued that the establishment of such an organization would be beneficial to Poalei Zion, since a women's organization (called in the report *fareynen* [societies] or *klubn* [clubs]) would attract hundreds of members to

Poalei Zion who could not be active in the party but would be connected to it and take part in its work for Palestine. Those opposed argued that if a network of women's organizations concentrating on work for Palestine were founded, membership in it would be regarded as more prestigious than membership in Poalei Zion. Their concern was that a more distinguished group of women would be set up, dealing only with Palestine-related matters, and this would adversely affect women who were already members of the party and were charged with carrying out much of its work. This new group might also have a damaging effect on the work of the party's branches. "We are a political party," the opponents argued, "and therefore we have no need to establish auxiliary organizations for *Eretz Yisrael.*"[91] They recommended instead that special branches be established in the framework of Poalei Zion for women only, which meant, of course, going back to the organizational pattern that had already been set in the Idish natsyonaler arbeter farband.

The controversy that arose at the Poalei Zion convention regarding a women's organization has interesting implications for the topic of this article. An independent organization, even if it is affiliated with another organization and even if the areas of its activity are peripheral, will generate an administration and a leadership. Consequently, it can serve as fertile soil for the emergence of a leadership that will subsequently bring about the organization's public involvement. Nonetheless, during the discussion at the convention this issue was not even hinted at. It would seem that the opposition to the establishment of a women's organization derived not so much from the concern about women organizing into a political force as from traditional views about the place of the woman in the home. However, all the arguments voiced in the discussion were instrumental. The advocates regarded a women's organization as a means of increasing Poalei Zion's influence; the opponents feared that the organization would deplete the party's strength. The issue of equality between the sexes in Poalei Zion in America was not even in the background of the discussion, and this was reflected in the following wording of the resolution:

> The committee affirms that the Central Committee will begin the work of establishing a women's organization, to be part of the Poalei Zion movement. Its chief aim will be to *enhance the position and life of the working woman in Eretz Yisrael.* The women's clubs will pay a Poalei Zion shekel, "trumah" [dues for "kapay" — the fiscal institute of the world confederation of Poalei Zion] and reduced party dues. The constitution of these clubs will be formulated by the party's Central Committee, in conjunction with the existing women's organizations.[92]

It is interesting that this decision does not refer to an independent women's organization, but makes it clear that the Central Committee will establish the women's organization, which will be part of the Poalei Zion party, and will also be involved in writing its constitution. Moreover, the organization's purpose, in the view of Poalei Zion, would be to assist the working woman in Palestine. The status of the working woman in America was not even up for discussion. It can be assumed, then, that the heads of Poalei Zion perceived Pioneer Women not merely as a possible means for expanding the party's ranks, but first and foremost as an organization that would engage in, and strengthen, the party's activity on behalf of Palestine. During the 1920s there were close ties between Poalei Zion of America and Ahdut ha-Avodah in Palestine, and this cooperation was expressed mainly in the United Hebrew Trades campaign for the Histadrut, from February 1924 for the next several years.[93] By the same token, Pioneer Women could also have been perceived as another channel for the activity carried out on behalf of Palestine, for the concrete purpose of helping *Mo'etzet ha-Po'alot*, or as its opponents put it, as "an auxiliary organization for *Eretz Yisrael*."

However, the founders of the organization wished to establish an organization that would be affiliated with Poalei Zion, but at the same time independent,[94] and a review of their aims sheds light on another facet of women's status within Poalei Zion in America. I assume that their desire to expand their initial response to the request made by the women of Palestine was an important factor in the organization's establishment. Probably, too, the growing number of women's organizations established in America had an impact on Jewish and Zionist society. But I believe there was another important element at work here, one that was manifested in a number of ways at the new organization's first convention.

The Pioneer Women and Its Founders

The first convention of the new women's organization, which already numbered nearly 900 members,[95] was held in New York on 29–31 October 1926. The organization's aims, as they were enunciated then, are of great interest. Leah Biskin, the organization's secretary, opened her keynote address by presenting its aims. She spoke at length about the organization's contribution to working women in Palestine, but also emphasized another aspect:

> We feel a pressing need to organize Jewish working women in America in order to raise their social and cultural level, to enable them to play an active role concerning Jewish social issues and in building *Eretz Yisrael* according to socialist principles ... for many long years, Jewish women, as an organized force, have, unfortunately, not been allowed to participate in the national liberation....[96]

The declaration of the organization's principles was worded in a similar vein. It was decided to name the organization Pyonerin — froyen organizatsye far di khalutzot in Erets Yisroel (Pioneers — Women's Organization for the Pioneers in Palestine). This was, then, a clear declaration of the organization's primary Zionist-Palestine orientation. But its aims were broader, and included the enhanced status of the working woman in Palestine, participation in building the national home according to cooperative principles, and so forth:

> The women's organization strives to improve the economic and cultural condition of the working Jewish woman here in America. To this end, the organization engages in a propaganda and educational effort centering on the social, national and cultural problems of the Jewish masses in general and of the Jewish woman in particular, and aspires to interest its members in Jewish and general social activity that is consistent with our principles.[97]

These declarations show that the establishment of the women's organization conformed with the overall objective of Poalei Zion, i.e., to expand and strengthen its Palestine-oriented work. But it is also abundantly clear that the founders of Pioneer Women had another, no less and perhaps even more important, objective in mind: the creation of a means by which women could be integrated into public life.

As I noted, the nucleus of the Pioneer Women's founders was composed of the wives of key figures in Poalei Zion. But the woman who was the living spirit and driving force of the organization, Sophie Udin, was not merely the wife of a Poalei Zion leader but an impressive personality in her own right, with public and professional achievements to her credit and a profound awareness of women's status. Udin was younger than Mintz-Aberson and, unlike her, had grown up and been educated in the United States.[98] After graduating from high school, she went on to study library science, which was one of the few professions open to women at the time, and worked in the New York public library thereafter.[99] She was already a member of Poalei Zion during her high school years in Pittsburgh, and in June 1918 became an active member, and later the national secretary of the Red Mogen Dovid of America, a short-lived women's organization founded to help the families of volunteers to the Jewish Legion in the First World War.[100] At the time, those men who joined the Legion and went to Palestine were regarded as having carried out the supreme Zionist act, the crowning glory of the activity of Poalei Zion in America. But this was an option available only to its male members.

Thus, Udin embarked on her public life not only in a woman's organization, but in one whose very raison d'être underscored the fact that it was men who played the key role, while the women were their helpers. Udin did find her own way to fulfill her Zionist beliefs. In 1921–22 she lived in

Palestine, where she worked at the Jerusalem library.[101] But her own experience probably taught her early on that women could only make their way into public life if special tracks were created for them, where they could work alongside the activists at the center, or perhaps on the sidelines as well. Udin headed the founding group of the new organization until March 1925, when she again left for Palestine to become the chief librarian in the Jerusalem library, which in the meantime had become the library of the Hebrew University.[102] She was replaced as the organization's leader by Sarah Feder, who had joined the Pioneer Women upon its establishment. Feder was also younger than Mintz-Aberson and, like Udin, had grown up and been educated in America. While still at school in Milwaukee, she had been a member of the local Poalei Zion branch, which was very active.[103] She studied education at Columbia University, and sociology at the University of Missouri, and then received her Ph.D. at the University of Chicago. At the same time, she became interested in the suffragette movement.[104]

These two women, who were also successful in their professions — Feder as a lecturer and researcher, and Udin as a founder of the Zionist archives in New York and later of the Israel State Archives — differed from Mintz-Aberson in two, possibly interconnected respects. Although like her, they had been born in Eastern Europe and lived in the East European immigrant society in America, they had come to America as children, received their schooling there and apparently were far more imbued with the attitudes of American Jewish society, including ideas about the place of women. Unlike Esther Mintz-Aberson, who tried by dint of her talents and knowledge to act within the male establishment, these two younger women apparently understood the special status of women in public life, and acted accordingly.

In a brief article that Udin published on the thirtieth anniversary of Poalei Zion in America, she explained why it had been necessary to establish a separate organization for the women of Poalei Zion: "The Jewish woman, in her separate organization, took an example from the American life she saw around her."[105] Indeed, in mid-nineteenth century America, women began to organize in order to engage in public activity, and towards the end of the century, Jewish women began adopting the same pattern.[106] The Jewish women's clubs were generally involved in matters regarded as "feminine," such as education and child care, and when the mass immigration from Eastern Europe began, they started providing philanthropic aid to the immigrants.[107] In 1893, the first national women's organization was founded in America — the National Council of Jewish Women.[108] Its aims were to further Jewish studies in addition to providing philanthropic aid particularly in education, as well as to constitute a forum for exchange of views by Jewish women.[109] In 1912, the largest, most important Jewish women's organization in the United States, Hadassah, was founded, and by the 1940s it had already become a political power base for its leaders.[110] And in 1913, the women of the Reform movement founded a national organization of their own.[111] This trend, of women organizing for public activity in separate frameworks, was widespread both in American society in general and in the Jewish community. Udin, in the article I mentioned above, explicitly cites the influence of Hadassah on Pioneer Women. She also adds that: "The Jewish woman had ... to learn ... how a woman's organization could contribute to a woman's life."[112]

Both Feder, who lectured at the University of Missouri on issues relating to the status of women,[113] and Udin were clearly aware of the situation of Jewish women in America. This consciousness led them to channel their public activity in a completely different way to that of Esther Mintz-Aberson. They were both highly educated (Udin completed her graduate studies at Columbia)[114] and well acquainted with American Jewish society, and acted accordingly. They understood that since the existing social conventions made it impossible for a woman to make her way up the public ladder alongside men, she had to create channels of her own. They both built personal careers for themselves, which enhanced their public status. They took steps to organize women in order to involve them in public life, and perhaps also because they realized that this would provide them with a power base in the future.

This understanding was reflected in the mode of action they chose, in the decisions of the new organization's convention, as well as in Udin's article as cited above. But, in an inverted manner, it was also reflected in Esther Mintz-Aberson's career, which showed that a woman with no external power base had no chance of surviving in the political system of Poalei Zion in America, or perhaps in any sector of Jewish public life there.

Conclusion

In her book, *Gender and the Politics of History*, Joan Wallach Scott claims that gender is the main indicator of the ratio of forces.[115] On the basis of that claim, Paula Hyman argues that because anti-Semites at the turn of the century described the Jew as physically weak, using feminine images for that purpose, "Jewish men, first in the countries of western and central Europe and later in America, constructed a modern Jewish identity that devalued women, and regarded them as the Other within the Jewish community."[116]

However, the cases I have discussed here seem to suggest that Poalei Zion in America did not regard women as the "other." On the contrary, the party regarded them as an indivisible part of public life, but one with a distinct role of its own. They accepted women as members in the branches, but apart from Esther Mintz-Aberson, there is no mention in this period of any other woman who served as a branch secretary, certainly not as a member of the Central Committee. Poalei Zion believed women filled a paramount function in the family, as the ones who educated the children and could influence family members to join the party. As in the family, women fulfilled an important role in Poalei Zion, but only in "feminine" matters — assisting the families of volunteers to the Jewish Legion, helping working women in Palestine, promoting education, and similar activities.[117]

Esther Mintz-Aberson's actions did not conform with this concept; rather, they were underpinned by her ideological-political views. But in Poalei Zion in America, and in the American Jewish immigrant society too, this realm was perceived as an exclusively male province. Mintz-Aberson was 23 when she came to America, and she began her political activity immediately. She may have known about the activity of women in the ranks of the Bund, who perhaps served as her role models; and more likely yet, she may have assumed that the equal participation of women was an intrinsic element in the revolutionary ethos of the founders of Poalei Zion in America, to which she belonged. However, Poalei Zion in America did not adopt a revolutionary socialist ideology, but proclaimed a program oriented towards the center of the Jewish immigrant society. Consequently, its attitude towards the woman's place in the public arena was also shaped by the paramount importance attributed to family values in Jewish life, and by the role assigned to women in that society.

This attitude was clearly exemplified in Esther Mintz-Aberson's career. Although she did occupy some important positions, she was only able to do so when the party was at a low ebb or when she was active on its fringes — the geographical-peripheral fringes, when she was in Chicago, or the developmental fringes, when the party was faltering. However, Mintz-Aberson did not seem to be concerned with the issue of women's status. She acted naturally, perhaps one could say naively, according to her own world-view. And this kind of activity was doomed to failure.

The founders of Pioneer Women, on the other hand, were at least a decade younger than Mintz-Aberson. They were educated in America and had absorbed the values of American Jewish society. They had also acquired higher education and had a profound understanding of issues pertaining to women's status and place in public life. As a result, they — unlike Esther Mintz-Aberson — realized that women could not participate directly in general public activity and that they had to create their own channels of activity, which would conform with society's perception of women's place in public life. Moreover, they also understood that the creation of such female channels on the fringes of public activity would have a twofold advantage: not only would those channels be accepted by the general "male" sphere of activity and might also pave the way for the acceptance of women as full, influential partners, but at the same time they would prepare women to take their place in that sphere and to fill key positions in it. In other words, they understood that activity on the fringes could lead to the center, while any attempt at acting directly at the center would undermine the possibility of any women's activity in the first place.

It is interesting, then, to note that despite Esther Mintz-Aberson's many talents, her leadership qualities and her devotion in the early years of Poalei Zion in America, the members of her party did not remember her public service as her most important accomplishment. On 1 July 1955, the news of her death was published in the *Idisher kemfer*. "Who among the founders of Poalei Zion does not remember the name of Esther Mintz, the first secretary of the party?" it asked, and continued:

> In those days she was the only or one of the very few women members that fought for the cause of Poalei Zion in America ... *when khaver Aberson, as a theoretician, was preoccupied with propaganda and debates, Esther Aberson stood on an additional front, to earn the family livelihood.*[118]

The author of this news item indeed remembered that Esther had been the party's secretary, although she was wrong in stating that she had been the first secretary. But the major emphasis in these few lines was not on her public work, but rather on her role as a wife and mother. Thus, in the memory of Poalei Zion in America Esther Mintz Aberson was engraved as a woman who in the distant past had tried to become a leader, but whose most real important contribution to the party had been as the wife of one of the male leaders.

NOTES

*   I should like to thank Mrs. Leah Aberson-Harpaz of New York, for placing at my disposal her parents' letters and other documents, and to Professor Deborah Bernstein of Haifa University for her valuable comments. This essay was first published in Hebrew in *Iyunim Bitkumat Israel*, Vol. 10 (2000), pp. 207–33.

1   See Rachel Rojanski, *Bein ideologiyah le-etos: Po'alei Tziyon be-Amerikah, 1905–1931* (Between Ideology and Ethos: "Poalei Zion" in America 1905–1931) (Sde Boker, forthcoming). On Women in the Bund in Eastern Europe and later in America, see Norma Fain Pratt, "Transition in Judaism: The Jewish American Woman through the 1930s," *American Quarterly*, Vol. 30, No. 5 (1978), pp. 688–9.

2   See L. Shpizman, "Etapn in di geshikhte fun der tsyonistisher arbeter bavegung in di fareynikte shtatn," in *Geshikhte fun der tsyonistisher arbeter bavegung in tsofn Amerike* (New York, 1955), p. 111; Meir Brown, "Tsu der entshtehung fun poaley tsyon in Amerike," in *Yubiley bukh tsu der fayerung fun tsvantsig yor poaley tsyonism in Amerike* (Philadelphia, 1925), p. 12; Baruch Zuckerman,"Al shnei rishonim be-Amerikah" (About Two of the Founders in America), *Davar*, 21 November 1956. Shpizman and Brown do not mention Glazer's first name, and Zuckerman does not mention her at all.

3   Mendl Zinger, *Be-reshit ha-tziyonut ha-sotzialistit*, (At the beginning of Socialist Zionism) (Haifa, n.d.), p. 188; Shpizman, *Geshikhte* p. 136.

4   Shpizman, *Geshikhte*, p. 136. Pevzner left America for Palestine, but kept close contacts with Poalei Zion in America.

5   See "Overcome in Address," *The Washington Post*, 29 March 1909.

6   On Shoshana Bukhmil, see Shpizman, *Geshikhte*, pp. 230–2.

7   See Golda Meir, *My Life* (London, 1975), p. 45; Memoirs of Louis Perchunok, the Secretary of the Poalei Zion Society in Milwaukee, manuscript in the American Jewish Archives, Cincinnati Ohio, Microfilm no. 1616.

8   Shpizman , *Geshikhte*, p. 137.

9   Interview with her daughter, Leah Aberson-Harpaz, New York, 1996, and an interview with Nomi Zuckerman, the daughter of Baruch Zuckerman, Jerusalem, 1998.

10 With the exception of some inaccurate information in Shpizman's book, she is not mentioned in the literature on Poalei Zion.

11 Paula E. Hyman, *Gender and Assimilation in Modern Jewish History: The Role and Representation of Women* (Seattle and London, 1995) , p. 112.

12 Ibid., p. 114. On the kosher meat boycott, see idem, "Immigrant Women and Consumer Protest: The New York City Kosher Meat Boycott of 1902," *American Jewish History*, Vol. 70, No. 1 (September 1980), pp. 91–105.

13 Joyce Antler, *The Journey Home: Jewish Women and the American Century* (New York, 1997).

14 Rey Malus, "Tsu vos darfn froyen shtimrekht," *Di tsayt*, 2 November 1920. See also articles published during October. Due to financial cuts the women's section was canceled. On *Di tsayt* see Rachel Rojanski, "The Rise and Fall of *Di tsayt*: The Fate of an Encounter Between Culture and Politics," *Jewish History*, Vol. 14, No. 1 (2000), pp. 83–107.

15 "Ha-haverah Golda Meir al ha-pe'ulah be-Amerikah, hartza'ot ha-ptihah be-mo'etzet ha-po'alot" (Comrade Golda Meir on the Activity in America, Opening Speeches), *Yediot Kapai shel Po'alei Eretz Yisrael*, 12 November 1929.

16 For a different reading, see Nick Mandelkeren, "The Story of the 'Pioneer Women'," *The Pioneer Woman*, September 1980, pp. 2–20; November 1980, pp. 6–8; January–February 1981, pp. 13–16; March–April 1981 pp. 6–9; Mark A. Raider , "Pioneer Women," in Paula E. Hyman and Deborah Dash Moore (eds.), *Jewish Women in America* (New York and London, 1997), pp. 1017–77.

17 According to an application for an American passport in 1949 (no day or month given), which is in the possession of her daughter Leah Aberson-Harpaz, Long Island, New York.

18 Interview with Leah Aberson-Harpaz, New York, 27 April 1996.

19 Application for American passport. Nearly all the documentation at my disposal relates to Mintz-Aberson's life in America. The main source of information about her life prior to her emigration is her daughter, and she knows very little about that period.

20 On Esther's early activity see Shpizman, *Geshikhte*, p. 124. On the early days of the Jewish labor movement in Eastern Europe, see Moshe Mishkinsky, *Reshit tnu'at ha-po'alim ha-yehudit be-Rusiya: Megamot yesod* (The Beginning of the Jewish Labor Movement in Russia: Basic Trends) (Tel Aviv, 1981), pp. 252 ff.

21 Shpizman, *Geshikhte*, pp. 126, 128; and Brown, "Tsu der entshtehung," pp. 18–20. On the establishment of the first Poalei Zion circle in New York, see Shpizman, *Geshikhte*, pp. 110–20; and Bezalel C. Sherman, "The Beginning of Labor Zionism in the United States," in Isidore S. Meyer (ed.), *Early History of Zionism in America* (New York, 1958), p. 279.

22 Baruch Zuckerman, *Zikhroynes* (New York, 1962), Vol. 1, p. 201.

23 Yoel Rozovsky, *Di yudishe freiheit* (Summer 1905), p. 42; Isroel Applebaum, "Fun Filadelfia biz Boltimor," *Der idisher arbeter* (10 October 1930), pp. 40–1.

24 Appelbaum, "Fun Filadelfia biz Boltimor," p. 40.

25 Shpizman states that the society was established in early June 1905, but he does not cite the source for this information. In any event, he notes that this society had existed even before the Seventh Zionist Congress (*Geshikhte*, pp. 132–3). Brown, on the other hand, states that it was established several months before the Baltimore Convention, but after the Seventh Zionist Congress, namely, after 2 August 1905 ("Tsu der entshtehung," p. 20). Zuckerman does not specify an exact date in his memoirs, but he relates that it was established a very short time after the convention in Philadelphia (*Zikhroynes*, p. 204). Another source dealing with the establishment of this society is an article written on behalf of Branch No. 1 in New York. This article states that the Society was founded in 1905 following the split with the

territorialists, without noting an exact date. The article (which calls the Society Branch No. 1, but is actually referring to the same Society, since the names of the founders it cites are the same as those mentioned by Shpizman) has a number of inaccuracies, and states that this Society was founded immediately after the first societies in New York and Philadelphia. This information does not correspond with the other sources. See "New Yorker Fareyn Brentsh 1," *Tsente yerlikhe convention* (Boston, 1916), p. 39.

26   Ibid., p. 38.

27   See a survey of the party's history (in English) in the papers of Poalei Zion in America, Lavon Institute, Tel Aviv, Section III-24-73 (hereafter PZ papers), folder no. 1/A; and also Shpizman, *Geshikhte*, p. 137; Meir Brown, *Mit idishe oygen* (New York, 1958), p. 281; Zvi Yosef Cohen, *Fuftsik yor poaley tsyonism in Amerike* (New York, 1953), pp. 23–4.

28   The ideological platform of the Poalei Zion Party in America was published in eight installments in the party newspaper, *Der idisher kemfer*: 30 March 1906, p. 2; 13 April 1906, p. 2; 20 April 1906, p. 2; 27 April 1906, p. 2; 4 May 1906, p. 2; 18 May 1906, p. 2; 8 June 1906, p. 2; 15 June 1906, p.2; as well as in a special booklet, *Program fun der sotsyalisher organizatsyon poaley tsyon fun Amerike*. The source does not show place and year of publication, however in an article published by Yoel Rozovsky in September 1906, he notes that a pamphlet entitled *Undzer program* had recently appeared: "Fun undzer bavagung," *Der idisher kemfer*, 14 September 1906, p. 4. This suggests that the pamphlet was published in the summer of 1906, and no later than early September. It also included the party's organizational by-laws, but it does not describe the process by which they were adopted at the conference, nor does it state who worded the party's program.

29   See A.S. Waldstein to Kalman Marmor, editor of *Der idisher kemfer*, 8 April 1906, YIVO Archives, Marmor Collection; and Yoel Rozovsky, "A kapitl poaley tsyion geshikhte in Amerike, *Der idisher kemfer*, 20 April 1906, p. 2. In his memoirs Baruch Zuckerman states that the first program of Poalei Zion in America was formulated at the Baltimore conference by a group of members, headed by Dr. A. S. Waldstein, who was a "radical Hebraist." See interview with Zuckerman conducted by Dov Levin and Yosef Schatzmuller on behalf of the Institute of Contemporary Jewry, Hebrew University of Jerusalem, 17 May 1960, third session, p. 20. Although Zuckerman did not attend the Baltimore conference, and belonged to the territorialist camp from May 1905 until 1909, once he joined the party he entered the top ranks of its intellectual and organizational leadership. He was also the one who more than any other member of the party was engaged in documenting and recording its history. Zuckerman published three books: *Oyfn veg* (New York, 1956); *Zikhroynes*, Vols. 1–3 (New York, 1962, 1963, 1966); and *Esseyen un profiln* (Tel Aviv, 1976). These are in addition to a very large number of articles printed in the Yiddish press in America and in Israeli newspapers.

30   For the ideological platform of Poalei Zion in America, see *Program*, pp. 3–14.

31   Shpizman, *Geshikhte*, p. 161.

32   For a detailed discussion of this issue, see Rachel Rojanski, "Bein ideologiyah le-metzi'ut politit: Yahasam shel Poalei Zion be-Amerikah le-yidish, 1905–1933," (Between Ideology and Political Reality: The attitude of Poalei Zion in America to Yiddish, 1905–1931), *Yahadut Zemaneinu*, Vol. 11–12 (1998), pp. 51–72.

33   "Shlos fun'm barikht," *Der Idisher kemfer*, 25 January 1907, p. 1.

34   Ibid.

35   On the Czernowitz conference, see Matityahu Mintz, "Tziyonim u-po'alei tziyonim ba-'shprakh konferents' be-Tshernovits, 1908," (Zionists and Poalei Zion at the Chernowitz Conference 1908), *Shvut*, Vol. 15 (1992), pp. 135–47.

36   Notes for a lecture, undated, private papers of Leah Aberson-Harpaz, New York (hereafter PP).

37   *Program*, p. 13.

38   "Tsveyte konvenshn," *Der idisher kemfer*, 4 January 1907, p. 2.

39   Matityahu Mintz, *Igrot Ber Borochov, 1897–1917* (The Letters of Ber Brochov, 1897–1917) (Tel Aviv, 1989), pp. 69–70.

40   Esther Mintz to Kalman Marmor, 2 February 1908, YIVO Archives, Marmor Collection, Part I.

41 Marmor to Esther Mintz (in the margins of a letter to Aberson), Jericho, 10 March 1908, YIVO Archives, Marmor Collection, Part I.
42 See Shpizman, *Geshikhte*, p. 165; Meir Brown, "Antshteyung un antviklung fun idish natsyonaler arbeter farband," in *Idish natsyonaler arbeter farband* (New York, 1946), p. 8.
43 Circular to party members, 28 February 1908, signed by Esther Mintz, Secretary, PP.
44 Circular to party members, 5 December 1907, unsigned, in Esther's handwriting, PP.
45 "Kritik fun Idisher kemfer," *Der idisher kemfer*, 28 December 1906, p. 3.
46 Circular to party members, 5 December 1907.
47 Circular to party members, New York, 28 February 1908, PP.
48 Nomi Zuckerman, the daughter of Baruch Zuckerman, one of the founders and leaders of Poalei Zion in America, and of Nina Avrunin-Zuckerman, one of the founders of Pioneer Women, told me that Mintz-Aberson was etched in her childhood memory as someone who was regarded in Poalei Zion as an educated woman. Conversation with Nomi Zuckerman, 28 May 1999.
49 Esther to Aberson, New York, 1 June 1908, PP; Esther to Kalman Marmor, 14 September 1908, YIVO Archives, Marmor Collection, Part I.
50 Esther to Aberson, 1 June 1908, PP.
51 Esther to Aberson, 27 June 1908, PP.
52 Esther to Aberson, September 1908, no day mentioned, PP. On the *Teglekhe yidishe presse*, see J. Chaikin, *Yiddishe bleter in Amerike* (New York, 1946), p. 202
53 Esther to Aberson, 13 November 1909. The exact date of their marriage is not known, but in a letter to Aberson of 7 September 1908, she speaks about the wedding that was to take place in a few months, and in the letter of 13 November 1909, she writes that she is looking forward to the approaching birth of her child. Both letters in PP.
54 Esther Mintz to the Central Committee, 17 August 1911, PZ papers, folder 40; see also Shpizman, *Geshikhte*, p. 182.
55 See her signatures on letters to the Central Committee, 4 and 20 September 1911, PZ papers, folder 41.
56 Esther Mintz to the Central Committee, 17 August 1911, PZ papers, folder 40.
57 Esther Mintz to Central Committee, 4 September 1911, PZ papers, folder 40 (emphasis added).
58 Esther Mintz to the Central Committee, 20 September 1911, PZ papers, folder 41.
59 Esther Mintz to the Central Committee, 4 September 1911, PZ papers, folder 41.
60 J. S. Hertz, *Di yiddishe sotsyalistishe bavegung in amerike* (New York, 1954), p. 141.
61 Esther Mintz to Hirsh Ehernreich, the secretary of Poalei Zion in America, 4 December 1915, PZ papers, folder 136.
62 Circular of the Central Committee of Poalei Zion in America [n.d.], summary of the sixth conference held on 8–12 October 1911, PZ papers, folder 42.
63 Esther Mintz to the Central Committee, 20 September 1911; 28 September 1911, PZ papers, folder 41.
64 Esther Mintz to the Central Committee, 9 February 1912, PZ papers, folder 47.
65 See "Fareyns barikhtn," *Unser lebn*, 18 February 1916, p. 2.
66 Esther Mintz to Hirsh Ehernreich, 26 November 1915, PZ papers folder 104.
67 Shpizman, *Geshikhte*, p. 325.
68 According to the stationary she used: "Aberson Cottages, light airy rooms, modern cuisine, and an address in Lakewood, New Jersey."
69 "I am filled with envy of you for still being engrossed in party affairs or matters of significance, while I am engrossed in petty everyday things." Esther Mintz-Aberson to Isaac Hamlin, 17 October 1922 (after the 14th Party Convention, Toronto, 14–16 October 1922), PZ papers, folder 412.
70 Interview with Leah Aberson-Harpaz, New York, May 1996, and a circular by the branch secretary, Esther Aberson, to the members, 19 September 1940, PP.
71 See, for example, Esther Aberson to Isaac Hemlin, 17 October 1922, PZ papers, folder 412.
72 Joel Entin, Secretary of the school network, to Esther Aberson, 24 October 1936, PP.
73 Silia Ginzburg, "Khavera Esther Mintz oleha hasholem," *Der idisher kemfer*, 1 July 1955, p. 14.

74 "Aberson, bakanter poaley tsyonist geshtorbn," *Forverts*, 23 November 1929.
75 One of her few articles that I found is Esther Mintz, "Idishe ertsiung in Amerike," *Idishe teglekh prese* (Chicago), 30 October 1908.
76 Meir Brown, "Antshteyung un antviklung," pp. 14–18.
77 "Di finfte yerlikhe konvenshn fun idish natsyonaler arbeter farband," *Der idisher kemfer*, 28 June 1919.
78 "Rezolutsyes fun der 5ter konvenshn fun'm idish natsyonaln arbeter farband," *Der idisher kemfer*, 19 July 1918. For the convention see: Brown, *Idisher natsyonaler arbeter farband*, p. 54.
79 See L. Segal, "Der idish natsyonaler arbeter farband fun 1924 biz 1945," in *Idish natsyonaler arbeter farband*, pp. 297–301.
80 Brown, "Antshteyung un antviklung," p. 54.
81 Segal, "Der idish natsyonaler arbeter farband," pp. 297–300.
82 Ibid., pp. 300–1. Segal does not indicate a date but he calls Poalei Zion "Poalei-Zion-Tseirei-Zion," which was their name after 1931.
83 Ibid, p. 301.
84 Brown, "Antshteyung un antviklung," p. 54.
85 Segal, "Der idish natsyonaler arbeter farband," p. 301.
86 See the speech by Leah Brown in 1965 on the occasion of the 40th anniversary of the organization, private documents of Dina Keler, the daughter of Leah and Meir Brown; Nick Mandelkeren, "The Story of the 'Pioneer Women," *The Pioneer Woman*, November 1980, pp. 6–8. The sources refer to a well in Ein Karem, but at that time the agricultural school for girls was in Talpiot. See Thea Keren, *Sophie Udin: Portrait of a Pioneer* (Rehovot, 1984), p. 36. For the circumstances of the acquaintance between Yanait and Udin, see ibid., p. 12.
87 See Leah Brown's 1965 speech; and S. Kamenetski, "Zeks yor arbet," *Di pionern froy*, No. 23 (October 1931), pp.1–2.
88 See the booklet on the occasion of the organization's 35th anniversary.
89 Blokh to Udin, 23 April 1923, PZ papers, folder 453.
90 See Keren, *Sophie Udin*, p. 37.
91 See the short review of the discussion in "Barikht fun dem fuftsenter konvenshn," *Der idisher arbeter*, 6 February 1925, p. 2.
92 "Rezolutsyes ongenumen fun der 15ter konvenshn fun undzer partey" *Der idisher arbeter*, 9 January 1925, p. 9 (emphasis added).
93 On the UHT campaign see Rachel Rojanski, "Magbit 'hageverkshftn' veha-tmurot be-kerev Poale-Zion be-Amerikah" (The United Hebrew Trades Campaign and the Changes within Poalei Zion in America), *Iyunim Bitkumat Israel*, Vol. 7 (1997), pp. 190–218.
94 See Keren, *Sophie Udin*, p. 37.
95 Leah Biskin, "Finf yor pyonern froyen organizatsye," *Der idisher arbeter*, 10 October 1930, p. 29.
96 "Barikht fun der natsyonal ekzekutiv tsum ershtn tsuzamenfor fun der froyen organizatsye far di khalutsot in erets Yisroel," *Di pyonern froy*, December 1926, p. 10.
97 Ibid, p. 14.
98 According to Thea Keren, Udin was born in 1896 and arrived in America at the beginning of the twentieth century (*Sophie Udin*, pp. 4–7). The same date is also given by Judith Friedman Rosen, "Sophie Udin," in Hyman and Dash Moore (eds), *Jewish Women in America*, p. 1425. According to Udin's son, Yehuda Paz, she was born in 1891/2 (conversation with Yehuda Paz , July 2000). It seems that the date in Keren's biography is wrong as she herself relates that Udin participated in the founding convention of the Farband in 1910 at the age of 16. I tend to accept Paz's calculation of her birth date.
99 See Keren, *Sophie Udin*, p.16.
100 See J. E. Neumann, "The Jewish Battalion and the Palestine Campaign," *American Jewish Year Book*, Vol. 21 (1919), p. 128. Red Mogen David was founded in 1918 and in 1923 merged with Hadassah. See Keren, *Sophie Udin*, p. 12.
101 Keren, *Sophie Udin*, p. 22.
102 See "Barikht fun der natsyonal ekzekutiv," p. 11.

103 One of the members of this branch was Golda Mabovitch, later Meir, who was Feder's close friend. On the Milwakee branch of Poalei Zion, see Memoirs of Louis Perchunok (n. 7 above). Feder was born in Poland in 1900. See Judith Friedman Rosen, "Sara Rivka Feder Kheifetz," in Hyman and Dash Moore (eds.), *Jewish Women in America*, pp. 398–9

104 Friedman Rosen, "Sara Rivka Feder Kheifetz."

105 Sophie Udin, "Di pionern froyen organizatsye un undzer bavegung," *Der idisher kemfer*, 20 December 1935, p.124.

106 William Toll, "A Quiet Revolution: Jewish Women's Clubs and the Widening Female Sphere, 1870–1920," *American Jewish Archives*, No. 1 (1989), pp. 7–8.

107 Linda Gordon Kuzmack, *Woman's Cause: The Jewish Woman's Movement in England and the United States, 1881–1933* (Ohio, 1990), p. 30.

108 On the circumstances of its establishment, see Faith Rogov, *Gone to Another Meeting* (Tuscaloosa and London, 1993), pp. 9–35.

109 See Kuzmak, *Woman's Cause*, p. 33.

110 See Evyatar Friesel, *Ha-tnu'ah ha-tzyonit be-Amerikah ba-shanim 1897–1914* (The Zionist Movement in the United States 1897–1914) (Tel Aviv, 1970), p. 175; Deborah Dash Moore, "Hadassah," in Hyman and Dash Moore (eds.), *Jewish Women in America*, p. 572. On one of its leaders, Rose Jacobs, see Zohar Segev, "Ha-hanhagah ha-tzyonit be-Artzot ha-Brit, 1938–1948: Pe'ilut ba-zirah ha-amerikanit ha-tzyonit veha-eretz yisre'elit," (The Zionist Leadership in the United States, 1938–1948: Its Activities in the American Zionist and Palestinian Arena) (Ph.D. diss., University of Haifa, 1999), pp. 91–103.

111 Michael Meyer, *Responses to Modernity: A History of the Reform Movement in Judaism* (Oxford, 1988), p. 285.

112 Udin, "Di pionern froyen organizatsye."

113 Friedman Rosen, "Sara Rivka Feder Kheifetz."

114 Keren, *Sophie Udin*, pp. 54–5.

115 Joan Wallach Scott, *Gender and the Politics of History* (New York, 1988), p. 42.

116 Hyman , *Gender and Assimilation*, p. 135.

117 Strengthening education in Yiddish was also one of the aims on the Pioneer Women's program. "Rezolutsyes fun der grindungs konvenshn fun der froyen organizatsye far di khlutsot in erets Yisroel," *Pyonem froy*, December 1926, p. 14.

118 Silia Ginsburg, "Khavera Ester oleha hasholem," p. 1 (emphasis added).

The Legend of Sarah:
Gender, Memory and National Identities
(*Eretz Yisrael*/Israel, 1917–90)*

Billie Melman

Forgetting, I would even go so far as to say historical error, is a crucial factor in the creation of a nation, which is why progress in historical studies often constitutes a danger for [the principle of] nationality. … [T]he essence of a nation is that all the individuals have many things in common, and also that they have forgotten many things.

Ernst Renan[1]

Can there be a surfeit of memory? wonders the historian Charles Maier, referring not only to the collective preoccupation with preserving the past and commemorating certain fragments of it, but also to the burgeoning of the history of memory and commemoration during the last two decades. Students of history and culture, including historians, Maier points out wryly, act as though they were assigned the task of metaphorically dipping their madeleines in the memories of the past.[2] He means, of course, the famous cookies dipped by the narrator in the first volume of Marcel Proust's *Remembrance of Things Past*; their taste, which reminds the narrator of the taste of the linden leaf tea that he drank in his childhood, was enough to carry the weight of "the immense edifice of memory."[3]

This excessive preoccupation with memory, bordering on the obsessive, both within and outside the academe, is also characteristic of Israeli culture.[4] Like the discourse elsewhere, so the Israeli discourse, both in the historiography of *Eretz Yisrael* before and after the establishment of the state and in the broader public debates, is marked by an intense interest in collective memory, in methods of commemoration, and in the preservation of certain narratives of the past and the forgetting of others. This interest is also a re-examination of national identity: of its boundaries and of what it includes and excludes. The "lieux de mémoire" (to use Pierre Nora's term) of Israel and *Eretz Yisrael* have been diligently mapped since the second half of the 1980s. These sites include commemorative sites such as cemeteries and monuments, rites, official and "spontaneous" memorial literature (Emmanuel Sivan's term), the Zionist calendar of Jewish history, as well as old-revived or "invented" traditions of sacrifice for the nation such as the tradition of Tel Hai and the story of Masada.[5]

The ongoing fascinating discussion of memory and commemoration is thus, on the one hand, an examination of identity itself and, on the other hand, an elucidation of the question of which groups and which historians own memory and commemoration of the past. To paraphrase on Natalie Zemon Davis, this discussion is about "who owns history?"[6] Nevertheless, the war over memory between so-called "old" and "new" historians, and between them (or some of them) and sociologists of various schools, is somewhat flawed, or deficient. Its deficiency stems from the fact that the concern with the relationship between the memory and myths of "Eretz Yisraeli-ness" and Israeliness, and the formation of national identities is separated from the historical study of male and female gendered identities. With a few exceptions, the "general" discussion of memory has not yet taken into account the ways in which gendered identities formed the boundaries of the collective memory. This lapse can be seen in important studies of identity and commemoration, such as those of Yael Zerubavel, which are gender-blind. The cult of Joseph Trumpeldor and the myth of Tel Hai, which have occupied historians and students of culture more than any other single cult in Israel, are examined without much attention to the fact that Trumpeldor was an exemplar of Zionist masculinity. Similarly, classic studies of *The Yizkor Book* of 1911, the prototype of the new, secular way of commemoration, ignore the fact that the first secular *Eretz Yisraeli* saints were also models of the new man in the nation-in-the-making. Nor does the assemblage of important studies that examine the changes in myth and memory in terms of "the revolutions of Israeli consciousness" consider the possibility of studying the changes from the perspective of gender.[7]

This separation of the history of memory and the study of gender characterizes not only "general" historical study, but also the historiography of women and gender. This historiography has important and impressive accomplishments, but apparently has not yet been integrated into the discussion of collective national memory. As I have pointed out elsewhere, until recently feminist historiography of the period of the *Yishuv* (the pre-state period and pre-state Jewish community in Palestine) has focused on various aspects of women's material experience of the Zionist project. Only very recently has this historiography even begun to show interest in the relationship between the construction of femininity and masculinity, and the formation and representation of the *Eretz Yisraeli* ethoses and identities. The study of a gendered memory as the social dynamic and public action of individuals and collectives that "create, express, and consume" the memory of the past or its commemoration (which Jay Winter and Emanuel Sivan call "public remembrance" or "public recollection") is only just beginning.[8] The scarcity of such historical studies is not manifested simply in the absence of women from the history of memory. Thus, it may not be corrected by simply appending heroines of the past to histories and making a place for them in the national pantheon, although this is important in and of itself. While a more inclusive version, a kind of "herstory" of the history of memory, may serve as a "corrective" to the larger history, it will also perpetuate the distinction between the two areas of study: gender history and the history of memory.

The gendering of the history of collective memory is important because it may help us draw a less homogenous and monolithic map of this memory than the one we have today. Indeed, historians of national memory have been unanimous that this memory is never monolithic, that its very essence, like the essence of a nation, lies precisely in the lack of uniformity, that indeed every nation is characterized by a constant negotiation between its components. At the same time, as Alon Confino has pointed out, one failure of historians of memory is precisely their tendency to homogenize the collective that remembers.[9] These historians still tend to regard the act of remembering (or forgetting) in terms of politics and ideology, and merely the reflection of the political hegemony of movements, ideologies or establishments. National memory is still identified with omnipotent entities — the state, the party, the movement, the dominant elite — on whom these historians bestow all-encompassing power as chief agents of culture.

The bias towards the political and towards the apparatus of the state is sometimes accompanied by a reneging on the social and cultural. Such a bias, and with it the homogenization of diverse publics and their perception into a single entity — the "Yishuv" — is salient in the discussion of the *Eretz Yisraeli* culture of memory and commemoration. The claim that the collective memory in the period of the *Yishuv* and the first decades of the state was statist and created by "Labor" elites and circles, whose hegemony was fractured and broken only in the second half of the 1970s, still persists. Even historians who locate memory in cells within civil society (and not within the state and its bureaucracy) believe that this memory, at least till the 1950s, was not spontaneous and was governed by the state and officialdom.[10]

Paradoxically, even those who call for including different groups and identities in the Zionist and *Eretz Yisraeli* ethos do not adequately consider the potential that lies in the history of gender, not only in and of itself but also for history in general — namely, the potential to make that history more varied and pluralist.[11] Collective memory, as some of its early students, first and foremost among them Maurice Halbwachs, have taught us, is not formed by general and universal images and practices; rather, this memory is historical and particular. It is made out of the experiences, perceptions, and imaginings of groups. As John Gillis has pointed out, national memory in particular is formed in terms of specific identities, such as those of class, gender and ethnicity.[12]

This type of memory developed in the *Yishuv* and even more so in Israel after 1948. It may be described in terminology from the world of vocal music, borrowing the concept of "polyphony," which Mikhail Bakhtin coined to describe the polyphonic quality of "voices in their full value" that are sounded and heard together but maintain their uniqueness. Emanuel Sivan too made use of the image of polyphony in relation to memory in Israel. Describing memory as a "chorus," he suggested that alongside the so-called "official," "central" or "establishment" memory, other voices were also heard: of political groups, of social sectors united by specific cultural experiences, and of groups concentrated in a particular locus — for example, as I show later, the memory that crystallized in the urban "Civic Sector" (*hugim ezrahiim*), as opposed to the socialist Labor sector — or in the *moshavot* (agricultural villages).[13] The polyphonic character of national memory was gendered. The one-armed hero of Tel Hai was perceived and represented not only as the new Zionist, but also as a new man. So were the fallen of the 1948 war. Similarly, women who died for the nation were perceived not only as national figures, but also as models of appropriate "national" female behavior. Put differently, the chronicles of deaths for country and state can also be examined in terms of the development of constructions of masculinity and femininity. Moreover, the gendering of the history of memory makes it possible not only to render a less homogenous account, but also to re-examine familiar questions, such as the question of the relationship between elites at the center and groups at the margins, between the culture of the establishment and sectorial and local culture, and between these and popular culture.

To focus the discussion and to elucidate the ways in which the polyphonic chorus of memory evolved in gender terms, I shall examine a single case: the forgetting (and the suppression) of the memory and commemoration of Sarah Aaronsohn (1890–1917), one of the leaders of the secret pro-British espionage network, known within British intelligence as "A Organization" and locally as "Nili," which operated under Turkish rule in Syria and Palestine in 1915–17. I shall examine her image from the time of her death, in October 1917, through the growth of the "legend of Sarah," as Avigdor Hameiri termed it, in the 1930s and 1940s, up to its annexing, starting in the late 1960s, into the national pantheon, an annexation which brought about a crucial change in the image.[14] Since the focus of this study is acts of public commemoration, I shall deal with the story of Aaronsohn's actual life and death only insofar as is necessary. As I have shown elsewhere, Aaronsohn regarded her suicide as a conscious and public act, and her death was the first example in the history of *Eretz Yisrael* of an active female death with secular and national overtones. I also argued that her death departed radically from existing models of female heroism, both from the classic Jewish model of female martyrdom that had developed after the waves of violence and persecution raging in Central Europe in 1096 and from the secular, national model of death which developed in *Eretz Yisrael* at the time of the First *Aliyah* and after.[15] Moreover, her death even deviated from the colonial model of female self-sacrifice for the nation, which evolved in anticolonial nationalist movements in the Middle East and South Asia, and which has been studied by Rajeswari Sunder Rajan, Gayatri Spivak and Beth Baron.[16]

My focus on Sarah Aaronsohn has another motive as well. The changes in her status as a national hero can be compared to the transformations in the political and cultural status of the legend of Tel Hai and the myth of Trumpeldor. This comparison between a central and formative myth and a memory that was initially peripheral and sectorial, but which subsequently became an alternative myth, may serve as an example for the comparative study of memory. Such a study forces us to raise a number of questions. Was memory homogeneous? Was it controlled by practically omnipotent elites? How did prevailing perceptions and representations of femininity (or masculinity) shape the narrative of the history of the Jews and of Zionism "written" by various groups? What were the features of a national heroine represented as a historical agent? And, finally, how did memory take form in various periods? Was it homogeneous until the 1970s and perhaps the 1980s, or had its fracturing or splitting (what some term its privatization) already begun in the early *Yishuv*?

To address these questions, I shall focus on two stretches of time which were major junctions in the evolution of "the legend of Sarah": from the beginning of her public commemoration in 1932 to the end of the Second World War, when the memory of Sarah Aaronsohn was nurtured by various right-wing groups within the Civic Sector (both urban and rural), as well as in popular culture; and after 1967, when local, sectorial and popular memory was appropriated into the mainstream national memory, which changed and reshaped it, but was also altered by it.

To elucidate the possibilities in gendering of memory I have applied a two-pronged methodology, using a dual reading. First, I examine memory, ignoring gender, even though the object of commemoration was a woman. Thus, in the first part of this article, I survey and attempt to reconstruct the political and social uses of Aaronsohn's memory. This survey is a "herstory": the "hero" of the story is female, but my rendition is deliberately blind to the ways in which different and dynamic perceptions of femininity (and masculinity) shaped the ethos of the national heroine. Only afterwards do I pursue a "gender reading" of narratives about Sarah, a reading that is sensitive to the ways in which the various and often competing definitions and notions regarding the role of women in the nation-in-the-making shaped the collective memory and commemoration.

1917 and 1932–47: Forgetting and Remembering

In contrast to the battle for Tel Hai (1 March 1920), the death of Sarah Aaronsohn about two and a half years earlier had made no immediate impact on the collective, public memory or upon that of specific groups or sectors in the *Yishuv* such as the *moshavot*. Her violent taking of her own life for her people and country did not immediately become a model of national heroism: its anniversary was not publicly commemorated, and her death did not stand out as a turning point or a formative event in the history of the *Yishuv*. In fact, in different milieux, both Labor and Civic, Nili's espionage activities were regarded as irresponsible (and by some as mercenary), and not as manifestations of devotion to the national cause. True, Sarah's suicide, which was also interpreted as a conscious choice of self-sacrifice for the nation, sometimes rescued her from the pejorative image that stuck to her colleagues in the leadership of the Nili underground. At least during the first decade after her suicide, her image as a heroine was rather equivocal. There is reference to her heroism in writings of that time (notably in the writings of her contemporaries in the *moshavot*, the socio-economic group in which she grew and among whom, as I show later, her memory as a national heroine was molded), and in the Jewish press in Palestine and elsewhere, but it is scattered and hardly constitutes a tradition of memory.[17] The "invention" of such a tradition, to use Eric Hobsbawm's well-known term, was deferred.[18] In contradistinction to the construction of Trumpeldor as a national icon immediately after his death, the ethos and myths of Sarah Aaronsohn present a delayed memory, evolving slowly and belatedly.

The appropriation of her heroism into a peripheral and distinctly sectorial remembrance began only 15 years after her death with the first "aliyah la-regel" or pilgrimage to her grave on 10 October 1932. The 35 ceremonial pilgrimages that preceded the first official state ceremony in her memory and that of the other dead members of Nili, held in Zikhron Yaakov in 1967, were constructed as a "tradition," as their organizers emphasized from the very beginning. They saw themselves as the agents of a tradition which had the potential to preserve a segment of the national past, create its symbolic patterns and commemorate it.

A close reading of the detailed descriptions of the pilgrimages allows us to examine not only the dynamics of the construction of public memory, but also to observe, in miniature, the remembering community and the social and political changes that occurred within it. Paraphrasing the anthropologists Clifford Gertz and James Clifford, we may describe the annual ceremony, held around the last day of the holiday of Sukkot in Zikhron Yaakov, as a "synecdoche," that is as a part representing the whole. This is a part, or perhaps a segment, of a culture, or of a cultural activity, that embodies the cultural, social (and political) whole of the observed community.[19] In the case at hand, the community is the Civic Sector of the *Yishuv* during the 1930s and 1940s.

Two thousand women and men of this community took part in the second pilgrimage to Sarah's grave on Tuesday, 10 October 1933. It served as a model for those that took place afterwards. 500 of the participants belonged to two leading organizations within the community: Bnei Binyamin, the Young Farmers' Federation, the best-organized and most dynamic body within the private agricultural sector, and the Revisionist organization, Betar. The other 1,500 participants included residents of Zikhron Yaakov and guests from the large cities and other *moshavot*. The "day of the popular procession," as the organizers called it, was described as a mass pilgrimage. The fact that in some of the *moshavot* it was a half-day holiday helped to make it successful.

At the head of the parade rode representatives of the First *Aliyah* and veterans of the *moshavot*, along with members of the "first" native-born "generation": Avram Shapira, his daughters, and the daughters of the Zviatitski family of Petah Tikvah, dressed in riding habits. After them came riders from Brit ha-Rokhvim (Riders' Club) and members of Bnei Binyamin from Zikhron Yaakov, Haderah, Shefeyah, Bat Shlomo, Binyaminah and elsewhere. Leisurely following them on foot came members of the Bnei Binyamin executive, schoolchildren, members of Betar, and the "kahal" (general public).[20] In their procession, the pilgrims retraced parts of the last three journeys that Sarah Aaronsohn had made on the way to her death and burial; from the house of her father, Efrayim Fischel, to the improvised jail where she was interrogated and tortured; from the jail back to the home of her brother, Aharon, where she tried to commit suicide; and from her father's house, where she lay dying for three days, to the cemetery where she was buried. On reaching the important stations in their itinerary, the pilgrims stood to honor the memory of the dead Sarah.

The most prominent cohort of pilgrims, the first native-born generation from the cities, the established *moshavot* and the new, private capitalist agricultural settlements, had an ambiguous collective status. This ambiguity dated back to the period before the First World War and to the time of the war itself, when this generation was socially and economically marginal, yet at the same time occupied a central and even iconic place in the Hebrew *Eretz Yisraeli* discourse, in which they were elevated to a model of a new national experience — masculine and feminine.[21] During the 1930s and 1940s, this relationship between economic marginality and iconic place in the national discourse was reversed. After the economic crisis of the early 1920s, the *moshavot* saw a period of certain expansion, including the founding of new agricultural colonies and urban settlements. During this period, the organizational infrastructure of the agricultural and urban Civic Sector was constructed, and what came to be described as the "Civic culture" developed. Yet "bnei ha-aretz" (literally, "sons of the Land," a term designating the first generation of native Hebrew speakers) lost their iconic place in the discourse on the nation and were consigned to the periphery.[22] The members of Nili, who represented this generation, especially Sarah Aaronsohn, were seized upon by "the remembering group," that group which sought to commemorate its own cultural heroes, as the site of authentic *Eretz Yisraeli*-ness. In contrast to Trumpeldor, who was an outsider affiliated with the Labor movement, Aaronsohn's conduct and action could become role models and she was reconstructed and represented by the Civic elites (and particularly by the native-born young elite) as both a sectorial and a national myth. The tension between sectorialism and nationalism is expressed in the first memorial pamphlet published by the Bnei Binyamin executive in 1932:

> Sarah Aaronsohn is a national heroine unrivaled in the annals of the Hebrew revival.... . Aaronsohn is not only the greatest national heroine in this period of our revival, she is also our own heroine, the heroine of the class of the *Boazim*, people oriented to building the collective through building the individual and through individual responsibility, whose value [others] try to play down at every opportunity, denying them any idealistic tone and any desire and power for national sacrifice; Sarah is not a solitary heroine in our ranks; she was the bearer of a large movement, a wide-ranging organization of Civic farmers, who made sacrifices and invested physical and mental energy in their outstanding devotion to the liberation of the homeland and in extending frequent aid to the *Yishuv* in its most difficult moments.[23]

As the "heroine of the homeland" and a "heroic sacrifice,"[24] as "a saint in her life and death" and as a "symbol of national sacrifice and pride,"[25] Aaronsohn became a model of national activism. Her tomb became a site "rousing audacity and sacrifice on the altar of liberation and the war to defend the *Yishuv* and the land .... "[26] The potential inherent in her commemoration was dual. She clearly represented a particular group or "class," and thus was not perceived as a unifying symbol by the peripheral young elite, her own milieu, and certainly not by the dominant "Labor" elite. The story of her heroism was not a part of what Hayden White called a "metanarrative," a meta-story organizing the history of the community as a whole and representing homogeneity.[27] Aaronsohn's story was divisive. She was constructed as a heroine of the *Boazim* — an appellation given to the native-born farmers belonging to the landowning sector within the *moshavot*, named after their prototype, the biblical Boaz — and as an icon of Civic culture, urban and agricultural alike, which saw itself as a "native" culture. The emphasis on "class" in the literature dedicated to Aaronsohn's memory competes with and was an alternative to the Marxist concept of class and to the reality of a strong organized Labor sector and a hegemonic Labor movement. Bnei Binyamim were known for their blunt anti-Labor rhetoric and for their fierce opposition to socialism and collectivism.[28] However, the members of the commemorating group also wished to "speak for" and in the name of the nation as a whole. Thus, Aaronsohn was described as both a "Boazit" heroine and as a national figure embodying the entire *Yishuv*. Her discovery and the promotion of her memory as a "saint" of the Civic Sector reflected the need of groups within it to correct the dominant Labor narrative of the recent Zionist past, from which they felt they had been excluded. Thus the representative of Bnei Binyamin stated on the fourth commemoration of her death (October 1935) that:

> It has always been falsely said of the farmers and their sons, who in fact served as the foundation for the Balfour Declaration and as the first stones for building the Land, that they were concerned only with their own gain. The story of Sarah has removed this accusation. They [the farmers] knew how to sanctify the Hebrew name and Hebrew honor. On this anniversary, and on every day of the year, we teach our youth to remember that, apart from all else, there is national honor and that in case of need, one must withstand the trial and act like Sarah and her friends.[29]

In Sarah Aaronsohn the commemorating group found their very own saint, who could also be represented as an icon of the nation as a whole. What is more, the organized commemoration transformed the activism of Nili, and especially the active death of Aaronsohn herself, into a model for the youth of the Civic Sector. The emphasis on sacrifice and exemplary death was particularly salient during the Second World War. In wartime memorial ceremonies, the comparison is repeatedly made between the willingness of the older generation of *Boazim* in the First World War to sacrifice themselves for their nation and the hedonism and complacency of the Civic youth in the 1940s. In the ceremony of 1944, Arieh Samsonov of Zikhron Yaakov appealed to the young men of the towns and the *moshavot* and to the "youth of Israel" to volunteer to serve in the British Army in order to prove "that you deserve to be called people of Zikhron, the place where Sarah, the spirit of Nili, was born, raised, and educated!" From this year, the recruits were sworn in on Aaronsohn's grave in a ceremony before a local audience and representatives of the British Army.[30]

The representation of Aaronsohn as a model of *Eretz Yisraeli* nationalism is not unique to the memorial ceremonies organized by the Bnei Binyamin Federation. It recurs in the eulogies for her in the daily Civic press (by writers who were not necessarily identified with Bnei Binyamin), in the children's press of the Civic Sector, such as *Ha-Boker le-Yeladim* (Morning for Children), as well as in stories, plays and skits written in the 1930s, 1940s and 1950s.[31] The discussion of her death and its symbolism makes a rich and dense fabric of texts characterized by what Raphael Samuel has called "a density of description and attention to the object of remembrance."[32] This density, along with the multiplicity of various texts, drawing on each other, representing writers of different political orientations, published in different platforms and directed towards different audiences, is what helped construct Sarah Aaronsohn as a cultural icon. The discussion of her life and death, both for those who had taken an active part in them and those who had not, was in fact a debate about the nature of *Eretz Yisraeli*-ness, about who owned national history and who had the right to interpret it.

It was precisely the absence of homogeneity in the collective memory of Sarah Aaronsohn that helped transform her into a "heroine for all," for different groups and at different times. For the older private agricultural sector, represented in the ceremonies by such veterans as Avram Shapira, Aaronsohn was an exemplar of "the farmer's way." For members of her own generation and for Bnei Binyamin youth, who from the beginning presented themselves as the true "natives of the Land", her "national espionage" accorded with the fulfillment of the Zionist project and "building the Land." As Oded Ben-Ami put it in 1932, she was "the one on whose grave we built the great building of the Land." Ben-Ami, like other activists in the Bnei Binyamin Federation, emphasized both Aaronsohn's local connections and her territoriality, the connection to the Land and people of Israel in general, acquired through her unmediated knowledge of nature, the terrain and its flora and fauna. As he presented her, she was a daughter of the Land and a true representative of the authentic native-born generation: "Nor did the *Yishuv* know how to appreciate the value of Sarah and her heroic friends, through malevolence, malice, and envy — because they were children of the Land."[33] Aaronsohn was a "territorial heroine," in accordance with the model that characterized the native Hebrew culture from the beginning, as Itamar Even-Zohar and others have shown.[34]

In contrast to the narrative of Aaronsohn's life and death molded by circles close to Bnei Binyamin, Revisionist as well as maximalist right-wing narratives emphasized blood sacrifice and revolt, which were promulgated as ideals in and of themselves and sometimes divorced from concepts of territoriality and of settling on the land. From the beginning, the Young Maccabi movement, Betar and Betar Youth took an active part in commemorating Sarah Aaronsohn. From the very first memorial ceremony, representatives of Betar attended the annual commemorations officially and in uniform; and their presence became especially conspicuous during the Second World War. Moreover, aside from the annual public ritual organized in

Zikhron Yaakov, Nili and Sarah Aaronsohn in particular became models of activism and revolt among both revisionists and right-wing maximalists. In the eyes of the Stern Group and of activists associated with Brit ha-Biryonim, her activities were not only a symbol of heroism and of "deeds" (presented as the opposite of the passivity and sterile verbosity of the intellectuals), but also part of a messianic myth. As Joseph Heller has convincingly shown, the zealot (*kanai*), rebelling against a sovereign ruler, had a central place in the Stern Group's eclectic messianic ideology. His/her historic role consisted of self-sacrifice that would bring on "the kingdom of Israel" — not by parliamentary means or through agreement (with colonial and international powers such as Britain), but by violent action. Thus, paradoxically, Nili, with its definitively pro-British orientation during the First World War, became the ideological and operative model for the anti-British Lehi in the Second World War. The maximalist right appropriated Sarah Aaronsohn and the story of her death and set her (along with Tomáš Masaryk, Marshal Piłsudski, and Eamon de Valera) in an eclectic pantheon of national rebels. They even turned her death into an alternative national narrative of the history of Israel — the chronicles of the acts of the zealots.[35]

The children's and youth culture of the Civic *Yishuv*, on the other hand, had no place for the model of the zealot and the saga of apocalyptic violence invented by the extreme right, or even for the sectorialism and the version of class identity that characterized the narrative fostered by Bnei Binyamin. The literature published by the children's newspapers of the Civic Sector sought to present Sarah Aaronsohn as an exemplary national figure. Like Trumpeldor, so too Sarah was represented as a hero of the nation as a whole. Her death had added pedagogical value as an example of a "boundless love for our people and our homeland" and of "self-sacrifice and devotion, all in faith and confidence," as pointed out in *Ha-Boker le-Yeladim* of 25 September 1945.

Unlike Trumpeldor, Nili and Sarah Aaronsohn were not included in the curriculum —either the curriculum of the general educational system or that of schools affiliated with the Labor movement. Her slow appropriation by the state educational system began only after 1967 (see below). Until then, and even in the 1950s, Aaronsohn and Nili were absent from school curricula and from the Hebrew school calendar, while the anniversary of Trumpeldor's death, the 11th of Adar, was made a day of ceremonies and the first national secular holiday. Given this absence, Aaronsohn's emergence as a national heroine for youth in the peripheral juvenile culture that emerged in the 1940s is particularly significant.

First occasionally, then more frequently, Sarah Aaronsohn's name and the story of her death appeared in fiction and memorial sections of the Civic children's press. A typical story was published in *Ha-Boker le-Yeladim* on 9 October 1946 (the eve of the traditional pilgrimage in Zikhron Yaakov). In the didactic "frame" story, serving as a setting for the inner narrative, a grandmother explains to her grandchildren why masses of pilgrims throng to the grave of the saint from Zikhron Yaakov every year. As befitting the genre, the story focuses on Sarah Aaronsohn's patriotic childhood and death and, typically, no mention is made of her adolescence or adult years. As the following brief excerpt shows, her death is described in territorial terms and through images of mourning that focus on the landscape and nature ("the heavens wept", "the first hard rain of the year") commonly found in Hebrew children's literature. These clichéd tropes, however, are now inserted into a new narrative of heroism for youth:

> When Sarah was brought to burial in the cemetery of Zikhron Yaakov, the first drops of the first hard rain of the season started to fall. Not only the people cried, the sky too wept for the death of Sarah ... saintly and pure, who sacrificed herself for the redemption of her people and country. Even the Turkish officers and governors who attended her funeral declared, "She was like a daughter of kings."[36]

The various narratives of Sarah Aaronsohn's life and death reflect the polyphony of collective memory. And this polyphonic quality was in tune with the different and often competing agendas and needs, mainly political but also cultural, of different groups. But despite their differences and plurality of voices, these groups belonged to the same community of memory and may be located in the Civic Sector and the national Civic culture that emerged during the 1930s and 1940s. However, this functional explanation of the polyphony of the remembering community is insufficient. First, there was not always a direct connection between the political affiliation of those who fostered the memory and commemorated the past, and the actual practice of memory. For example, unorganized, popular forms of commemoration, which were not partisan or connected to organizations sprang up (see below). Moreover, an explanation that reduces memory to a simple relationship between needs (mainly political) and organized social activities (such as public mourning and commemoration ceremonies) errs in ignoring the complexities of the object of the memory, its images and the reconstruction of this object by individuals and groups. This kind of functional explanation also ignores the relationship between gender, memory and identity.

How, then, was the discourse on Sarah Aaronsohn made into a gendered memory? Was she invented as a national *hero* of *Eretz Yisrael* who *happened to be a woman*, or, put differently, was her "femaleness" relevant to the myth of *Eretz Yisraeli*-ness that she represented? I shall argue that the memory of Sarah Aaronsohn cannot be understood outside of gender, since her construction as a model of *Eretz Yisraeli*-ness by the groups examined above, as well as by other groups, was related to the identification between nationalism and the active sacrifice and historical action of women. To examine the associations between gender, identity and memory, I shall consider, from the perspective of gender, the same narratives that were examined above in a functional and neutral way. In addition, I shall discuss other sources — plays, high and popular literature, and the practices of memory in daily life, such as the custom of giving girls and boys "national" names associated with the history of Nili.

1917–67: Memory and Gender

The most salient feature of the formation of the memory of Sarah Aaronsohn's life and death is the identification of nationalism with activism and femininity. This identification is manifest, first and foremost, in Sarah's very centrality in the many varied narratives of the history of Nili, its rise, deeds and fall. The typical plot of the 1930s and 1940s did feature the central male figures in the anti-Ottoman underground: Aaron Aaronsohn, her older brother, and Avshalom Feinberg, presenting both of them as models of *Eretz Yisraeli* masculinity (Feinberg was described as "the first Sabra").[37] But Sarah Aaronsohn, the only woman in the Nili leadership (though not the only female member of the organization), who coordinated and from late 1916 practically ran the organization and the wider network that supported it, was the only activist to be elevated to a paragon of sacrifice and a model of national conduct. The relative marginality of the underground men within the memory undoubtedly had technical reasons, to do with the local-territorial aspect of every presence of the past in private and collective memory. Sarah Aaronsohn had a *site* of memory and even "sacred" relics, which the pilgrims to her grave visited in their ritual processions. Aaron Aaronsohn and Avshalom Feinberg had no place of burial or relics. Their death was not final because their bodies disappeared and this disappearance was shrouded in uncertainty: the plane in which Aaronsohn flew to the Versailles Conference vanished over the English Channel; Feinberg disappeared on his unfortunate journey to Egypt in 1917, and the remains of his body were recovered by chance only in 1967.

As historians of memory such as Pierre Nora, Raphael Samuel and Frances Yates have noted, the act of remembering the past, whether to preserve an individual past or to reconstruct a public myth, is related to the practices and techniques of recall as a spatial art — remembering, preserving and memorizing places or individuals in a space. The technique of recall is based on memorizing the exact location and arrangement of the disparate items that those that remembered "saw" at a particular site. This also characterizes the building of sites of commemoration. Without place, Frances Yates has pointed out, there is no practice of memory.[38]

Since Sarah Aaronsohn's death and burial she had a *place* of memory. The presence of her remains in the local space of Zikhron Yaakov aided in the "arrangement" and formation of the narrative of her activities and its incorporation into the history of the heroism of the nation, both by those who perpetuated her memory and by the groups who made pilgrimages to Zikhron Yaakov on the anniversary of her death. Her memory was preserved in the series of sacred places and relics: the room where she was tortured, the place where she committed suicide (the bathroom of Aaron Aaronsohn's house in the Aaronsohn family's back yard), the "instrument" of death (the gun), the blood-stained suicide letter, the white dress in which she committed suicide, and her grave. Every year from the 1940s, a *sukkah* was erected in the Aaronsohn yard, which the local schoolchildren and the general public were encouraged to visit throughout the festival of Sukkot and on Shmini Atzeret, the eighth and last day, when Jews in Israel no longer sit in the *sukkah*. At the center of the *sukkah*, on a table decorated with branches and flowers, stood Sarah Aaronsohn's photograph. In this iconic presentation of the dead "saint," in a public *sukkah*, the local ritual of the pilgrimage to Sarah's grave was combined with the tradition of the three pilgrimages to the Temple in Jerusalem at Passover, Shavuot and Sukkot.

Aaronsohn's centrality in the narrative of Nili, and of *Eretz Yisraeli* heroism as a whole, however, is rooted in her complex gender identity. Sarah Aaronsohn's femininity was defined and interpreted in various ways, according to available models of gender, particularly the model of the "new" *Eretz Yisraeli* woman, which had already emerged before the First World War and were refined during the interwar years. Both the definition and the memory contained an unresolved (and insoluble) tension between two perceptions of femininity and between two practices of *Eretz Yisraeli* female public behavior, which cohabited in the national discourse and in particular in the culture of the Civic Sector.

One perception may be termed "maternalist." This was based on the assumption that women were mothers of the nation, in two senses of the word: literally, by virtue of their reproductive capacity they were responsible for reproducing the nation, and also in the sense that they were the conduit for the transmission of the national culture through teaching their children the Hebrew language. This twofold contribution to the nation was seen not merely as a "natural" (biological) role but also as a social and cultural activity.[39] The other perception, which cohabited with the maternalist definition, blurred gender differences and detached national female identity from motherhood. This perception was conspicuous, as I have demonstrated elsewhere, among women of the first native Hebrew-speaking generation and especially among Nili members and their female supporters. Sarah Aaronsohn's own conduct was an eloquent manifestation of this perception.[40] I shall now discuss each of these components in the gendered memory.

First, the national-maternalist perception and memory. As is well known,

Zionist gender ideology in the first decades of the twentieth century was no different from Western nationalist ideology in general. Like nationalism in the West, so too Zionism "invited" women into the budding community of the nation and bestowed upon them historical agency by virtue of their essence as mothers. The vast body of studies on maternalism, most notably the writings of Gisela Bock, Patricia Thane, Sonia Michel and Seth Koven on western Europe and of Beth Baron and Fatma Müge Göçek on the Ottoman Empire, clearly shows how maternalism enabled the recruitment of women to nationalist movements. Yet, this selfsame image of femininity, which served to include women in the nation, at the same time led to their exclusion from what was perceived as the apotheosis of national liberation: blood-sacrifice for the nation and participation as combatants on the battlefield.[41] "Translated" into *Eretz Yisraeli* terms, the maternalist model prevented women from acquiring (and in Hebrew *kniyah*, literally "buying") the land with their blood. Until Sarah Aaronsohn's death, this possibility was restricted to men, for example, the martyrs of Ha-Shomer. Although women also died in the battle for Tel Hai, blood sacrifice "for the Land" was identified with a new Hebrew hero, Trumpeldor, and with masculine characteristics.[42] Of course, the maternalist perception of the *Eretz Yisraeli* woman, as the embodiment of motherhood and of the family of the nation, did leave a certain space for women to act as agents of the national revival. Indeed, this space is one of the components of the memory of Sarah Aaronsohn. Various versions of the story of her heroism emphasized characteristics that were considered feminine, among them her devotion to her family, her willingness to sacrifice herself, and, lastly, her capacity for emotional identification with human suffering, as clearly manifest in her attitude towards the genocide of the Armenians (the latter being considered a major factor for her joining a political movement). These feminine traits turned her story into a part of a repertoire of alternative, feminine, versions of the story of Jewish heroism.

In one such version, Aaronsohn's act of nationalism was described as a part of a domestic, family drama. This displacement of heroism from the public realm to the home, and its presentation as part of a feminine biography is quite conspicuous in the hagiographies of Aaronsohn that were written under the aegis of the Aaronsohn family, especially of her brother Alexander. A typical example may be found in the volume dedicated to Sarah in Yaari-Polskin's work on Nili, which relates in detail the story of the growth and *Bildung* of an *Eretz Yisraeli* heroine. This story of pioneering, represented as a source of heroism and sacrifice, is distinctly gendered:

> The pioneers had to create and develop everything. Isolated among their Arab neighbors, whose language and customs they did not know, they were forced to learn the work … to adapt to everything. And how

difficult the life of these women pioneers was! They had to do everything with their own hands. They took care of their children by themselves, because there was no "daycare" yet. And every mother cooked, baked, washed, and sewed for her household; for in those days the pioneers had not yet come to believe that they could give up their personal lives and families.... Sarah grew up in a life of work, heroism, and sacrifice. From childhood, she worked, like all the daughters of the pioneers. Hand in hand, shoulder to shoulder with her mother, she washed floors, scrubbed tables and chairs … .

After specifying the various household chores, he continues:

And Sarah also inhaled spiritual heroism daily in her life with her mother.... From her she learned to suffer in silence, to dry her tears quickly, and to present a laughing face … to do her daily chores despite the ache in her body, in her heart. From her mother she learned that there was no obstacle, no hindrance, no power on earth that could keep the soul from rising and exalting above all and soaring, soaring to the heavens![43]

From her father, Yaari-Polskin points out, Sarah Aaronsohn learned a more earthly and territorial love: love for the land, a land identified with the space outside the home and the female sphere.

The relationship between memory and group or class, emphasized in the first part of this study and given social and political interpretations, is a gendered relationship. The "class" of farmers is endowed with qualities or a history which, in the view of Yaari-Polskin and other members of his group, had been expropriated from them: namely, a history of pioneering. Just like the people of the Labor movement, so too the Aaronsohns and the farmers of Zikhron Yaakov are "pioneers," insists Yaari-Polskin. And, most relevant here, this pioneering is gendered. Women's pioneering is domestic and spiritual. This spirituality is embodied in the Aaronsohns' mother, Malkah, and in her daughter Sarah, and does not characterize the men of the family, who represent the material connection to the land.

In another version of the maternalist narrative, Sarah Aaronsohn's life is detached from the domestic and familial framework and integrated, as an epic and a public story, into a clearly feminine narrative of the history of heroism. In this version, Sarah is described as a link in the chain of mothers of the nation, which includes the biblical Sarah, Deborah and Yael, and sometimes even mothers from the Jewish apocrypha. In the necrologue, "Sarah Aaronsohn" by Avigdor Hameiri, which was first published in the newspaper *Doar ha-Yom* (Today's Mail) in 1923, Sarah is presented as a "Judith," a "great and gigantic" mythical heroine. Her mythological status and power are conveyed through images of femininity, seduction and sexuality, which remain only symbolic: "And Judith bestows Greek compliments on Holophernes ... and her eyes [Sarah's] were light, her face always smiling, and her lips full and somewhat obdurate."[44] Judith the tyrant-slayer is a founding mother of the nation. The fact that, Sarah Aaronsohn, like Judith, was never a mother and, stricty speaking, did not fulfill wifely duties, since she abandoned her husband and home, has little or no significance. For maternalism identified all women as mothers, regardless of their biological or family status.

Alongside this genealogy of national mothers and daughters, there evolved another memory of Aaronsohn's heroism and death, in which her role as an agent, in Jewish history and that of the *Yishuv*, was severed off from the maternalist notion of action. This memory, in which the boundaries of femininity are blurred, took shape between the early 1920s and the end of the 1950s. Yet, at the same time, this non-maternalist (sometimes even anti-maternalist) image draws on the images of femininity and on social behaviors of the women of the native-born elite before and during the First World War.

The blurring of gender boundaries and a pointed criticism of the identification of national femininity with motherhood were salient features of Aaronsohn's own writings and public conduct. Aaronsohn occasionally wore men's clothing and used the masculine form when writing about herself. She also criticized the way in which her male colleagues in the underground perceived femininity and represented women as mothers, saints or asexual creatures. And she herself was a very sensual woman. Her challenge to notions of femininity and its boundaries culminated in the way in which she designed her death, in the last letter and in her behavior until the moment of suicide.[45]

After her death, and especially after the early 1930s, right-wing movements and youth organizations within the private agricultural sector adopted the non-maternalist and open-ended definition of *Eretz Yisraeli* femininity formulated by Aaronsohn herself and other women of her generation. This model was not entirely political, however, for it also penetrated into popular culture, especially into popular women's culture. In this alternative narrative, memory operated as a sieve that sifted features identified as feminine and domestic out of Sarah Aaronsohn's biography, retaining details that were not perceived as purely feminine or that could be deemed "masculine." For example, a great many descriptions emphasized her physical prowess, her freedom of movement outside her home, her horsemanship, her mastery of various weapons, as well as qualities such as her unperturbability, unemotionality, contempt for pathos, and the desire to "do" rather than talk. Some of the traditional maternalist biographies also included these characteristics. Yaari-Polskin, for example, gives Sarah's love of riding a central place:

[She loved] horse riding and life in nature.... She bore a sword and galloped in the mountains.... How beautiful she was ... as she rode her noble and gleaming horse, rejoicing in gatherings and competitions with our Arab neighbors. Sarah was perhaps one of the first Hebrew women in the land [to participate] in heroism and horse racing and even in raids on a caravan of camels in the dark of the night.[46]

This portrayal of Aaronsohn as a horseman, a *man* of nature and the land, is very similar to descriptions of her by the historian Joseph Klausner. The portrayal is intriguing precisely because of the analogy between the Sabra woman and the Bedouin man, involving a broad notion of gender and elements of orientalism, an approach that idealizes the oriental man while blurring his gender.[47] Such comparison of the first Sabra women to Bedouin men and heroes was most common from the turn of the twentieth century, as was the custom of *Eretz Yisraeli* women to dress up as Arab men. Moreover, the compound of masculine traits, activities and appearance attributed to the female "hero" would be applied to the Sabra male. It was precisely at this time that the masculinist ethos of the native-born male, a man of deeds, lacking pathos, was promulgated.[48]

The authenticity of Aaronsohn as a daughter of the Land, her love of nature, her contempt for verbiage and her admiration for action were contrasted to the behavior of the men around her. Thus, this narrative of her heroism was based not only on the blurring of gender (as in the analogy to the Bedouin man), but also on the reversal of gender behaviors. Aaronsohn's behavior is presented as diametrically opposed to the feminine conduct of the men in Nili. Such a reversal is salient in the writings of Moshe Smilansky, who deserves attention as an exception among the activists in the farmers' and nationalist bloc. Although Smilansky served as the President of the Hebrew Farmers' Association and as editor of its newspaper, *Bustana'i* (Orchardist) till the early 1920s, he detached himself from the ideology of the organization and from Bnei Binyamin. And it was at the time that the memory and the commemoration of Nili and of Sarah Aaronsohn were being shaped that he began to formulate his own special views about Hebrew labor and about the relationship between Jews and Arabs.

What is unique about Smilansky is that his rendition of the myth of Sarah Aaronsohn was neither political nor strictly partisan. In the play *Rohele* which he wrote in 1933, underground leader Rohele — Sarah Aaronsohn — prefers an active political life to family and the love of a man, while her male colleagues (who are portrayed as feminine) long for home, family and the love of a woman. The heroine reproaches them: "Go without asking, without enquiring, with eyes shut, through fire and water, in blood and in death, always forward. Death with honor in an instant is better than a life of shame of the vanquished."[49] For "life of shame" read a comfortable domestic life. Rohele/Sarah's death is depicted as an especially "active" death. In the last scene of the play, Smilansky describes a duel between equals — between the heroine and Hassan Beck (the Ottoman interrogator). Rohele stabs Hassan Beck, and only then kills herself and dies on the spot.[50] Such reversal of gender roles and the relegation of the men in the underground to the margins of the narrative reach their peak in the article on Sarah that Smilansky wrote in 1935. The article ends with the sentence: "If there is truth in the statement that there is a next world, and that in the next world there are two parts, one for Paradise and one for Hell, and her male friends chance to go to Paradise, may her place be in Hell, and may she not meet them there."[51]

The blurring of the boundaries of femininity and the reversal of gender images characterize not only the statements of a "rebel" like Smilansky, but also the memory and acts of commemoration of Bnei Binyamin and the revisionist and maximalist organizations of the right. Indeed, Aaronsohn's biography was integrated not only into the genealogy of the rebels and zealots discussed above, but also into an alternative history of Western female heroism.

From the early 1930s, Aaronsohn was commonly compared to non-Jewish female warriors or heroines whose myths were marked by gender ambiguity. These myths commemorated "masculine" traits such as courage on the battlefield and soldiering, on the one hand, and idealized female qualities such as sexual purity and sometimes even virginity, on the other hand. The two most common analogies in the memorial literature dedicated to Aaronsohn in the interwar years were to Joan of Arc, the Maid of Orleans, born in 1412, captured by the Burgundians and burnt by the English in 1431, and canonized in 1920, and to Edith Cavell, the British nurse who was executed in Belgium for anti-German espionage during the First World War. Cavell, executed in 1915, promptly became a national saint in Britain and a propaganda asset for the Allied forces.[52] Her blood sacrifice was associated with the sacrifice of occupied Belgium, which was routinely feminized and described as a woman in the propaganda. It is noteworthy that no comparison was made between Sarah and the best-known spy of the First World War, Mata Hari. The reasons are clear. Hari spied, apparently, for personal gain and not for any nation. Moreover, by the first decade of the twentieth century she was already a sex symbol and an orientalist icon of sensuality and exotic eastern femininity. Saint Joan and the nurse Cavell, in contrast, were symbols of a national femininity, distinctly nonsexual and asexual. The military nurse and the virgin-warrior crossed the gender lines without endangering the prototype and ideal of the female saint. A similar tendency to desexualize the heroine and distance her from an ascribed gender role also characterizes the memory of Sarah Aaronsohn and bears little relation to her "real" life.

The comparisons to Christian myths and images of womanhood are especially important because they manifest not only the tension, enhanced by the blurring of the borderlines of gender, between definitions of femininity and nationalism, but also the syncretism of the national symbols of the center and right-wing circles in *Eretz Yisrael*. Some of the images of femininity taken on by these circles were not Jewish but Catholic or Protestant Evangelical. The use of the myth of Joan of Arc in relation to Sarah Aaronsohn is an examplar of such syncretism. Joan was a virgin, and her virginity endowed her with exceptional power in contrast to other women, though her special power also derived from her assumption of the role of a soldier and cross-dressing as a man. As a man-woman who deviated from the boundaries of gender, Joan became a symbol of national as well as many political and social movements: Catholic and Protestant, right-wing royalist movements and radical movements on the right and left in France, anti-feminist movements and militant feminists such as the WSPU (Women's Social and Political Union, the British suffragette organization).[53]

The analogy between Sarah Aaronsohn, the woman farmer and native of the land, and Joan of Arc, the French peasant of Lorraine, was quite prevalent in the political rhetoric of Bnei Binyamin and various right-wing circles. The heroism of Aaronsohn, who "invited" the British to her land, was compared to Joan of Arc's anti-Burgundian and anti-English patriotism. Moreover, both women were depicted as soldiers and at times referred to in the masculine gender. Already in the second pilgrimage to Aaronsohn's grave, in 1933, Bnei Binyamin activist Ze'ev Neiderman, also a native of Zikhron Yaakov, compared Aaronsohn's acts to the "nobility and heroism of this daughter of Orleans, 'Joanna of Arc'": in the pilgrimage "to the holy grave of Sarah of Zikhron, we today went up to this holy place to stand at attention before the same exalted soul and to remind future generations of this heroine of Zikhron Yaakov, like the heroine of Orleans."[54] In the pilgrimage of 1941, Aaronsohn was called a heroine "greater than Joan of Arc,"[55] and, speaking at her grave in October 1946, Betar member Baruch Weinstein called her "the Hebrew Joan of Arc ... Commander of Nili." But here the resemblance ends

> between Joan of Arc, the Frenchwoman, and Sarah, the Hebrew. They made their appearance in different national frameworks, in different periods, and under different conditions. Joan of Arc — among her own people, sitting on their own land, healthy in body and soul ... who saw her, the heroine, as their emissary — their leader — of their own flesh. Joan of Arc made her appearance in an atmosphere of sympathy and admiration. The French people understood the value of her mission, gave her their assistance and backing for her actions. And our Sarah? She [appeared] under conditions of a cruel foreign government [and in

a society] that had not reached a stage of complete national development ... . Under these conditions, Sarah the Commander appeared.[56]

Weinstein's typical speech is marked by his alternating use of the masculine and feminine gender, especially in his description of Joan-Sarah as a military commander. Joan of Arc, as noted, donned a uniform, and was depicted in uniform in the religious and secular iconography of both the right and left in the early twentieth century, as well as in feminist iconography. However, another source of her power was her virginity. In Western Christian culture virginity was perceived as a source of female power and, more important, of authority.[57] Beginning in the early 1930s, Aaronsohn was described as a (female) commander or as a (male) soldier and officer. The militarizing of her image and concomitant blurring of her sexuality (and femininity) culminated during the Second World War. Already in 1935 a Betar boat and naval unit were named after her,[58] and from 1941 representatives of the British Army attended her memorial. From 1942 her graveside eulogies became army recruitment speeches, and a number of recruits swore allegiance to Sarah Aaronsohn and committed themselves to avenging her sacrifice by freeing *Eretz Yisrael* and world Jewry from the National-Socialist threat. These recruits included not only members of Betar, but also members of *moshavot* whose political affiliation may not be determined with certainty.[59]

With the end of the Second World War, there was no longer a need to militarize Sarah Aaronsohn or to imagine her as a soldier. However, her blurred sexuality and sexual identity remained a part of her image as the alternative national saint of the Revisionist right. Thus, in 1958, the historian Joseph Klausner found it necessary to point out:

> Another people would have bestowed a laurel wreath on her. I do not know what the world view of the French was, but the French people as a whole fall on their knees before Joan of Arc, who, in actuality, did not bring about victory and permitted the desecration of her body. And how do we treat Sarah? And this after the State has already been established.... How many books have been written about Sarah? To what extent are her history and heroic act taught in schools?

Klausner in fact urged women to constitute an alternative memory of the "heroine": "Women should have established something special in her memory."[60] Women and girls did indeed take an active part in the pilgrimages to the grave, both as members of the organizations involved in the commemoration, such as Young Maccabi and Betar, and as members of women's organizations, such as the Federation of National Women affiliated with the New Zionist Federation. However, women's participation, like the blurring of gender in the political memory of Sarah Aaronsohn, may not be taken as proof of an egalitarian outlook on gender relations within the Civic Sector or in its dominant political movements. As several historians of gender have shown, integral nationalist movements identified with the right, whether the radical or the traditional right, tended (more than liberal or left-wing movements), to foster non-maternalist images of femininity. In some of the former, women succeeded in carving out major roles for themselves.[61] However, the process by which access to the nation and the right to act on its behalf were extended to women did not involve egalitarian politics, nor a liberal universalist notion of rights. Thus, in the *Yishuv*'s right-wing circles and in the various farmers' organizations, the radical view of femininity that characterized the myth of Aaronsohn did not manifest itself in practice. Bnei Binyamin, for example, did not accept women as members. Moreover, its rhetoric (except for Aaronsohn's memorial rituals) celebrated male brotherhood, as one of the organization's publications noted.[62] Thus, Bnei Binyamin carried on the pre-First World War tradition of the "Gidonim" (after the biblical Gideon, the semi-military, all-male organization of the native-born from which Nili eventually emerged) and, unlike other youth movements, excluded women. Mixed organizations as well as nationalist women's organizations which criticized the militarism and militaristic rituals of the exclusively male organizations were established before, during and after the war. Nili itself was a mixed organization, in which the borderlines of the definition of femininity and nation were stretched in an unprecedented manner, especially in Sarah Aaronsohn's activities.[63] However, as Mary Louise Roberts and Rajeswari Sunder Rajan have shown, a gender model that blurs the difference between what is considered "feminine" and what is accepted as "masculine" may develop, and is actually more likely to develop, within hierarchical communities with a patriarchal tradition lacking gender equality. It is precisely in such communities that images of exceptional and extraordinary women, embodying ideal qualities that are not necessarily "essentially" feminine, can develop.[64] What needs stressing in the anti-maternalist narrative reviewed here is not the disparity between this narrative and the actual position of women in the Civic Sector in the *Yishuv*, but women's conspicuous presence in the nationalist discourse and the ways in which this presence shaped the collective memory.

This narrative should not be seen as a political "invention" manufactured by bodies with clear programs and political affiliations. Obviously, the narrative was political. However, it seeped into the popular memory and created that fabric of representations and practices which Raphael termed "the density of memory." These practices testify to the extent to which Sarah Aaronsohn — as a symbol of active female heroism that challenged the definitions of femininity — was identified with Nili. A clear case of this permeation of the myth into the collective memory was the practice of naming girls "Nili." Choosing a name is a way of bestowing identity, both on those who choose it and on the person for whom it is chosen. Nili was a national and native name, an acronym that stood for the biblical phrase "Netzah Yisrael lo yeshaker" (the Strength of Israel will not lie [1 Sam. 15:29]).

Prior to the second half of the 1930s, the name Nili was chosen rarely and sporadically. Yet, as the data on Hebrew names gathered by Sasha Weitman shows, it appeared on the population register regularly from 1936 onwards. Between 1936 and 1979, 2,889 girls were named Nili. In contrast, only 1,300 boys were given the name Avshalom, which was both biblical and native, and was not exclusively identified with the underground figure Avshalom Feinberg. The name Nili was most popular in the early 1940s: it was given to 75 girls in 1940, to 106 in 1942, to 150 in 1943, and to 141 in 1944. In the early 1950s, its popularity declined, rising again at the end of the decade, with an increase from 46 in 1955 to 59 in 1958. A further increase occurred in 1967, when 71 baby girls were named Nili.[65] The value of these figures is rather limited since there is no way of breaking them down and analyzing them by ethnic origin, economic and social status or political affiliation of the families that named their daughters Nili. However, the clear national character of this name and the fact that it was most popular during periods of national emergency (like the Second World War and the Six Day War) and security crises (during the 1950s) point to the feminization of the memory of heroism. Oral testimonies indicate that the choice of the name Nili was not limited to right-wing circles.[66]

The domestication of the memory and its appropriation to the daily life of women and girls are also manifest in Sarah Aaronsohn's legitimization in the women's press, where her biography began to appear in the second half of the 1940s. In one commemorative article published on the 30th anniversary of her death (1947) in the weekly magazine La-Ishah (literally, For the Woman) — which would become a prototype for writing about her in this press — Sarah's story served as a way of inverting a conventional gender fairy tale: the story of the rescued princess. This biographical article, entitled "Captain without Stars," completely reverses the customary image of the princess. Sarah is not rescued or saved by any of the men around her, but rather frees herself of them. She chooses to liberate herself from an unsatisfying marriage and the burden of home and family and becomes the "captain of her fate" as well as the captain of the underground.

As captain, she rejects the suggestion of her older brother, Aaron Aaronsohn, to escape on the British warship Managem, which had been sent to retrieve the activists in the espionage network. And as "captain" of her ship, she commits suicide.[67] It is precisely on a platform like the weekly women's magazine, which perpetuated cults of femininity and domesticity, that Aaronsohn's military behavior is portrayed not as a contradiction of feminine ideals but rather as a possibility for a correct gendered nationalist behavior. This kind of diffusion (and internalization) of the story of Nili raises doubts about the assumption, still widely accepted in the debate on memory, that centers and elites mold the national ethos by means of cultural hegemony, and have an omnipotent power over the collective memory. Memory became part of the everyday, here the everyday of women and girls. It developed in the arena outside the core of hegemony — outside the ceremonial and the distinctly political space of official rites of commemoration and in "sites" outside unifying systems with repressive powers. This very process serves as proof of the tenacity and durability of a gendered memory that is both marginal and peripheral.

1967: Into "the National Pantheon"?

In the debate on memory and identity in Israeli society, the year 1967 has the special status of an *annus mirabilis* (or, depending on the interlocutor's politics and ideology, an *annus horribilis*). It is generally described as heralding a profound change and as the beginning of an ongoing process of the disintegration of collective ethoses and of a uniform, hegemonic and cohesive culture of memory. Above all, the period beginning in 1967 is associated with the process of the "privatization of memory" and its expropriation from the nation and from national needs to groups and individuals within the nation.[68] However, an examination of the evolution of the memory of Sarah Aaronsohn as a gendered process may change our perspective on the broader changes in Israeli culture and society, as well as on the relationship between periphery and "center" within the national community.

The year 1967 indeed represents a surfeit of memory and commemoration; but, in contrast to the practices of the 1930s and 1940s, the commemorations of the 50th anniversary of the death of Sarah Aaronsohn were marked by her appropriation into the mainstream ethos and consensus and her consolidation as a popular figure. Along with these developments, there also occurred a perceptible change in her status as a heroine. These changes were related, of course, to the political and cultural changes of the times. The Six Day War, with the arrogance that followed in its wake, happened to occur in the 50th anniversary year of the eradication of Nili. It was in this year that Sarah Aaronsohn first received official state recognition by the representatives of the hegemonic and ruling Labor movement culture. In 1967, the men and women members of the Nili underground who had been killed were recognized as soldiers in uniform who had died in action, and those who had survived were decorated with the "Nili Medal." That same year, the bones of Avshalom Feinberg were discovered by chance and brought to burial in a full military ceremony. In tandem with these events, the first official state ceremony was held at the grave of Sarah Aaronsohn in Zikhron Yaakov.

In the memorial ceremonies conducted between 1967 and the death of Rivkah Aaronsohn in 1981, Sarah's younger sister and the force behind her local commemoration, the local Zikhron Yaakov tradition and the state tradition intermingled in the annual pilgrimage to Sarah's grave. The revised syncretic ceremony had a clear feminine element: members of the Bnot Brit Organization of Zikhron Yaakov gathered together with women from the adjacent *moshavot*, many of whom had been active in the Bnot Binyamin Federation, the women's equivalent of Bnei Binyamin.[69] They gathered in the Aaronsohn family home before the public ceremony and marched to Sarah's grave, led by Rivkah Aaronsohn.

Such signs that the peripheral memory was penetrating the central and official tradition were not restricted to the ceremonies. The peripheral memory was legitimized in the gender discourse within the Labor movement itself. Already in November 1967, after the jubilee ceremony, Rachel Katzenelson, editor of *Dvar ha-Po'elet* (Word of the Woman Worker), the flagship magazine of women's activity in the movement, published a lead article on Sarah Aaronsohn in which she described Aaronsohn as the first *Tzabarit* (female Sabra) and a national heroine. More important, she also settled accounts with the leadership of the *Yishuv* during the First World War and with the pre-state and Israeli Labor leadership on the suppression of the story of the Nili heroine. Katzenelson even called for reburying Aaronsohn — metaphorically, of course — in the state pantheon:

> From now own, she shall belong not only to the national pantheon of the renewed *Eretz Yisrael* [!]. She shall also be incorporated into the innermost soul of the nation ... . So, now, after some fifty years of silencing, they win the recognized title of admired heroes of the nation, a model for coming generations. Indeed, Sarah's home in Zikhron Yaakov still remains something of a "private national museum," a family heirloom, administered as a national asset and serving as a sanctified site for mass pilgrimages, by the young and old of all kinds.[70]

Katzenelson's sermon was undoubtedly inspired by political motives. As one of the founders of the Livneh group, the first adherents of the idea of a Greater Israel in the Labor movement, Katzenelson may have been attracted to the territorialism and political activism of the heroes of the "native" culture in general and of Sarah Aaronsohn in particular. But a narrow biographical-political explanation does not suffice here, as Aaronsohn and Nili were rehabilitated within the Labor movement as a whole, and not only in its Greater Israel circles. Even before Katzenelson's article, *Davar*, the Labor daily and the most authoritative platform of official discourse, had devoted some columns to the debate on Sarah Aaronsohn and her actions. From October to December 1967 the newspaper published a series of articles by writers of both the Revisionist right and the Labor movement on the Nili affair, the attitude towards the underground, and the association between this attitude and the formation of the collective memory. Yehuda Slutsky claimed that the "Nili group" was "from a social and historical perspective ... the first sign of independent political activity on the part of the 'Sabra'." He saw Nili as a reflection of the native-born hero Yoash, "the new Jew of *Eretz Yisrael*" in the story by this name by Joseph Luidor (1912). Slutsky, who evidently was not a member of the Labor movement, portrayed Aaronsohn as a moral authority and as "the first link in the chain of the fallen for the establishment of the State of Israel."[71] However, the fact that his voice was heard from a platform such as *Davar* is evidence of the change in Labor's attitude towards this chapter in the history of the *Yishuv*. Nonetheless, one of the responses to the article leveled criticism at the attempt — attributed to the right, but also to voices identified with the Labor movement — to "falsify our history" and to include in it persons, like Nili members, who harmed the security of the *Yishuv*.[72]

The debate on the death and memory of Aaronsohn thus became at once a negotiation over her inclusion in the official national ideology and a discourse on the development of the nationalist memory of Labor itself — her exclusion in the past from this discourse, on the one hand, and the integration of different kinds of heroic ethos into the discourse on the other. Katzenelson, for example, found it necessary to compare Sarah Aaronsohn to "the female workers" and female socialist settlers of the Second *Aliyah*, Manya Shochat and Dvorah Dayan. Dayan, who was perceived as one of the female saints of the pioneer Labor settlement, was the mother of a national *Sabra* icon, Moshe Dayan.[73]

The rehabilitation of the memory of Sarah Aaronsohn, and the efforts to bring her memory to bear on the history and ethos of Hebrew labor and settlement, did not impair her appeal as a popular, and not necessarily political, heroine. In contrast to the memory of Trumpeldor and the myth of Tel Hai, the memory of Aaronsohn and Nili survived outside clearly political and official sites of memory. In fact, the single most important feature of the narratives of her heroism fashioned after 1967 was the depoliticization of her national activity. Depoliticization was accompanied by another crucial change: Aaronsohn's feminization — an emphasis on the feminine and domestic essence of her activities, on the one hand, and the sexualization of these activities, or her representation as a product of the relations between the sexes and sometimes as a product of female identity and sexuality, on the other. Before 1967, and especially before 1948, there had been a concerted effort to blur Aaronsohn's sexuality and the gender boundaries of her activities. However, after 1967 she was pushed to the margins of the story of Nili, while efforts were made to include her in the national pantheon. Her involvement in national affairs was interpreted as the outcome of her position in her family and in the extended "family" of the Nili underground.

These two changes, occurring simultaneously, are especially striking in the shaping of Aaronsohn's image as a "historical" and didactic heroine for juveniles. Nili gradually made its way into the curriculum of the mainstream state school system, as well as into the special curricula of the kibbutz movement. From the second half of the 1960s, the moralizing position regarding Nili's activities was almost totally abandoned, and discussion of Nili was no longer political. At the same time, Sarah Aaronsohn's role in the underground was rarely mentioned, while the deeds of the men were discussed in great detail. She was rendered mostly in terms of her familial and gender affiliations: as the younger sister of Aaron, "father" of the underground, and as a loyal daughter. This feminization of her image is striking, for example, in the second edition of *The History of the People of Israel in Our Generation* by Shimshon Leib Kirshenbaum (1965), in the nine editions of his book *The History of Israel in Recent Generations* published between 1968 and 1973,[74] as well as in *A Brief History of Israel in Recent Times*, by Shlomo Horowitz, which was used by teachers and pupils of the Reali High School in Haifa (1973).[75]

Sarah's marginality is also manifest in the guidelines for teachers issued by the curricula division of Ha-Kibbutz ha-Artzi, the kibbutz movement of the left-wing Ha-Shomer ha-Tza'ir. These guidelines stipulated that the Nili affair was to be taught in the movement's schools by means of reenactment games with the triple aim of first, "encouraging the consideration of and thinking about Nili as a social-historical group"; second, rousing debate "on the moral image of Ha-Shomer" and of the Labor movement in general, given the history of Nili and their treatment of this organization; and third, "expressing feelings and opinions about concepts such as 'the politically persecuted'." In the detailed quiz that accompanied the program, Sarah was mentioned only marginally and characterized by the gendered trait of "nobility" (described as a feminine quality), rather than by her actions or ideas.[76]

It is difficult to assess the influence of these schoolbooks on different juvenile readerships. It is easier to appraise the distribution and impact of texts such as *Sarah giborat Nili* (Sarah, Heroine of Nili) by Dvorah Omer, which contributed more than any other book to spreading the memory and myth of Aaronsohn as a heroine for young people and as a model of *Eretz Yisraeli*-ness. Between 1967, when it was published, and 1990, the book went through 25 printings, and between 1970 and 2000 it sold 88,009 copies. It was a "steady seller," its sales never falling below 1,500 or rising above 3,300 copies a year.[77] In the wake of its success, Omer wrote a play with the same title, which ran for fifteen consecutive years at the Theater for Children and Young People.

The book deserves special note since it was the first monograph written for children on Sarah Aaronsohn and Nili, a subject which until then, as already noted, had been treated only in the children's and juvenile press of the periphery. Moreover, the book is a clear example of the penetration of spontaneous and apolitical popular memory into the hegemonic mythology of *Eretz Yisraeli* heroism, and also of the complex relationship between dominant, official myths and those evolving in the periphery. A test case of this set of relationships between the center and periphery in Israeli culture, the success of *Sarah giborat Nili*, raises questions about the power of establishments or of so-called "central agents of culture." Moreover, the book also encapsulates the changes, noted above, in the relationship between gender and identity: that is, the feminization of the female national "hero," on the one hand, and the integration of this "hero" into an epic national narrative, on the other hand.

The book, like the *Ha-No'azim* (The Audacious) series of which it was a part, was the brain-child of the educator, editor and writer Uriel Ofek, who suggested it to Omer as an "educational story."[78] The very view of Sarah Aaronsohn as a model "educational figure" was totally new, since, until then, the activities of Nili and Aaronsohn had not been deemed "educating" or even properly nationalist outside Civic circles.

For Omer, who had been raised in a kibbutz and was identified, like Ofek, with the Labor movement and with the mainstream culture, Sarah Aaronsohn was a political and sexual adventuress. Omer and Ofek felt a need to provide young people with literature that would rescue "stories of *Eretz Yisraeli* heroism" from oblivion.[79] Thus the *Ha-Noazim* series, which included canonical figures such as Hannah Senesh and Manya Shochat, also made room for peripheral figures like Sarah Aaronsohn, the pugilist and spiritualist Raphael Halperin and Etzel terrorist/freedom fighter Dov Gruner. Not only was the book not published on the initiative of the establishment; it was not supported by it either. It was brought out by the small, politically unaffiliated Sherberk publishing house.[80] Yet it received no funding from the "local" commemorative apparatus based in Zikhron Yaakov, under the direction of Rivkah Aaronsohn, who helped finance a number of hagiographies of Sarah Aaronsohn and other Nili figures that were published from the 1930s. Rivkah Aaronsohn cooperated with Omer only after the book had proven a success, and even tried (with little success) to interfere in how her sister's image would be shaped, attempting to remove details that undermined Sarah's asexual image, such as the descriptions of her in the company of Turkish and German officers.[81]

The book's indisputable success led to its adoption both by the educational establishment and by the local memorial center. From the early 1970s onward, the Ministry of Education ordered numerous copies of the book through projects such as "A Book for Every Home" and "The Literature Fund for the

Children of Israel." From 1970, about 10,000 copies of *Sarah giborat Nili* (5,009 of them in 1970 alone) were produced for the Ministry of Education.[82] At the same time, the book's success also transformed the Beit Aaronsohn Museum into a flourishing center, especially for schoolchildren. As early as 1970, it was visited by pupils from the very sectors that in the past had excluded Sarah Aaronsohn and Nili from the collective memory and youth culture: namely, the kibbutzim and the Labor-affiliated agricultural settlements.[83]

It may seem that Sarah Aaronsohn in the 1967 version is the focus of Omer's novel and of the newly defined memory of Nili's heroic deeds. She bestows her name on the novel; indeed, the novel itself is the first *Bildungsroman* about a young *Eretz Yisraeli* girl. Without doubt, Omer had intended to tell the historical story from a female perspective. She preferred to narrate the epic of Sabra-ness through the figure of Sarah Aaronsohn and not through that of Avshalom Feinberg precisely "because she was a woman, and I could identify with her better" and because women were absent from [Israel's] history and youth culture.[84]

In addition, Omer's version of Sarah's life is in no way domestic. It is a story of adventures and heroism, a "thriller," in the words of the boy listening to the narrator in the "outer" story that frames the inner plot of the First World War heroism. Sarah is apparently a "hero." She possesses the traits of the non-essentialist woman, who is not a mother: physical prowess and the skills of a scout and warrior and horsemanship.[85] She and her younger sister Rivkah are even included in the quasi-military activities of the Gidonim (in fact, the Gidonim had excluded women and girls).[86]

However, this narrative of national political activity is undermined and even canceled out by a separate, albeit parallel, narrative. This is the story of one woman's personal drama, in which the personal engenders the political act in an almost deterministic way over which Sarah has no control. Sarah is driven to her activities for *Eretz Yisrael* through and by the men around her. "Girls don't fight, but you must know how to defend yourselves," her brother Alexander tells her. "It's good I was born a girl," Sarah declares. "I'm terrified of blood and afraid of every pain, even the tiniest."[87] And, elsewhere: "Only if she becomes a heroine will he [Avshalom] value her."[88] Sarah's death scene at the end of the book merges the feminine, essentialist narrative with memory itself: "I'm coming, Avshalom ... Remember me, don't forget ... ."[89]

From the Periphery to the National Pantheon

That the "legend of Sarah" took such a circuitous road from the periphery to the national pantheon of heroism clearly has a political reason and explanation. This article discussed the suppression of Sarah's death, and of the

Nili affair itself, as well as the delayed evolution and peripheral nature of her memory. All these were undoubtedly outcomes of her political, social and cultural affiliation to a group that was excluded from the hegemonic memory, and not the result of her gender. However, as the first part of the article argues, this political explanation is inadequate. For when the memory did evolve, it was distinctively gendered. It was shaped by different, and sometimes competing, perceptions of the national female-social identity. The survey offered here of these perceptions, of their dynamics, and of their representation in the dense fabric of memory may teach us some lessons that could prove useful for students of the history of memory, for those who map Israeli identity, and for historians of women and gender.

The first lesson concerns the dynamic and frequently changing presence of group — or collective — memory in culture and society. The memory of a voluntary death for the nation was shaped by the Labor movement establishment, as historians of the legend of Tel Hai and the story of Trumpeldor have shown. However, this memory was not homogenous, and not even hegemonic. Alongside this central and unifying myth other memories also emerged in "cells" or sectors of civil society, in what is generally viewed as the cultural and political periphery. Moreover, these memories had begun to crystallize before the disintegration of the Labor hegemony and a long time before the processes that are conventionally described as the segmentation and disintegration of the Israeli national ethos. The alternative memory of Sarah Aaronsohn, which started off as a marginal and sectorial compound of rites and practices of remembrance memory and evolved into a popular memory, was crystallized precisely during that same period which is seen as the zenith of Labor hegemony and cultural domination. However, the Labor establishment did not have unchallenged control over the narrative of the past or the contents of memory; these were subjects of a continuous negotiation, in which individuals and groups outside the center (whether or not they were identified with specific political groups) took part. It is thus quite clear that "center" and "margins" or periphery are relative and complementary, rather than binary entities.

The second lesson, which is closely related to the first, concerns not only the periodization of the history of the particular memory studied here — or of Israeli memory more broadly — but also the periodization of *Eretz Yisraeli* and Israeli culture as a uniform and cohesive entity. In the historiography and study of Israeli culture in general, the collapse of cohesiveness is still associated with the emergence of the critique of the Zionist project voiced in the 1980s and 1990s, as well as with the profound changes in Israel's social fabric after the 1960s. However, the example of Aaronsohn indicates that the sharp distinction between an "official" and central monolithic memory during the *Yishuv* era and the early years of the State, and the splitting and pluralization afterwards, has little or no validity. Pluralism and the "polyphonic" choir of memory characterized the discourse on Sarah Aaronsohn from the very beginning.

The third and most important lesson concerns the use of gender in the study of memory. This is considerably more than the mere "addition" of a forgotten historical female subject to a historical pantheon. It is an indispensable tool for analyzing nationalism and nationalist myths. It is also a valuable methodology, which provides us with additional — and perhaps new — understanding of the manner in which images and constructs of female identities formed the ways in which the past was remembered, represented and commemorated.

Precisely the fact that Aaronsohn was commemorated as a figure embodying competing, and sometimes conflicting, images of femininity, whose interrelationships changed over time, reinforces her enduring image as a national heroine. Aaronsohn embodied the maternalist ideal of female patriotism but at the same time crossed the boundaries of femininity. She represented essentialized female features and secular Zionist ideals of femininity, but also Western Christian perceptions that had undergone processes of secularization and syncretization. Once again the lack of compatibilities in gendered memory are apparent, the very contradictions within the national images of femininity and women, which cannot and need not be resolved. These "insoluble paradoxes" (Joan Wallach Scott's term)[90] are saliencies of gender constructs and of the definition of femininity in the modern nationalist age. The paradoxes do not detract from the power of the myth, but strengthen it, as illustrated above. Significantly, the paradox of the maternal woman and the sexless soldier, which cohabits in the discourse on Sarah Aaronsohn, was especially pronounced in times of crises and transitions, for example in the 1930s and 1940s. Moreover, at such times, the female image also served as a metaphor, a tool, and as the locus of a discussion of the broader issues concerning the relationships of individuals and groups with *Eretz Yisrael* and *Eretz Yisraeli* identity.

Yet Aaronsohn's survival as a female icon of the nation well into the so-called post-Zionist era also involved her transformation into a more conventional figure. From the late 1960s, with the rehabilitation of her memory, Aaronsohn's image became wholly essentialist. Paradoxically, the narrative of her heroism and death seeped into the narrative of sacrifice for the nation at the very same time as the story of her heroism was detached from the political and public sphere. As my analysis of the novel *Sarah giborat Nili* shows, the hierarchy between the political and the personal that characterized the 1930s and 1940s was reversed in the depiction of the character of the *Eretz Yisraeli* heroine. The story is made by the personal drama of the *Eretz Yisraeli* woman; and the public and political are explained in terms of the personal and intimate.

This reversal is even more striking in the 1993 television drama *Sarah*, whose creators enjoyed liberties that Omer, as the writer of a book for children and adolescents, never had. The depoliticization of the myth and the sexualization of Sarah are reinforced in various ways: the script of the teledrama, the contents of the introduction to the story, which is spoken in a male voice, visual images, props, dress and body language, and sentimental-romantic music. The new hierarchy is established in the polarities within the opening statement: "Sarah came to politics from love, and to love from politics." It is consistently reinforced through Sarah's appearances on screen, where camera shots of her face create a claustrophobic, domestic ambiance: in her tiny bedroom; in the kitchen, where she performs female chores like cooking and sewing; and on the balcony of the experimental agriculture station at Atlit, where she hangs out colored washing (to signal the British ship *Managem*), a shot that relays political and domestic meanings at one and the same time. Only for 2.39 minutes out of over 50 minutes of film is Aaronsohn seen in outdoor shots, in which she plays a secondary or passive role. In the opening and final scenes, which frame the story, the camera travels from her scarred and bloody legs to her unkempt hair, as she walks along the main street of Zikhron Yaakov. The historical Aaronsohn took care to tie up her hair, and various sources describe her walk from the interrogation room to her brother's house as proud and dignified. In the teledrama, neighbors denounce her with shouts of "whore, whore … ."[91] There may be no sharper contrast than that between this comparison of Aaronsohn to a prostitute in the early 1990s and the analogies to the Maid of Orléans in the 1940s.

We must be wary, however, of a simplistic and linear view of the gendered memory studied here that would describe it as a move from the periphery to the center, or from the right to the center, hence to the left. We must also be careful not to idealize the peripheral memory, for this will lead us to chart a decline in or a deviation from an original powerful image to one representing powerlessness, thus delineating a process in which a memory that features an activity that crosses the boundaries of gender turns into an essentialist and sexual memory. Such a reduction to a movement from Joan of Arc to the sexual Sarah ignores the complexity of the images during the two periods studied here, the "insoluble paradoxes" that characterize them. It may of course be argued that endowing Sarah Aaronsohn with masculine qualities and the rituals commemorating her as a "soldier" and as "Sarah, the [male] commander" actually reinforced inequality. For these images were shaped by political and military organizations that were highly patriarchal and excluded women from their activities. Yet it would be mistaken to reduce the blurring of gender boundaries to a manifestation of total repression or the silencing of women's voices. The emphasis on the absence of female sexuality, the erasure of the image of the "mother of the nation," and the blurring of gender — all these characterized native *Eretz Yisraeli* women's discourse until 1920. As I have shown in great detail elsewhere, the crossing of the borderlines of gender was particularly salient in the activities of Nili and those close to this group, and characterized the activities, writings and self-image of Sarah Aaronsohn herself.[92] In other words, the martial images that were so central to the commemorative rituals prior to the 1950s were not created by a "male elite." They were drawn from a reservoir of images and representations that were available to the men and women of the time, and especially to the men and women of the remembering group.

The appropriation of Aaronsohn's memory and her commemoration in the national pantheon, from the end of the 1960s, are closely related to an essentialist perception of women and femininity within the state. Nonetheless, this essentialism is not peculiar to the hegemonic culture or the so-called formal "agents" of this culture, but rather is conspicuous in feminist and postmodern interpretations of the female Zionist story, for example in Ben-Dor's and Landau's teledrama. The lessons related here may tell us that gender and memory are closely intertwined and are quite inseparable — whether as subjects for research or as possibilities for analyzing national culture. If we acknowledge this, we shall perhaps be able to write a history that will allow a different and more complex interpretation of Israeliness, of national memory and of national amnesia than is available to us at the present.

NOTES

*   This essay, which was first published in *Zion*, Vol. 65, No. 3 (2000), pp. 343–78, is dedicated to the memory of George L. Mosse, whose writings on memory, war, and masculinity have brought me to study the associations between gender, memory, and identity and *Eretz Yisraeli* culture. I thank Shulamith Shachar and Shulamit Volkov, who read an earlier version of the article. I owe special thanks to Natalie Zemon Davis and Avner Ben-Amos for their contributions to my understanding of the complexity of collective memory. I extend thanks to Deborah Bernstein, Yaffa Berlovitz, Dalia Ofer, and Margalit Shilo for their comments. The staff of the Beit Aaronsohn Archives in Zikhron Yaakov helped me find a variety of documents dealing with the commemoration of Sarah Aaronsohn in the 1930s and 1940s. I am also indebted to Dvorah Omer, Zohar Shavit, Yael Dar, Rima Shichmenter and Naama Sheik Eitan.

1   The quotation is from Renan's lecture at the Sorbonne, 1 March 1882, "Qu'est-ce qu'une nation?", *Oeuvres completes*, Vol. 1 (Paris, 1947–61), pp. 887–907, translated in Homi K. Bhabha (ed.), *Nation and Narration* (London, 1990), p. 11.
2   Charles S. Maier, "A Surfeit of Memory? Reflections on History, Melancholy and Denial," *History & Memory*, Vol. 5, No. 2 (Fall/Winter 1993), pp. 136–7.
3   Marcel Proust, *Du côté de chez Swann* (Paris, 1954), p. 57.
4   See, for example, Pierre Nora (ed.), *Les Lieux de mémoire* (Paris, 1984–92); Paul Connerton, *How Societies Remember* (New York, Cambridge, 1989); John R. Gillis (ed.), *Commemorations: The Politics of National Identity* (Princeton, 1994); Raphael Samuel, *Past and Present in*

Contemporary Culture, Vol. 1, *Theatres of Memory* (London, 1994); Frances A. Yates, *The Art of Memory* (London, 1984, reprint); Jay M. Winter, *Sites of Memory, Sites of Mourning* (London, 1996); George L. Mosse, *Fallen Soldiers: Reshaping the Memory of the World Wars* (New York, 1990); Natalie Zemon Davis and Randolph Starn, "Introduction," *Representations*, No. 26 (Spring 1989), special issue on collective memory and counter-memory.

5 Emanual Sivan, *Dor tashah: Mitos, dyukan ve-zikaron* (The Generation of 1948: Myth, Profile, and Memory) (Tel Aviv, 1991), especially pp. 169–231; Yael Zerubavel, "Mot ha-zikaron ve-zikaron ha-mavet" (The Death of Memory and the Memory of Death), *Alpayim*, No. 10 (1994), pp. 42–68; Anita Shapira, "Historiografiyah ve-zikaron: Mikreh Latrun tashah" (Historiography and Memory: The Case of Latroun, 1948), ibid., pp. 9–42; David Ohana and Robert S. Wistrich (eds.), *Mitos ve-zikaron: Gilguleiha shel ha-toda'ah ha-yisre'elit* (Myth and Memory: Transfigurations of Israeli Consciousness) (Jerusalem, 1996); Yael Zerubavel, *Recovered Roots: Collective Memory and the Making of Israeli National Tradition* (Chicago, 1995); idem, "The Historic, the Legendary, and the Incredible in Invented Tradition and Collective Memory in Israel," in Gillis (ed.), *Commemorations*, pp. 105–25; David N. Myers, *Reinventing the Jewish Past in Israel* (New York and Oxford, 1995); Nachman Ben Yehuda, *The Massada Myth: Collective Memory and Mythmaking in Israel* (Madison, WI, 1995). See also Idith Zartal, "Ha-me'unim veha-kdushim: Kinunah shel martirologiyah le'umit" (The Tortured and the Sanctified: The Creation of National Martyrology), *Zmanim*, No. 48 (1994), pp. 26–45; Eliezer Witztum and Ruth Malkinson, "Shkhol ve-hantzahah: Ha-panim ha-kfulim shel ha-mitos ha-le'umi" (Bereavement and Commemoration: The Dual Face of the National Myth), in Ruth Malkinson, Shimshon Rubin and Eliezer Witztum (eds.), *Ovdan ve-shkhol ba-hevrah ha-yisre'elit* (Loss and Bereavement in Israeli Society) (Jerusalem, 1993), pp. 231–58.

6 Conversations with Natalie Zemon Davis, 17–19 March 1998.

7 Zerubavel, "Mot ha-zikaron"; Ohana and Wistrich (eds.), *Mitos ve-zikaron*. On *The Yizkor Book*, see Jonathan Frankel's important study, "*The Yizkor Book* of 1911 — A Note on National Myth in the Second *Aliya*," in Hedva Ben Israel et al. (eds.), *Religion, Ideology and Nationalism in Europe and America: Essays in Honor of Yehoshua Arieli* (Jerusalem, 1986), pp. 355–84.

8 For the most recent reflection of the state of the research, see Margalit Shilo, Ruth Kark, and Galit Hasan-Rokem (eds.), *Nashim ba-yishuv uva-medinah be-reshit darkah* (Jewish Women in the *Yishuv* and Zionism) (Jerusalem, 2001), especially Deborah S. Bernstein, "Heker nashim ba-historiografiyah ha-yisre'elit: Nekudot motza, kavanot hadashot ve-kavanot sheba-derekh" (The Study of Women in Israeli Historiography: Starting Points, New Directions, and Emerging Insights), ibid., pp. 7–25; Billie Melman, "Min ha-shulayim el ha-historiyah shel ha-yishuv: Migdar ve-eretz yisre'eliyut (1890–1920)" (From the Periphery to the Center of *Yishuv* History: Gender and Nationalism in Eretz Israel [1890–1920]), *Zion*, Vol. 62, No. 3 (1997), pp. 243–79. See also Judith T. Baumel, "'In Everlasting Memory': Individual and Communal Holocaust Commemoration in Israel," in Robert Wistrich and David Ohana (eds.), *The Shaping of Israeli Identity: Myth, Memory, and Trauma* (London, 1995), pp. 146–70; Orly Lubin, "Ha-emet she-bein misgerot ha-emet: Otobiografiyah, edut, guf ve-atar" (The Truth between the Frameworks of Truth: Autobiography, Testimony, Body, and Place), in *Aderet le-Vinyamin: Sefer ha-yovel le-Binyamin Harshav* (Jubilee Book for Binyamin Harshav), Vol. 1 (Tel Aviv, 1999), pp. 133–49; Hannah Naveh, *Be-shevi ha-evel: Ha-evel be-re'i ha-sifrut ha-ivrit ha-hadashah* (In the Thrall of Mourning: Mourning in the Mirror of the New Israeli Literature) (Tel Aviv, 1993). For more on the definition of the areas of the history of memory, see Jay Winter and Emanuel Sivan (eds.), *War and Remembrance in the Twentieth Century* (Cambridge, 1996), pp. 6–40.

9 Alon Confino, "Collective Memory and Cultural History: Problems of Method," *American Historical Review*, Vol. 102, No. 5 (1997), pp. 1386–1403.

10 See Confino's critique of Zerubavel in ibid.; see also Emanuel Sivan, "Private Pain and Public Remembrance in Israel," in Winter and Sivan (eds.), *War and Remembrance*, pp. 177–205.

11 See, for example, Ilan Pappé, "Seder yom hadash le-historiyah hadashah" (A New Agenda for a New History), *Teoriyah u-Vikoret*, No. 8 (1996), pp. 130–31.

12 See Gillis (ed.), *Commemorations*; Maurice Halbwachs, *Les Cadres sociaux de la mémoire* (Paris,

1925), English translation with Foreword by L. A. Ciser, *On Collective Memory* (Chicago, 1992).

13   On polyphony as the proliferation of independent voices and consciousness, see M. M. Bakhtin, *Problems of Dostoevsky's Poetics* [1929], trans. R. W. Rotsel (Ann Arbor, 1973); Sivan, *Dor tashah*, especially p. 138.

14   Avigdor Hameiri, "Sarah Aaronsohn," *Do'ar ha-Yom*, 10 October 1923; "Sarah Aaronsohn," in *Sarah ve-Aaron Aaronsohn le-mle'ot 15 shanah le-motah mot giborim* (Sarah and Aaron Aaronsohn, in honor of Fifteen Years since her Death as a Hero) (Tel Aviv, 1932). This is the first official commemorative book whose revenues were dedicated to the construction of a memorial for Sarah Aaronsohn. Beit Aaronsohn Archives, Zikhron Yaakov (hereafter BAA), newspaper clippings files, numbering unclear.

15   See Melman, "Min ha-shulayim," pp. 243–79.

16   See ibid., pp. 275–7; Billie Melman, "Introduction," in idem (ed.), *Borderlines: Genders and Identities in War and Peace, 1870–1939* (London and New York, 1998), pp. 1–25; Rajeswari Sunder Rajan, *Real and Imagined Woman: Gender, Culture, and Postcolonialism* (London, New York, 1993); Gayatri C. Spivak, *In Other Worlds: Essays in Cultural Politics* (New York, London, 1988), pp. 241–69; and Beth Baron, "The Politics of Female Notables in Postwar Egypt," in Melman (ed.) *Borderlines*, pp. 329–51.

17   On the immediate impact of the events at Tel Hai on the public memory, see, for example, the works of Zerubavel and others cited in note 5. For references to her death in the 1920s, see Hameiri, "Sarah Aaronsohn"; Peretz Pascal, "Sarah Aaronsohn," *Do'ar ha-Yom*, 27 October 1920; Zipora Chon, "A Hero of the New Zion," *Jewish Tribune*, 22 May 1922; Benjamin Yablons, "New Palestine's Jean d'Arc," *Jewish Daily Bulletin*, 27 January 1925; Yirmiyahu Jaffe, "Yoman Zikhron Yaakov, April 1917–April 1918" (Zikhron Yaakov Diary, April 1917–April 1918), BAA. See also Aharon Ever-Hadani's play *Shomrim* (Guards), in which Nili's espionage is condemned in Act 3, Scenes 4–9. The play opened in the Habimah Theater on 24 August 1937, but was promptly removed because of strong public protest. See A. Ever-Hadani, *Kitvei ne'urim* (Juvenile Writings) (Tel Aviv, 1944), p. 320.

18   Eric Hobsbawm, "Introduction: Inventing Traditions," in idem and Terence Ranger (eds.), *The Invention of Tradition* (Cambridge, 1983), pp. 1–15.

19   Clifford Geertz, *The Interpretation of Cultures* (New York, 1973), especially his analysis of the Balinese cock-fight, pp. 412–55; James Clifford, *The Predicament of Culture: Twentieth Century Ethnography, Literature, and Art* (Cambridge, MA., 1988), pp. 31–2.

20   "Ha-aliyah al kever Sarah Aaaronsohn zal" (The Pilgrimage to the Grave of Sarah Aaronsohn of Blessed Memory), 10 October 1933, BAA, Sarah, Box 2.

21   Melman, "Min ha-shulayim," pp. 243–79; Rachel Elboim-Dror, "'Hu holekh u-va be-kirbenu ha-ivri he-hadash': Al tarbut ha-no'ar shel ha-aliyot ha-rishonot" ("He is come, from amongst us he is come, the first Hebrew": On the Youth Culture of the First Waves of Immigration)," *Alpayim*, No. 12 (1996), pp. 104–35.

22   Yigal Drori, "Reshitam shel irgunim kalkaliim be-Eretz Yisrael bi-shnot ha-esrim" (The Beginning of Economic Organizations in *Eretz Yisrael* in the 1920s), *Cathedra*, No. 25 (1983), pp. 99–112; idem, "Ha-hugim ha-ezrahiim ba-yishuv ha-eretzyisre'eli bi-shnot ha-esrim" ("Hachugim Ha'ezrachiim" in the Jewish "Yishuv" in Eretz Israel, 1920–29) (Ph.D. diss., Tel Aviv University, 1981); see also Amir Ben-Porat, *Heikhan hem ha-burganim ha-hem? Toledot ha-burganut ha-yisre'elit* (The Bourgeoisie: The History of the Israeli Bourgeois) (Jerusalem, 1999), especially pp. 72–80, for the distinction between the urban and rural bourgeoisie. See also Yaacov Shavit, "Ha-roved ha-tarbuti he-haser u-milu'av: Bein 'tarbut amamit rishmit' le-'tarbut amamit lo rishmit' ba-tarbut ha-ivrit ha-le'umit be-Eretz Yisrael" (Supplying a Missing System: Between "Official" and "Unofficial Culture" in Hebrew National Culture in *Eretz Yisrael*), in B. Z. Kedar (ed.), *Ha-tarbut ha-amamit* (Studies in the History of Popular Culture) (Jerusalem, 1996), pp. 327–45.

23   *Sarah ve-Aaron Aharonson, le-mle'ot 15 shanah* (1932), p. 7.

24   "Ha-aliyah al kever Sarah," BAA, Sarah, Box 2, pp. 3–5.

25   18th Anniversary Ceremony (1935), BAA, Sarah, Box 2, p. 1.

26   *Sarah ve-Aaaron Aharonson le-mle'ot 15 shanah*, first page (unnumbered).

27 Hayden White, *Metahistory: The Historical Imagination in Nineteenth-Century Europe* (Baltimore and London, 1973).

28 Elboim-Dror, "'Hu holekh u-va'"; Drori, "Reshitam shel irgunim kalkaliim."

29 A. Zilber, on behalf of the Bnei Binyamin Federation, description of the 18th Memorial Day, 1935 (no exact date), BAA, Sarah, Box 2 (no pagination).

30 "Yom ha-aliyah le-kever Sarah, 14.10.41" (Day of the Pilgrimage to Sarah's Grave, 14.10.41), BAA, Sarah, Box 2.

31 On the juvenile press, see Zohar Shavit (ed.), *Toledot ha-yishuv ha-yehudi be-Eretz Yisrael me'az ha-aliyah ha-rishonah: Bniyatah shel tarbut ivrit be-Eretz Yisrael* (The History of the Jewish Community in *Eretz Yisrael* since 1882: The Construction of Hebrew Culture in Eretz Israel), Part 1 (Jerusalem, 1989); for the children's press, see ibid, pp. 455–61. For a discussion of Sarah's depiction and representation in the children's press, see below. For plays and stories, see the play by Moshe Smilansky, *Rohele*, in *Kitvei Moshe Smilansky* (The Writings of Moshe Smilansky) Vol. 4, *Sipurim* (Stories) (Tel Aviv, 1934), pp. 155–92; Ever-Hadani's play *Shomrim* (note 17 above); Aharon Avraham Kabak, *"Ha-meragelet"* (The Spy) *in Bein ha-midbar u-vein ha-yam* (Between the Desert and the Sea) (Tel Aviv, 1959); the prose poem by Y. Cohen, *Megilat Avshalom ve-Sarah* (The Scroll of Avshalom and Sarah) (Tel Aviv, 1948), pp. 29–50; "Sarah Aharonson: Arba'im shanah le-motah" (Sarah Aaronsohn: Forty Years since her Death), was broadcasted on Kol Yisrael radio station on Saturday, 26 October 1957 with Hannah Rovina as Sarah.

32 Samuel, *Past and Present in Contemporary Culture*, Vol. 1: *Theatres of Memory.*

33 "Ha-aliyah al kever Sarah Aharonson," 10 October 1932, BAA, Sarah, Box 2, pp. 3–5.

34 Itamar Even-Zohar, "Ha-tzmihah veha-hitgabshut shel tarbut ivrit mekomit ve-yelidit be-Eretz Yisrael, 1882–1948" (The Emergence and Formation of Local and Native Hebrew Culture in *Eretz Yisrael*, 1882–1948), *Cathedra*, No. 16 (July 1980), pp. 165–89.

35 Y. Heller, *Lehi, 1940–1949*, (Jerusalem, 1989), Vol. 1, pp. 25–6, 61, 81–8, 99, 101, 121–2, 131, 154–5, 172.

36 *Ha-Boker le-Yeladim*, No. 161–62, 9 October 1946, pp. 10–11; see also ibid., No. 107–108, 20 September 1945, p. 27. A sample of elementary school primers between 1950 and 1960 indicates that the story of Nili was not included in the school curriculum or in the organized collective memory. This, of course, is in contrast to the story of Tel Hai. See also Aviezer Yellin Archives of Jewish Education in Israel and the Diaspora, Tel Aviv University; and Keren Kayemet Archives, Tel Aviv, the Leah and Dov Aloni collections.

37 See, for example, *Sarah ve-Aaron Aaronsohn le-mle'ot 15 shanah le-motam*, p. 30.

38 See note 4 above.

39 Melman, "Min ha-shulayim," pp. 255–60; A. Bar-Adon, "'Ha-imahot ha-meyasdot' u-mnat helkan be-tehiyat ha-ivrit be-hithavtah, 1882–1914" ("The Founding Mothers" and Their Role in the Hebrew Language Revival: 1882–1914," *Lashon ve-Ivrit*, No. 3 (1990), pp. 5–27.

40 Melman, "Min ha-shulayim," pp. 255–60.

41 Pat Thane and Gisela Bock (eds.), *Maternity and Gender Politics* (London, 1991); Seth Koven and Sonia Michel (eds.), *Mothers of a New World: Maternalist Politics and the Origins of the Welfare State* (New York, 1993); Melman, "Introduction," in Melman (ed.), *Borderlines*, pp. 1–25; Fatma Müge Göçek, "From Empire to Nation: Images of Women and War in Ottoman Political Cartoons, 1908–1923," in ibid., pp. 47–73; Beth Baron, "Mothers, Morality, and Nationalism in Pre-1917 Egypt," in Rashid Khalidi (ed.), *The Origins of Arab Nationalism* (New York, 1991), pp. 271–88.

42 Billie Melman, "Re-Generation: Nation and the Construction of Gender in Peace and War — Palestine Jews, 1900–1918," in Melman (ed.), *Borderlines*, pp. 121–41.

43 Yaakov Yaari-Polskin, *Nili, Sarah be-hayeha uve-motah* (Nili, Sarah in Life and Death) (Tel Aviv, 1951), pp. 57–9.

44 Hameiri, "Sarah Aharonsohn."

45 Melman, "Min ha-shulayim," pp. 260–7, 274–6.

46 Yaari-Polskin, "Mi-hayei Sarah Aharonson (Biografiyah ve-epizod)" (From the Life of Sarah Aaronsohn [Biography and Episode])," in *Sarah ve-Aaronsohn*, p. 18.

47 Joseph Klausner, "Sarah Aharonson: Ha-giborah ha-le'umit" (Sarah Aaronsohn: The National Heroine), *Ha-Mashkif*, September 1942; see also his eulogy on the 45th anniversary of her death in 1962, BAA, Sarah, Box 2, undated and unpaginated.
48 Melman, "Min ha-shulayim."
49 Smilansky, *Rohele*, p. 181.
50 Ibid., p. 191.
51 Moshe Smilansky, "Ha-ishah: Ner le-nishmat Sarah Aharonson" (The Woman: A Candle for the Soul of Sarah Aaronsohn), in *Kitvei Moshe Smilansky*, Vol. 8, (Tel Aviv, 1935), p. 22.
52 See below. On Aaronsohn as "the Jewish Edith Cavell," see, for example, "A Tribute to Sarah Aaronsohn," *Jewish Daily Bulletin*, 27 January 1925.
53 On the images of Joan of Arc and on memory, see M. Winock, "Jeanne d'Arc," in Nora (ed.), *Les Lieux de mémoire*, Vol. 3, *Les France* (Paris, 1997), pp. 4427–73. On evangelism and the suffragette movement in Protestant countries, see Martha Vicinus, *Independent Women: Work and Community for Single Women, 1850–1920* (London, 1985), pp. 20, 266, 270.
54 BAA, Sarah, Box 2, 10 October 1933.
55 Ibid., 14 October 1941.
56 Ibid., 15 October 1946.
57 Ludmila Jordanova, *Sexual Visions: Images of Gender in Science and Medicine between the Eighteenth and Twentieth Centuries* (Madison, WI, 1989), pp. 81–111.
58 Ceremony, 1935, BAA, Sarah, Box 2.
59 Ceremony, 1941: "Every Betar club is a temple for your teachings, Commander Sarah! We stand at attention before you — our Commander"; Pilgrimage Ceremony, 1942. BAA, Sarah, Box 2.
60 Pilgrimage Ceremony, 1958, "Professor Klausner" [*sic*!], unnumbered. BAA, Sarah, Box 2.
61 Melman, "Introduction," in idem (ed.), *Borderlines*.
62 Reports on the activities of Bnei Binyamin in late 1927 and early 1928 record 1,500 "young men" as members of the organization. The English-language report emphasizes "a fine spirit of brotherhood." See "Doh al pe'ilut Bnei Binyamin be-Palestinah" (Report on the Activities of Bnei Binyamin in Palestine), BAA, Alexander Aaronsohn Box, Bnei Binyamin 213. According to the Regulations of the Bnei Binyamin Federation, "The purpose of the organization [is] to unite and to organize the youth of the *moshavah*." A similar point is made in the 1927 report, in connection with the organization's athletic activities, whose purpose is to "attract our young men" (ibid.).
63 On the organizations, see Rachel Elboim-Dror, *Ha-hinukh ha-ivri be-Eretz Yisrael* (Hebrew Education in *Eretz Yisrael*), Vol. 1 (Jerusalem, 1986); Melman, "Min ha-shulayim," p. 266.
64 "Essentialism" refers to the perception of femininity — and of gender in general — not in social-historical terms, but as a natural, unchanging essence. On "androgynous" images, see Mary L. Roberts, *Civilization without Sexes: Reconstructing Gender in France, 1917–1927* (Chicago, 1994); Billie Melman, *Women and the Popular Imagination in the Twenties: Flappers and Nymphs* (London and New York, 1986); Sunder Rajan, *Real and Imagined Woman*. It is clear that in cultures like these the worship of women, especially of women leaders as mothers of the nation, can also develop.
65 I am grateful to Sasha Weitman who permitted me to use his data. On the choice of Hebrew national names, see Sasha Weitman, "Prénoms et orientations nationales en Israël, 1882–1890," *Annales ESC*, Vol. 42, No. 4 (1987), pp. 879–901; idem, "Shemot pratiim ke-madadim hevratiim: Megamot bi-zehutam ha-le'umit shel yisre'elim, 1882–1980" (First Names as Social Indicators: Trends in Israelis' National Identity, 1882–1980), in Nurith Gertz (ed.), *Nekudot tatzpit al tarbut ve-hevrah be-Eretz Yisrael* (Perspectives on Culture and Society in Israel) (Tel Aviv, 1988), pp. 141–51.
66 Conversations with Yaffa Berlovitz and Nili Friedland, June 1998.
67 R. Tkhelet, "Kapitan lelo kokhavim" (Captain without Stars), *La-Ishah*, 2 October 1947. See also "She'oteha ha-aharonot shel Sarah" (Sarah's Last Hours), *Olam ha-Ishah*, 16 October 1947, p. 5. For a different version, see "Shtei nesikhot ra'ah Avshalom be-neshef ha-masekhot" (Avshalom Saw Two Princesses at the Masked Ball), *Shiva Yamim, Yediot Aharonot* weekend supplement, 5 November 1954; "Ka-zeh hayah sofam shel Sarah ve-Avshalom"

(Such was the End of Sarah and Avshalom)," ibid., 12 November 1954.

68 Ohana and Wistrich (eds.), *Mitos ve-zikaron*, pp. 21–7. These authors locate the "fracture in the collective Israeli experience" in 1973, and point out that the mythology of the "Sabra" and Israeliness, which had already collapsed at the end of the 1960s, was finally buried. See Ben-Porat, *Heikhan hem ha-burganim ha-hem?*, pp. 130–31.

69 For this information, I thank the staff of Aaronsohn House, and especially the acting director Esther Cohen, as well as David Shoham.

70 Rahel Katzenelson,"Giborat Nili: Sarah le-veit Aharonson" (Heroine of Nili: Sarah of the Aaronsohn Family)," *Dvar ha-Po'elet*, 11 November 1967, p. 359.

71 Yehudah Slutski, "Nishmatah shel Nili: Hamishim shanah le-motah shel Sarah Aharonson" (The Soul of Nili: Fifty Years since the Death of Sarah Aaronsohn), *Davar*, 27 October, 1967.

72 Y. Manor, "Ha-agadah veha-metzi'ut shel Nili: Ha-reka hu ha-noten partzuf emet le-historiyah" (The Legend and Reality of Nili: The Background Is What Shows the True Face of History), *Davar*, 1 December 1967.

73 Katzenelson, "Giborat Nili," p. 361.

74 S. Kirshenbaum, *Toledot Yisrael ba-dorot ha-aharonim* (History of Israel in Recent Generations) (Tel Aviv, 1968), p. 78.

75 See also Ministry of Education, Curricula Division for the General School System, *Ha-ra'ayon ha-tziyoni ve-hakamat Medinat Yisrael* (The Zionist Idea and the Creation of the State of Israel) (Jerusalem), p. 162; Moshe Lifshitz, *Toledot am Yisrael ba-dorot ha-aharonim* (History of the People of Israel in Recent Generations), Vol. 1, *Ha-tnu'ah ha-le'umit* (The National Movement) (Tel Aviv, 1985), pp. 75–6.

76 Yisrael Pazi, *Me-emantzipatziyah le-tziyonut: Migvan darkhei hora'ah le-kitot 10–11* (From Emancipation to Zionism: A Variety of Teaching Methods for the 10th and 11th Grades) (no place [Tel Aviv?], 1975), pp. 255–8.

77 I wish to thank Sherberk Publishers, which made its archives available to me; my special thanks go to Ze'ev Namir.

78 Conversation with Dvorah Omer, 1 August 1999.

79 Ibid.

80 Ibid.; conversation with Ze'ev Namir, 1 August 1999.

81 Conversation with Dvorah Omer, 1 August 1999.

82 Sherberk Publishers Archives; conversation with Ze'ev Namir, 1 August 1999.

83 BAA; conversations with Esther Cohen, acting director, Aaronsohn House, the Nili Museum, April 1998.

84 Conversation with Dvorah Omer, 1 August 1999.

85 Dvorah Omer, *Sarah giborat Nili* (Tel Aviv, 1990), pp. 37–40.

86 Ibid., pp. 21–2.

87 Ibid., p. 33.

88 Ibid., p. 35.

89 Ibid., p. 198.

90 Joan W. Scott, *Only Paradoxes to Offer: French Feminists and the Rights of Man* (Cambridge, MA, 1996), pp. 1–19.

91 *Sarah*, directed by Orna Ben-Dor, produced by Orna Landau.

92 Melman, "Min ha-shulayim."

"Teacher, Tiller, Soldier, Spy"?
Women's Representations in Israeli Military Memorials*

Judith Tydor Baumel

They dot the landscape almost wherever one looks. One finds them at roadsides, in the middle of barren fields, inside public parks, at crossroads, and even under densely foliated overgrowth. They are almost always stark in color and texture, tending towards black, white or gray; on a rare occasion they express themselves in unusual bursts of color, usually variations of metallic blue, brick-red or silver. Ranging in height from ground-level slabs to towering obelisks they may include abstract or figurative images. There is no exact count as to their number; experts estimate that several thousand are found throughout the country. They are memorials for Israelis who have lost their lives since the beginning of Jewish settlement in the country: war monuments, memorials for civilians killed in terrorist attacks, and more recently, markers commemorating the victims of the "scourge of modernity," road accidents.

Israel is a commemorating nation, noted the late historian George Mosse on one of his last trips to the country.[1] Unlike its European or American counterparts which tend towards more centralized forms of commemoration, this state of soldier-citizens in which "every man has a name" proliferates with individual memorials as well as group monuments for both civilian and military casualties. Whether this is a product of the Jewish dictum to "remember" (*zakhor*) or the result of an attitude that almost sacralizes various groups within Israeli society, one thing is certain: Israel holds what appears to be a world record in individualized military commemoration in comparison with other countries of the industrialized world. The tendency towards individual commemoration that has long characterized Israeli society — and stands in stark contrast to the collectivist nature of the state during its early years — has also spilled over into patterns of nonmilitary commemoration. The most tangible examples are visible along the many roads crossing the country, from major thoroughfares to winding country trails: memorials for accident victims that target the automobile, and not the tank, as the ultimate vehicle of death. The form and content of these memorials are often similar to those of a more military framework and the wreaths laid at their base on certain dates often confuse the bystander as to their true nature. However there is at least one major difference in the public conception of the two types of monuments. Unlike military memorials, which the general public automatically associates with young males in their prime who gave up their lives for their country, there is no automatic gender distinction with regard to civilian road victim memorials, as auto accidents do not differentiate between men and women.

Although the latter statement is certainly true, an examination of Israeli military monuments shows that while it is not commonplace, both individual and collective women's commemoration certainly exists. Furthermore, apart from the official and unofficial monuments erected in memory of women who perished while on military service and in battle, women's abstract and figurative representation also plays an important role in certain memorials built primarily in memory of men.

In what ways do military memorials for women differ from those put up for men? Does the paradigm which states that monuments commemorate myth and not reality also apply to women's images appearing in Israeli military commemoration? If so, which myth — or ethos — do these statues attempt to promote regarding Israeli women? In this article, which is part of a larger study dealing with women's military commemoration in the State of Israel, I will examine the continuous representation of women in Israeli military memorials and analyze the changing forms that this representation has taken since the establishment of the state. As a first step I will discuss a typology of the various gender motifs appearing in Israeli military commemoration and the dynamics of their generational development. Building upon this typology I will juxtapose history with memory, asking whether the forms in which women are depicted actually mirror their military or civilian status as alluded to by my title: "Teacher, tiller [of the soil], soldier, spy." Finally, I will explore the tensions between myth and reality, history and memory, and local culture versus international influences as expressed in the gendered narrative emerging from Israeli military monuments. By doing so, I will also allude to a broader issue that is of growing interest to both historians and social scientists: the connection between nationalism, space, militarism and gender stereotypes in developing nations.[2]

Memorials Commemorating Fallen Soldiers in the State of Israel

Commemoration, and particularly plastic commemoration such as statues, monuments and cenotaphs, expresses the human need to deal with issues that are "larger than life," and particularly those centering on human mortality. Functioning simultaneously on several levels, commemoration fulfills a number of social, educational, national, psychological and theological needs. The common action of erecting a memorial stone is a source of unification and continuity. Simultaneously, commemorative forms act as tools to develop a national ethos or strengthen national identity. Finally, the memorial site metamorphoses into "sacred space," acting as a ceremonial platform which can integrate with or substitute for existing patterns of belief.[3]

Contemporary research considers monuments to be a system of symbols through which one can examine a society's culture and ideology.[4] Some studies concentrate upon a monument's history; others choose to analyze its artistic effect; a third type of study deals with its impact on the public. Like all "texts," plastic commemoration must be read within its surrounding "context," the interactive triangle taking shape between the group commissioning the memorial, the artist, and the viewer. To this we must add situational variables which also influence the texture of public memory. Commissioning entity, artist and viewer rarely achieve cognitive synchronization; more often than not they view the event being commemorated through different prisms. Consequently, each interprets the memorial according to his/her own understanding and personal vision. Furthermore, as plastic commemoration simultaneously faces the present and future, it almost always serves the interests of the commemorators while not necessarily meshing with the former agendas of those being commemorated. Any analysis of plastic commemoration must therefore take a plethora of variables into account when trying to correctly interpret the memorial dynamics portrayed by commemorative statuary.

The scope of plastic commemoration can also teach us much about a society's essence. Boasting military memorials in hundreds of cities, towns, villages and rural settlements throughout the country, Israel provides commemorative researchers with a fascinating challenge.[5] In addition to the scope of its monuments, a closer look at the Israeli commemorative scene highlights the unique character of its plastic commemoration: the broad chronological range of its memorials, the particular cultural and religious constraints of their context, the intensely national flavor of their framework and the unusual demographic composition of their potential viewers.

A common pitfall of studies covering large numbers of memorials is their tendency to become quantitative catalogues or inventories rather than qualitative examinations. In this case, the dilemma is compounded by the dynamic and ever-growing nature of the Israeli memorial landscape, making it impossible to ensure that all existing military memorials be included in such a survey. In order to avoid these traps and focus upon the cultural dimensions and historical implications of memory, I have explored the wealth of Israeli military memorials through a gender destratification based upon typology — repetitive patterns — and not an individual survey of each of the hundreds of memorials I encountered.

Three books published in the last decade have listed and partially analyzed close to 1,000 memorials spread throughout Israel, but devoted little space to the gender component in plastic commemoration.[6] However, the centrality of plastic commemoration in transmitting social and cultural messages to future generations makes it imperative to explore this theme, and not only in order to examine gender images in commemorating a sector that is traditionally considered masculine. The development of female motifs in military commemoration points to the gender dynamics inherent in a developing society, to the connection between gender construction, nation and state, and to the role of women in a developing national society. Simultaneously, it acts as an indication of the various cultural tensions that have influenced Israeli society during its half century of existence.

This article is based on a survey of over 900 official and semi-official military memorials erected in Israel until 1998, which are under the auspices of the Division of Soldier Commemoration in the Ministry of Defense. 27 of them focus upon women in one way or another: some commemorate women alone, others commemorate both men and women, a third group commemorates men through the use of female images. Most of the memorials commemorate soldiers; a few were erected in memory of civilian war casualties or terrorist victims. 60 percent of the memorials involving women are figurative, while figurative commemoration is found in only 13 percent of the total number of war memorials in Israel. One possible explanation for the high percentage of figurative memorials portraying women is chronological: most were erected before the mid-1970s, during the period when figurative imagery was at its zenith. Another possible explanation stems from the uniqueness of women's images in a male sector, a phenomenon that practically demands a figurative expression. There seems to be little connection between the choice of genre — figurative or abstract imagery — and the artist's sex, as only four of the 27 memorials were sculpted by women.

The percentage of military memorials erected in memory of women or portraying female images mirrors the percentage of women soldiers who lost their lives in Israel. Defense Ministry figures from 31 January 1998 show that out of a total of 20,298 soldiers who lost their lives since the early days of pre-state Israel, 704 (or 3.5 percent) were women. 27 of the 900 memorials (3 percent) mention women or portray a female image while 2 percent of all military memorials were erected in memory of women who fell in battle, were killed in terrorist attacks or died in accidents. The largest number of memorials which refer to women were erected in the wake of the War of Independence, the war in which the largest number of women lost their lives. During that war 137 women soldiers were killed; the 1956 Sinai Campaign claimed only one female victim, and in the Yom Kippur War of 1973 there were 16 female casualties. The percentage of female soldiers who lost their lives as compared to their male counterparts has risen gradually since the

Lebanese War of 1982 and particularly since the 1987 *Intifada* (Palestinian uprising), as most were victims of terrorist attacks and accidents which, as opposed to wars, are not gender-differentiated. This has been vividly expressed since the beginning of the recent Al-Aqsa *Intifada*, beginning in late September 2000.[7]

Similar to all memorials throughout the world, every Israeli military memorial is the result of a meeting of cultures. These include the official dominant culture, the popular culture and the ethnic subcultures. During its first decade of existence, the fledgling State of Israel was characterized by a dominant political culture that both reflected a national ethos and encouraged its continuity. Alongside, a more popular *sabra* (native-born Israeli) culture flourished, promoting the same ethos, but viewing it through a softer, more tolerant and almost ironic prism. Both cultures were ideological — one official, the other popular. In addition, a third, almost clandestine culture continued to exist — the popular culture of immigrants that continued to weave its way in and out of their conscious lives. For several decades, those molding the national culture tended to ignore the existence of ethnic cultures that had been transplanted to Israel or preferred to dismiss them as "folklore," something akin to a faded photograph-print of what they considered to be true culture. Nevertheless, the ethnic subcultures slowly seeped into various fields, including plastic military commemoration of fallen soldiers.

Three of the memorials upon which I have focused are official monuments erected either by state or municipal authorities, and we can naturally assume that they reflect the elitist, dominant state culture in all of its forms. Most of the other memorials portraying women are found in agricultural settlements, and we would therefore assume that they reflect the official-popular culture. However both categories of memorials combine attributes of "statist"[8] culture with influences of either European or Oriental subcultures brought to Israel by immigrants from those areas. The cultural interplay expressed in public commemoration appears to embody a process characterizing the State of Israel since the late 1960s, during which the collectivist ethos — a linchpin of formative Israeli society — was slowly replaced by more individualistic expressions in both thought and deed. Gradually rupturing the iconographic discourse expressing glory and sacrifice, the "privatization" process also affected the gendered commemoration of both Israeli male and female soldiers.

Women in the Pre-State Fighting Forces and the IDF (Israel Defense Forces)

Israel is the only country in the world to institute a compulsory draft for women. Since the War of Independence women have not participated in battle; however, the socialist ideology of sexual equality and the pre-state tradition in which women and men shared all military tasks created an image of the fighting woman soldier who took her place alongside the armed men. Even during the days of pre-state sexual equality within the clandestine Haganah and the initially British-supported Palmah fighting forces, women's combat status was very complex. Although women had taken their turn in guard duties in all pre-state defense organizations and were even trained for command positions in the Haganah, full equality never became a widespread practice. Most women did not engage in battle but were integrated into the military support system of nursing and communications.[9]

The creation of the Palmah (special duty units) in 1941 triggered a series of debates over whether women should be trained for battle or auxiliary tasks. A crucial transition stage began in 1944 when agricultural trainees joined the Palmah, raising the percentage of women from 10 to 30 percent of all participants. Furthermore, during the Second World War over 3,000 women from the Yishuv (pre-state Jewish community in Palestine) volunteered for the British Auxiliary Territorial Service (ATS), and close to 600 women joined the Royal Air Force. Women soldiers served as wireless operators, clerks, radar operators, photographers, parachute inspectors, truck drivers, ambulance operators, mechanics, nurses and medical orderlies. With few exceptions women did not participate in battle. One notable exception was the parachutists' mission of 1944, which later became a symbol of Yishuv activity to assist European Jewry during the Holocaust. During this mission some three dozen volunteers from the Yishuv, all officers in the British army, parachuted into Europe in 1943–45. Almost all were new immigrants from Europe, most were kibbutz members. Some joined the mission straight from the ranks of the British army while others came from the Palmah. The parachutists were faced with a double mission: on the one hand they were to assist the Allied war effort and in particular to assist downed Allied pilots to escape from behind enemy lines. On the other hand they were to organize the Zionist groups within the Jewish communities and assist them to escape from the Nazi clutches where necessary. Seven parachutists were killed during the operation, among whom were two of the three female participants: Hannah Senesz from Kibbutz Sdot Yam was executed by a Hungarian firing squad, having been accused of spying for the enemy; Haviva Reik, from Kibbutz Ma'anit was murdered along with her mission partner Rafael Reiss from Kibbutz Huliyot (Sde Nehemia) and a group of Jews in the Kremnica forest in Slovakia. Of the seven it was the 23-year-old Senesz who became the operation's symbol, thus leaving her personal mark on the Israeli collective memory.[10]

After the end of the Second World War the Palmah was the largest military framework in which women from the Yishuv participated. During the years between the end of the war and the establishment of the State of Israel — a period during which the Palmah metamorphosed from a British military organization to an underground body — women in the Palmah engaged in four types of tasks. One group carried out operational duties such as manning battle stations, engaging in open warfare and accompanying convoys. A second group was assigned professional tasks in the fields of communication, nursing and as quartermasters. Other women soldiers served in the administration as clerks and division secretaries while a fourth group gave instructional training for field maneuvers, sport and weaponry. Three women Haganah members were sent for pilot's training but were not employed in battle during the War of Independence for fear of being shot down and captured by the enemy.[11]

The War of Independence was the last war in which women actively participated in battle according to the Palmah tradition. After a woman soldier's body was mutilated by Arabs near Kibbutz Gevulot early in the war, the Israeli High Command decided to remove women soldiers from the front lines and forbid them from participating in future battles. The compulsory nature of the IDF draft, as opposed to the voluntary nature of the Haganah and the Palmah, also encouraged the decision to relegate women to auxiliary tasks. Finally, the first women officers in the IDF had received their training in the British army where women were not permitted into battle, thus strengthening the reversal of previous policy. Even tasks to which women had been assigned in the British army such as truck driving were forbidden to women in the IDF for fear that they would lead to front-line assignments at times of war. Consequently, by the mid-1970s only 150 military classifications were open to women in the IDF as opposed to 571 which were available for women serving at that time in the American army. Today, some 500 military classifications are open to women in the IDF, of which 100 are reserved for officers.[12]

The means by which women were integrated into military frameworks prior to the establishment of the State of Israel and their motives for joining are reminiscent of a common pattern characterizing a large number of developing nations in a state of acute or continuous national struggle. In many Third World countries — even those with no socialist equalizing tradition — women often joined the national struggle as a means of emancipating themselves from the double burden of their female and their colonial status.[13] In Western countries as well, such as in Ireland during the "troubles," boundaries between the public and private were blurred, similar to the situation in the *Yishuv* during the revolt against the British. This process enabled women to join the gendered discourse of war, which simultaneously strengthened their traditional tasks while causing an imbalance in the social stratification of society, thus destroying the stability of these same tasks.[14] The dissonance between these two components provides a partial explanation for the changes in women's positions in the Israeli national discourse in general and within the Israeli military framework in particular. Applying Nira Yuval-Davis's categorization of the five roles through which women participate in ethnic and national processes in a civil society, it appears that the removal of women from front-line military positions and their transfer to auxiliary services was a stage in turning them into what she calls "national mothers," "biological reproducers of ethnic collectivities."[15] By ensuring the male character of most active military tasks, it was also possible to emphasize that a woman's true task was that of biological reproduction, cultural strengthening, delineating the boundaries of ethnic groups and as a symbol within the ideological discourse of ethnic construction. Only after a woman left her mark on these fields, states Yuval-Davis, could she integrate into a fifth role within a developing nation, taking part in the national, economic, political and — most important — the military struggle of her new nation.

Typology of Images

Although almost all women in the IDF served as auxiliaries, for several decades collective public memory retained the original image of the fighting woman soldier. This image, particularly with regard to the War of Independence, was strengthened by popular literature and women's autobiographies such as those of Netiva Ben-Yehuda and Tamar Avidar.[16] How was the public image of women in the IDF translated into plastic representation as seen in military memorials? An examination of Israeli military memorial sites pinpoints a number of recurring gender motifs:

(a) *Combat and Front-line Soldiers.* The female warrior image is initially rooted in Western European Christian culture — Joan of Arc, savior of humanity, or Delacroix's "Liberté." In addition, the principle of sexual equality and the pre-state policy of allowing women into combat imbedded an image of women combatants in the collective public memory. One would therefore expect a plethora of these figures in Israeli plastic commemoration, particularly in those monuments appearing in the wake of the War of Independence. However only two "fighting" women appear in Israeli iconography: one is part of a group of combatants in Batya Lishanski's statue commemorating the soldiers from Kfar Yehoshua (1949–53). The second is calling fighters into battle in Aharon Priver's relief at Kibbutz Tel Yosef (1952). There is also an earlier memorial to a "fighting" woman, also by Lishanski: her statue depicting Sarah Chizik (1937), killed at the Tel Hai battle of 1920. The monument, located in the Hulda forest, was erected over the grave of Chizik's brother, killed while defending Kibbutz Hulda. Citing the statue in Kfar Yehoshua, Levinger states that Lishanski was the only artist in her generation who gave women equal status in figurative art. However a

closer examination reveals that the Kfar Yehoshua model was not designed by
Lishanski but by Menachem Zaharoni, a member of the moshav (cooperative
settlement) and teacher of its fallen fighters. Although women from Kfar
Yehoshua were not killed in battle, they fought alongside the men and it was
self-understood that any plastic commemoration would include both sexes.
The relief at Tel Yosef, also designed by a man, commemorates the two women
from the kibbutz who were killed during the War of Independence.[17]

Aside from these three statues, women combatants do not appear in any
plastic commemoration after 1953. Descriptions of women's battle-related
activities received only a minor echo in plastic commemoration, even in those
monuments that were erected soon after the war's end. As women's combat
activities during the War of Independence were often a local phenomenon,
their plastic commemoration appears to have suited reality much more than it
did the myth of women's military equality which never truly achieved large-
scale practical expression.

(b) *Auxiliaries*. A second group of figures were auxiliaries, assisting the
combatants by providing medical assistance or communications facilities.
Similar to the previous category, the female auxiliary is a time-linked
phenomenon, appearing in three monuments erected in memory of soldiers
who lost their lives in the War of Independence and not reappearing at any
later date. In Kibbutz Nitzanim (1955) and Tel Yosef where women were killed
in battle, the auxiliary is depicted by a woman kneeling next to a wounded
soldier and proffering assistance; according to Aharon Priver, she symbolizes
the gendered characteristics of "assistance, love, sorrow, friendship and
human kindness."[18] The third auxiliary is part of Nathan Rapoport's
monumental memorial tableau at Kibbutz Negba (1953) portraying an armed
soldier flanked by male and female figures. Initially, the muscular woman
appears to be a combat soldier (in an essay appearing in the local kibbutz
newspaper *Voice of Negba* she is referred to as a "female combat member") but
in truth she is a medic carrying a first aid kit.[19] Although the IDF's practice of
automatically assigning women to auxiliary tasks was based upon British army
policy, these monuments are quite different than the British memorials
erected in memory of nurses and medical auxiliaries who lost their lives during
the First and Second World Wars. In most cases such commemoration in
Britain takes the form of a statue of a nurse in uniform, or more commonly as
textual commemoration — a list of names appearing under a cross or on a
memorial plaque. Such textual plaques are found in Salisbury, Canterbury,
Lewes and Winchester, just to mention a few.

As most female soldiers — both during the War of Independence and
throughout the history of the IDF — served as auxiliaries, one might assume
that the auxiliary fighter would be the most prominent figure to appear in
Israeli military memorials. The appearance of only three female auxiliaries in

over 900 such memorials teaches us how little impact this image had on the collective Israeli public memory of women in military settings, although it portrays the military reality of women, even during the 1948 war. Furthermore, although female combatants and woman auxiliaries are the only figures in Israeli military memorials that depict women in "military" situations, they never appear alone but only together with male soldiers. In this respect Israeli military commemoration differs from both British and American military monuments where women appear as solitary auxiliary figures, such as the Second World War Monument on the Pacific coast showing a nurse gazing out towards the horizon.[20] Could this allude to the gender bias long prevalent in Israeli society, which assumed that women could have no independent existence within a military framework? The explanation for this phenomenon could be cultural, ideological or simply practical. On the one hand, it may stem from the strong collectivist nature of the young state which imprinted itself on forms of plastic commemoration. On the other hand it may stem from the general (male) consensus that women had no independent military position in Israel. Finally, it may simply represent the fact that since the War of Independence no all-female combatant or auxiliary units have functioned within the IDF.

While the image of the Israeli woman soldier helped to promote Israeli culture in Hollywood, her disappearance from Israeli iconography during the mid-1950s — a phenomenon having both military and cultural roots — reflects a general trend in the dominant Israeli culture of those days. Commercial pictorial histories of Israel published during the 1950s and 1960s devoted an inordinate amount of space to pictures of women soldiers on parade or teaching new immigrants in an absorption camp. In contrast, the official Israeli album of that time — During the First Decade of Israel, edited by Abraham Harman and Yigal Yadin — did not contain even one picture of a woman soldier, despite the fact that an entire chapter was devoted to the IDF. The same reluctance to turn the spotlight on women soldiers was evident in other forms of Israeli culture (such as literature and cinema) during those decades. The few exceptions are the autobiographies of women who served in the Palmah, that of Moshe Dayan's daughter Yael, and the full-length movie classic Hill 24 Doesn't Answer.[21]

The disappearance of the image of women soldiers from the dominant Israeli culture seems to be connected with a two-dimensional, machoistic perception which was prominent in that society for several decades regarding the essence and purpose of the Israeli army (as per the slogan "the best boys are pilots and the best girls are for the pilots"). In a culture that equated the term "army" solely with a fighting corps, female soldiers, barred from combat status since the War of Independence, carried little weight. Hence, they were also excluded from figurative representation of fallen soldiers, as their death almost always occurred outside of combat, in accidents and the like. This dichotomy also had its semantic expression. Although the texts appearing on military tombstones were uniform with the only difference being the notation regarding the soldier's form of death, unconnected to the sex of the fallen soldier, the popular expressions used by newspapers and the media were different. While male soldiers were spoken of as having "fallen in the line of duty," women soldiers were "killed while on army service," etc. The metamorphosis within Israeli society regarding its "sacred cows" — including the military — and the large number of both male and female soldiers killed in terrorist bombings, have recently begun to change this perception. As of yet, however, this trend has received little figurative expression, as various constraints (primarily religious: see below, p. 104) have kept Israel from adopting the figurative genre which has gradually made a comeback in Western memorial statuary.[22] However, in view of the influences of the religious establishment, which eschews figurative statuary, upon Israeli public life it is difficult to imagine that such statuary will make a reappearance within the near future.

(c) *Young Mothers*. The mother image is usually seen as a variation of the universal Christian image of the Madonna. This is the most common figurative image of women appearing in plastic commemoration of fallen soldiers. At times it represents a flesh-and-blood mother, such as Hannah Orloff's statue at Ein Gev (1952) of a mother holding a baby in the air, erected in memory of Hannah Tuchman-Adlerstein, a kibbutz mother who lost her life during the 1948 war. In other cases, such as David Polus's statue at Ramat Rachel (1949) of a woman holding a torch and protecting two small children, she symbolizes the motherland. The original six-figure cast of the Negba monument, reduced to three figures due to financial considerations, also included a young mother embracing an infant. During the War of Independence the image of the fallen mother more suited the civilian reality than the military one: only two of the war's female military casualties (1.5 percent) were mothers while they composed 47 percent (170 mothers) of the civilian female casualties.[23] The motif of the young mother appears on later memorials such as Matanya Abramson's Kinneret monument commemorating an accident (1955) and Rivka Keren's memorial statue at Kfar Yuval in memory of the terrorist attack on that settlement (1975). The most unusual image of a young mother is that of a woman in the first stages of pregnancy who is also the mother of a grown soldier, appearing in the Givatayim military memorial (from 1978) which I will discuss in the following section.

(d) *Older Mothers*. The older mother sending her son to war, a common image in European iconography, appears in only two Israeli memorials. One is Nathan Rapoport's Beer Tuvia memorial (1957) and the second is Mordechai Cafri's Balfouria monument (1971). It is not surprising that this image does not appear in plastic commemoration of the 1948 War of Independence. Despite the fact that one of the hit plays of those days was Nathan Shacham's *They Will Arrive Tomorrow*, which deals with a mother sending her son to war, and one of the bestsellers at that time was Moshe Shamir's *He Walked in the Fields*, in which the relationship between a kibbutz mother and her son plays an important role, a great number of soldiers had immigrated from Europe either before or after the Holocaust, losing their parents in the European cataclysm. Consequently, the image of a mother sending her son off to war was inapplicable to over two-thirds of those participating in the War of Independence. Furthermore, in the days when "the entire country was a war front," as the popular slogan of those times went, mothers themselves were often part of the defense system. Only after the generational metamorphosis, which occurred between the Sinai Campaign (1956) and the Six Day War (1967), could one totally separate combatants from civilians and depict a mother sending her son off to war — like the mythological mother in Sparta who told her son to return "with his shield or upon it" — to be victorious or die in battle. The contrast between the diminutive elderly mother in a long gown and the young bare-chested soldier, embracing her with one hand and holding a rifle in the other, is clearly expressed in Rapoport's statue. Cafri claims that his depiction of maternal behavior reflects his own family's experience: the mother, based on his wife who had just parted from their paratrooper son, symbolizes all the mothers during the War of Attrition (1968–71) who sent their sons off to war while they remained at the home front.[24]

(e) *Weeping Women.* Or rather, mothers mourning their children, which is also a common motif in European iconography. The image of elderly mothers or weeping women also draws upon various Christian iconographic traditions. A prime example of weeping women in European iconography is the graveyard memorials found throughout Central Europe.[25] In Israel this motif appears twice: in Aharon Ashkenazi's memorial at Kibbutz Revadim (1954) of a kneeling, weeping woman holding her head in her hands, and in Batya Lishanski's relief at Kfar Yehoshua (1979) erected in memory of the Yom Kippur War casualties, depicting two weeping women with arms wrapped around themselves. As these memorials were meant to serve as quasi-tombstones for the bereaved families, the motif of weeping mothers ostensibly seems to be a natural one. However it appears that the contrast between the image of the weeping mother who symbolizes surrender to tragedy and the Zionist ethos of parents who stoically face bereavement prevented most of the early memorial designers from adopting this image.

The older, and particularly the weeping, mothers appearing in Israeli iconography from the late 1950s onward had a social and cultural significance far beyond that of expressing personal bereavement. Their inclusion in military commemoration indicates the continued existence of a popular immigrant culture that allowed mothers (and sometimes even fathers) to publicly and vocally mourn their children. Simultaneously, it was a first indication of the psychological transformation that would characterize Israeli society from the 1970s onwards, expressed in the public and private sectors through a softening of the heroic façade regarding the treatment of bereavement. This process is best expressed in the Kfar Yehoshua memorial, which indicates the impact of the Yom Kippur war with its 2,687 casualties upon all segments of Israeli society and highlights the cracks appearing in what was once a highly collectivist ethos. Designed by Batya Lishanski — the same artist whose statue erected at Kfar Yehoshua 30 years earlier had depicted a woman among the group of combatants — it depicts women as expressing a raw, individual grief, each embracing herself as a separate, and not collective, entity.

(f) *The Virgin*. The image of the "virgin" inevitably has Christian roots, often merging with that of the female warrior, as in the case of Joan of Arc, or with pagan images such as Athena, Diana and Aretmis. In Israel, the image of the innocent young girl appears only once, in Gershom Knispel's memorial relief at the Kfar Galim agricultural school (1970) depicting a teenage boy and girl carrying sheaves of wheat and flowers. The combination of innocence with the pastoral setting suits both place — an agricultural school — and time — the days between the Six Day War and the Yom Kippur War when many Israelis lived in the hope that active combat had become an issue of the past.

Several gender motifs are notably absent. The first is a Pietà-like image of a mother holding her dead son, common in both East and West European military iconography, particularly that of the Second World War. This uniquely Christian image was obviously rejected by a Jewish cultural framework, and it is found neither in Israeli Holocaust iconography nor in monumental military commemoration. With one exception that I will examine later, equally absent is the wounded woman soldier, although a wounded male soldier is a common memorial motif. Wounded women also fail to appear in European monuments: one of the few statues portraying a wounded female image is Fritz Kramer's and Will Lammert's Ravensbrück memorial where a wounded woman is carried by her comrades. This lacuna may stem from a universally accepted cultural reluctance to deal with the concept of female war casualties, although the phenomenon existed in reality, particularly during the War of Independence.[26]

An additional difference between the commemoration of male and female military casualties is semantic. The difficulty of finding a suitable phrase to accompany military memorials, which would denote both men and women who lost their lives in the armed forces, was raised in England soon after the First World War. In most cases, the more general phrase, "In memory of all those from [name of village] who lost their lives for their country," was chosen as a non-gendered alternative.[27] However, various gendered epitaphs also appear: "In memory of the sons and daughters" (Winchester); "In memory of the men and women who gave their lives for king and country" (Lewes; Canterbury); "In memory of the Men and Women who gave their lives in the service of others and especially during 1914–1918 and 1939–1945" (Salisbury).[28] Because of the gendered nature of the Hebrew language, female military casualties were incorporated into the masculine term "the fallen"; only in Haifa were the female military casualties referred to separately in a memorial garden dedicated to "Our Sons and Daughters who were killed in the War of Independence." Even in the abstract memorials, the phrases chosen to commemorate female soldiers indicate the collective image which the commemorators wished to project during certain periods. In most cases, gendered phrases expressing social or biological differences were not employed. Thus, Elyakim Ben Ari's Nitzanim memorial (1950), commemorating his wife Miri (a communications expert who died in battle), makes no mention of the fact that she was a mother who refused to leave the kibbutz with the other mothers and their children because of her military task.

The typology of gender images in Israeli military memorials is better understood within the context of several unique factors influencing Israeli military commemoration. As opposed to most countries whose iconographic system commemorates finite events or a series of well-defined wars often separated by decades or even centuries, Israeli military commemoration appears to be a never-ending process which began before the establishment of the State of Israel and continues until the present. From Melnikof's "Roaring Lion" (1932) in memory of the Tel Hai fighters[29] up to the recent memorial erected at Nitzanim commemorating casualties of the Women's Army Corps, Israeli iconography consists of an ongoing, developing system of semantic and figurative images. On the gender level, these images reflect the modulations of local attitude towards an interaction between the variables of gender and the military. No similar developing continuity of memorial imagery appears elsewhere, as plastic commemoration in most countries reflects a retrospective-static view of women and/or female combatants through the prism of a specific war.

Religious dictates are a second factor influencing Israeli commemorative iconography. From the medieval period onward, Jewish religious prohibitions stemming from a broad interpretation of the commandment "Thou shall not create a graven image" (Exodus 20:4) successfully eradicated any traces of figurative iconography in the cultural sphere. Aharon Priver, writing in Kibbutz Tel Yosef's newsletter in April 1952, states that "religious prohibitions, the yoke of exile, the suppression and negation of our people's rights, dried up this blessed source of creativity." Similar sentiments were expressed at the inauguration of the Negba monument a year later.[30]

Consequently, it is not surprising that close to 90 percent of the figurative memorials pertaining to women are located in secular kibbutzim and moshavim which were not curtailed by religious cultural prohibitions of this sort. It is also clear why these memorials, erected in settlements where only a purely Israeli identity could be considered suitable to commemorate fallen soldiers, bear no religious imagery. The exception to this rule is the Givatayim memorial, uniquely symbolic due to both its location and its content. The story of this memorial gives us a glimpse into the dynamics existing between the entity that commissions a monument, the artist and the viewers.

Four Memorials and Their Gender Representation

In the spring of 1978, Givatayim Mayor Kuba Kreizman commissioned an official municipal monument in memory of all the fallen soldiers from his city. Having already approached a well-known Israeli sculptor, Mordechai Cafri, Kreizman decided not to put out an open tender but instead asked Cafri to present three different models from which he and a committee of bereaved parents would make a final choice. As this was the "year of peace" with Egypt, Cafri suggested one model based upon a dove, a second one of a more abstract choice, and a third, figurative model, which was ultimately chosen. The winning model consisted of three figures: a tall elderly man wrapped in a prayer shawl and phylacteries, a woman in the first stages of pregnancy standing beside him, and a bare-chested young man standing slightly below the duo. Placed behind and above the young man, the man's and woman's hands rest on the lad's shoulders; he reaches back, grasping their legs, but is looking towards the horizon and striding forward. Behind the statue is a wall upon which the Hebrew alphabet appears in *Rashi* script (a medieval variant of Hebrew script), next to which is the phrase "For fame, for glory, and for praise," appearing in the traditional Friday-night Jewish prayer *Lekha dodi.*

The Givatayim monument, which was dedicated only in 1988 due to financial disagreements, is unusual in four respects: it is one of the last figurative statues to be erected in Israel when the abstract school was already at its zenith; it is the only monument located in a city that features a woman in full body; it is the only memorial that includes a pregnant female figure, and it is the only military memorial that contains overtly religious symbols.

"A war memorial is always erected in the name of national ideals and collective values, but an important aspect of any memorial is the freedom of thought it allows the individual within the collective," writes Esther Levinger in her study of women in Israeli military monuments.[31] The story of the Givatayim monument teaches us the need for careful cross-checking when deciphering commemorative codes. As the statue is located in a south

Givatayim park, near two religious neighborhoods which had seen many local casualties in the various wars, many of the locals were convinced that its "traditional" design was chosen by the Orthodox deputy mayor of Givatayim, a neighborhood rabbi. In truth, Cafri designed the monument long before the rabbi moved to the neighborhood and entered political life. When asked about the matter he admitted that the images which he incorporated into the monument had been triggered by his own imagination and personal background: the grandfather in prayer shawl and phylacteries symbolized the traditional Warsaw Jews among which the now secular Cafri had been raised prior to the Second World War; the pregnant woman was "the mother of all living creatures." As the park where the statue was to be placed was located directly in front of an educational complex composed of two secular schools, Cafri desired that the children "would see a bit of tradition, including Hebrew [*Rashi* script] letters, and would play with the letters in order to try and compose their own names." As for the young man in the group, Cafri saw him as "striding forward, freed from all restraints, also from religious ones." Cafri did not inquire as to whether he was commemorating male soldiers or a mixed-sex group. In either case he considered it imperative to include a female figure who would complete and complement the circle of female images appearing in military monuments since the state's founding. Thus he decided to include a young-old mother sending her son off to war, an auxiliary to the tableau while providing support for the next generation, averting her eyes from the future (her son) in order to gaze at the past (the grandfather) and be strengthened by it so as not to succumb to her tragic loss.

Simultaneously, there were viewers who later interpreted Cafri's symbolism as an ironic parody of the Israeli ethos and a kitsch interpretation of stereotyped Israeli machoism: the grandfather, deeply steeped in an anachronistic religious tradition, who tries in vain to transmit it to his grandson; the mother, a walking womb who prepares the new generation of soldiers even as she sends the present one off to war; the young man, a bare-chested soldier marching resolutely forward, paying no attention to the hands of past and present lying upon his shoulders, despite the fact that his fate is sealed and his replacement-continuation is already taking form under his mother's skirts.[32]

The story of the Givatayim memorial demonstrates the dichotomy that often arises between the artist's intentions, the desires of the commissioning body, and the viewer's interpretations. As most plastic memorials are not accompanied by an explanatory text penned by the artist, viewers invoke various personal factors in order to reach their own interpretations. Furthermore, neither the artist nor the viewer may fully understand the intentions of the individual or collective which commissioned the memorial. Every historian is a product of his own era, wrote Benedetto Crocce, and each viewer interprets a monument through the prism of his own internal world.

A second memorial, this time a private one erected in a public space by the family of a female military casualty, sheds light upon a different facet of gender commemoration: the juxtaposition between form and text. On Sunday morning, 25 February 1996, 20-year-old Sergeant Hofit Ayash stood at a soldier's hitch-hiking post at the Ashkelon junction waiting for a lift. Minutes after reaching the junction she was killed by an Arab suicide bomber, detonating himself and injuring 34 additional soldiers. Shortly after Ayash's death, her family, and particularly her mother, decided to commission a monument in memory of the young soldier which would stand at the Ashkelon junction. Battling both municipal and military authorities wishing to have a small marker set inland from the main road, Ayash's mother had the memorial set in a concrete base on the main highway, next to the hitch-hiking post where her daughter had passed the last minutes of her life. Having consulted with newly religious family members, she decided against a figurative representation and instead chose a six-foot reddish-brown stone upon which the name "Hofit" was set in bronze letters. In the center of the stone was a plaque noting her name and age, the circumstances and date of her death, the acronym H.Y.D. (Hebrew for "may the Lord avenge her blood," used to commemorate martyrs), the verse "Behold, the keeper of Israel neither slumbers nor sleeps," and its source, Psalms, 21:4. In spite of the fact that this verse is primarily used to commemorate (male) soldiers killed in battle, Ayash's mother insisted on its inclusion out of a combination of religious considerations and the feeling that her daughter was the casualty of an ongoing terrorist battle with growing numbers of victims. The debate over the monument's size and location and the verse's suitability that ensued between the Ayash family and the military/municipal authorities responsible for the memorial's upkeep (which had preferred a small, out-of-the-way stone for a lone female soldier) articulates the difficulty certain groups have in accepting commemorative equality. This includes battle versus terrorist casualties, military versus civilian casualties, and even male versus female casualties. Simultaneously, it points to yet another commemorative transition in Israeli society: the growing decision-making role of the family in "official" military commemoration.[33]

A third memorial, in memory of a group of women, is the newly inaugurated Women's Army Corps memorial complex found at the Shikma field school on the grounds of the former site of Kibbutz Nitzanim.[34] Inaugurated during Israel's jubilee year, the memorial is named *Yad la-ishah ha-ivriyah ha-lohemet* (Memorial to the Hebrew Woman Combatant). Ultimately meant to be an entire memorial complex, its first stage was the creation of a statuary tableau alongside a small amphitheater where military ceremonies of the Women's Army Corps would be held. The semi-abstract statues, sculpted by artist Shosh Hefetz, were placed together in several thematic groups which, according to the sculptor, herself the first medic of the *Nahal* army corps, represented what she felt to be the full gamut of female military experience. Yet a closer look shows this to be only a partial reflection of the facts. Among the groups one finds a woman supporting her female comrade, a mother protecting her small children, and even a male figure holding a wounded female soldier in his arms — the only such figure found in Israel. In spite of Hefetz's own personal history, there is not even one semi-abstract female combatant or auxiliary. In fact, although the original cast of the monument approved by the memorial committee included barbed wire, guns and a communications radio, Hefetz dispensed with these accessories in the final version, preferring, as she called it, "a minor representation of war."[35] Indeed, Hefetz admits that although it was meant to be a monument to all casualties of the Women's Army Corps, she decided to center the statuary around the story of the child (Danny Ben-Ari), evacuated from the kibbutz, and his mother, Mira, who remained behind and is commemorated in a nearby memorial. By telling one story, she was also muting a different one, in which women were marked not only by their biological/gendered function but by their full participation in battle.

What can we learn from the Nitzanim memorial? Even at the end of the twentieth century, when female recruits in the IDF were permitted to try out for positions which had not been open to women since the days of the Palmah, the female figurative image and accompanying texts remain relatively passive, reminiscent in form and motif more of Krammer and Lammert's sculptures at Ravensbrück than of the "Hebrew Woman Combatant," who, it appears, engages in everything other than combat itself. Despite the acceptance of women pilots and women in elite navy units, in Israel of the late twentieth and early twenty-first century it appears almost impossible — if not practically forbidden — to create a figurative connection between women and militarism. This is, of course, in spite of the fact that women stand at the center of a public discourse revolving around sexism, racism, violence in general and family violence in particular, not as an abstract image but as a concrete victim.[36]

The three memorials that I have highlighted here represent three types of women's representation in Israeli military commemoration. The first is the use of a female figure as part of a group in figurative commemoratory statuary, meant to represent both male and female casualties. The choice of the mother image makes it a universal form of representation with the hint of pregnancy alluding to an ongoing process of demographic proliferation. The second is a stone monument representing a single female casualty, with the only reference to the victim's sex being textual (her name). However the textual component is also misleading, due to the use of a phrase commonly associated with male soldiers who were casualties of battle. The third is a semi-abstract group memorial to hundreds of women soldiers who lost their lives in various circumstances. Among the bronze figures are both males and females, however the memorial focuses upon the figure of a mother and child, the mother a kibbutz member, a tiller of the soil more than a soldier. Together, the three memorials commemorate almost the entire gamut of soldiers — both male and female — killed in the Israeli military corps: those killed in war, those who were victims of terrorist attacks, and in the case of the last memorial, all women in the Israeli army who lost their lives while on active military duty.

One final group of women, depicted in a fourth memorial, deserves special mention: those who fell while serving in the intelligence corps or in one of the Israeli security services. The memorial to members of the intelligence corps, built next to the military base at the Gelilot junction in central Israel, has neither figurative nor abstract statuary. Instead it is built as a maze, a series of interconnecting walls upon which dates appear, beginning with pre-state intelligence operations. Israel's wars and military engagements are listed chronologically, under which appear the names of those intelligence corps and secret service members who lost their lives in the course of that war or between the various wars. No distinction is made between the men or women whose names and dates of death are mentioned, nor between those referred to collectively as belonging to operations that have still not been disclosed to the public. As one progresses through the maze from Israel's earlier wars up to the present, one notes a larger number of female names under recent dates, mute testimony to the growing number of women in the intelligence corps and security services killed in road accidents and through Arab terror.

Unlike the three previous memorials, this one is not a commemorative site solely for women, nor does it have any form of statuary. However it is interesting to note a true form of commemorative equalization. In spite of the extremely gendered nature of tasks often assigned to women in the security services in order to ensure an operation's success, this memorial, commemorating men and women side by side, makes no distinction between age, sex, rank and type of operation being commemorated.

Summary

"Landscapes are culture before they are nature; constructs of the imagination projected onto wood and water and rock," writes Simon Schama in *Landscape and Memory*.[37] An observer of the Israeli commemorative landscape will find it difficult to recover a single collective memory of either female military casualties or gender images which is embodied in Israeli commemorative culture. Instead one finds a developing series of images reflecting the emotional and physical maturation process of the young state and shedding light on the construction and transformation of Israeli gender identity during a period of over half a century.

An investigation of gender images in Israeli plastic commemoration shows the shift of images mirroring the interplay between private mourning and public commemoration. First we see how the auxiliary and the young mother grew seamlessly from the image of the female combatant, the only one appearing before the War of Independence and disappearing in the Israeli postwar reality. Mirroring the Israeli collectivist ethos, the early young mothers symbolized not only the dozens of mothers who lost their lives as civilian and military casualties in the 1948 war, but the motherland, the hope of continuity. As one progresses chronologically from the period in which women played an active role in military and civilian defense, the auxiliaries and young mothers are replaced by images representing the passive task relegated to most Israeli women after the Sinai Campaign: older and weeping mothers sacrificing their children for the motherland. The same image was chosen to commemorate both male and female soldiers, one of a woman who provides the nation with warriors as part of her biological task, and mourns them — as only mothers are permitted to mourn publicly — by gendered privilege. From this point onwards the elderly-mother image remains dominant in Israeli commemorative iconography, until figurative images disappear at the end of the 1980s.

Apart from expanding our conceptualization of the military and civilian metamorphosis of Israeli women, the transformation of the female image in figurative commemoration points to three widespread processes which defined and characterized the national-gender discourse in Israeli society from the establishment of the state until the present. The first is genderization and retreat from an ethos of socialist equality, which was expressed through the figurative commemoration of female military casualties and particularly by the transition from the female combatant and auxiliary images to that of the mother. In removing women soldiers from front-line tasks — and thus from Israeli commemorative iconography — the military was turned into an almost completely masculine sector, one example of the genderized process taking place in Israel society. Other sectors of Israeli society characterized by a similarly process of genderization were labor relations and allocation of public resources, both of which contradicted the equality ethos that the early pioneers had adopted as their credo. The struggle for equality in these fields began even before the establishment of the State of Israel and has remained one of the social, economic and political sources of tension throughout its 50-year history.[38]

The transition from auxiliary to mother image points to a second gendered process characterizing developing society: the need to turn women into "national mothers," birth machines that would ensure national continuity while simultaneously ensuring ethnocultural uniqueness.[39] This process was a central issue facing Israeli society and deeply concerning Israeli Prime Minister David Ben-Gurion during the early years of the state: demography. Ben-Gurion believed that only rapid demographic growth could assure Israel's continued existence and he therefore initiated a massive immigration campaign while investing both energy and resources in encouraging what he called "internal immigration." This determination was expressed in generous birth grants, child allowances, prizes awarded to mothers of large families and the creation of an ethos that placed a premium on viewing the Israeli woman as mother, particularly as a mother of soldiers. In his early speeches during the War of Independence Ben-Gurion allotted special honor to the mothers of fallen soldiers and spoke of their unique relationship with their sons and daughters who had sacrificed their lives for the motherland.[40] The transition in commemorative iconography from female soldier to mother (young or old), expresses the transformation of an Israeli ethos regarding how a woman should shoulder the national burden: not by protecting the motherland with her body but by supplying future protectors via her body. The gendering process of Israeli society, in both ethos and praxis, reflects the metamorphosis of the female image in Israeli figurative memorial iconography during the five decades of the state's existence.

Transformations of the mother image hint at yet another process which has characterized Israeli society since the 1960s, that of *decollectivization*. Similar to their European counterparts, the early mother images that appeared in Israeli plastic commemoration (Ramat Rachel, 1949) represented the motherland more than they did an individual mother. Beauty, purity, courage, and vision which the young mother expressed were supposed to reflect the motherland's collective qualities and act as a model for them. However, iconographical feminization of the motherland, well known in western and eastern Europe (Marianne in France, "Winged Victory" in Britain, the monumental statue in memory of the Stalingrad fighters in the form of a woman holding a sword), was barely absorbed by a country colloquially known in Hebrew as *Eretz hemdat avot* (the forefathers' beloved land). The difficulty in equating the motherland with a mother image led to the fact that the mothers who appeared in Israeli commemorative iconography from the late 1950s onwards did not represent a collective ethos but a personal one. Hence the transition from the young, beautiful and striking mother to the older and more minor figure, a flesh-and-blood image representing only herself. The decollectivization of a mother image in Israeli iconography predates the general trend of diminishing the collective ethos in Israeli society which expressed itself in the social, cultural and political spheres only a decade later.[41]

The third process affecting Israeli society expressed by commemorative iconography was the transition to multiculturalism. In spite of the broad cultural spectrum that new immigrants brought to Israel, for over two decades the official culture, reflecting the definitive Israeli ethos, was both dominant and all encompassing. Nevertheless, the richness and diversity of immigrant subcultures continued to express themselves in certain fields, particularly during major transitional events such as birth, marriage and death. In the commemorative sphere the tension between the official dominant culture and the immigrants' subcultures is expressed by the older and weeping mothers. "Who will understand the mother's pain; who will sweeten the sorrow of her mourning and heal her mortal wound, even when she hides all this in simplicity and courage from strangers!" wrote Ben-Gurion in the spring of 1950.[42] Even before the national ethos of concealing bereavement pain began to soften (a process that has recently reached a new zenith as evidenced by the pictures of Israeli soldiers weeping over their comrades' graves shown in daily newspapers and broadcast on national television), Israeli iconography recognized the bereaved family's right to mourn publicly, a central component in both East European and *Mizrahi* (Jews from Muslim countries) immigrant subcultures. Here, too, it appears that gender commemoration in Israeli iconography preceded a general trend later expressing itself in Israeli society.

Many assumed that the latter two processes — decollectivization and the transition to multiculturalism — would give birth to new forms of military commemoration which would reflect the various military and civilian tasks that women had fulfilled. By doing so, the commemorative forms would not only reflect the entire gamut of women's military activities but would also act as a factor in molding the national discourse regarding the future role of women in the military framework. However, the opposite trend is becoming evident: at the Women's Army Corps memorial mentioned earlier there is no plastic representation of either a female combatant or auxiliary. Does it look as if this process is undergoing any change? In a country where the national discourse is still molded by former commanders of elite army units, generals and other military figures, and the socio-economic discourse often emanates from the offices of clerico-patriarchal political representatives, it is difficult to believe that women in active combat positions will receive any form of commemorative expression in the near future.[43]

NOTES

*   This essay is an expanded and revised version of an earlier article published in Margalit Shilo, Ruth Kark and Galit Hasan-Rokem (eds.), *Ha-ivriyot ha-hadashot: Nashim ba-yishuv uva-tziyonut be-re'i ha-migdar* (Jewish Women in the *Yishuv* and Zionism: A Gender Perspective) (Jerusalem, 2001). It is also part of a larger study on Women's Military Commemoration in the State of Israel, supported by the Littauer Foundation, New York.

1   Cited in Tom Segev, "Mah osot ha-matzevot ba-lailah: Doh masa" (What Monuments Do at Night: A Travel Report), Ha'aretz, 27 April 1990.

2   See Nira Yuval-Davis and Floya Anthias, Woman-National-State (Houndsmill and London, 1989); Catherine Nash, "Men Again: Irish Masculinity, Nature, and Nationhood in the Early Twentieth Century," Ecumene, Vol. 3, No. 4 (1996), pp. 253–427; Lawrence Dowler, "'And They Think I'm Just a Nice Old Lady': Women and War in Belfast, Northern Ireland," Gender Place and Culture, Vol. 5, No. 2 (1998), pp. 159–76. Gail Zwerman, "Mothering on the Lam: Politics, Gender Fantasies and Maternal Thinking in Women Associated with Armed, Clandestine Organizations in the United States," Feminist Review, No. 47 (1994), pp. 33–56; Joy Elshtain, Women and War (New York, 1987); Alice McClintock, "Family Feuds: Gender, Nationalism and the Family," Feminist Review, No. 44 (1993), pp. 61–80; Kumari Jayawardena, Feminism and Nationalism in the Third World (London, 1986); D. Kendiyoti, "Identity and its Discontents: Women and the Nation," Millenium: Journal of International Studies, Vol. 20, No. 3 (1991), pp. 229–43; Tamar Mayer (ed.), Women and the Israeli Occupation: The Politics of Change (London and New York, 1994).

3   Regarding the meaning of commemoration see, James E. Young, The Texture of Memory: Holocaust Memorials and Meaning (New Haven and London, 1993), p. 15.

4   Clifford Geertz (ed.), Myth, Symbol and Culture (New York, 1971).

5   In a semiological study of Israeli war memorials sociologist Oz Almog states that "Israel has a ratio of one memorial per 17 fallen soldiers, whereas in Europe the ratio is one to 10,000 ... there isn't a city in Israel, not even the smallest town, which lacks its own memorial." Oz Almog, "Andartot le-halelei milhamah be-Yisrael: Nituah semiologi" (Memorial Statues for Israeli War Dead: A Semiological Analysis), Megamot, Vol. 34, No. 2 (1991), p. 182.

6   Esther Levinger, Andartot le-noflim be-Yisrael (War Memorials in Israel), (Tel Aviv, 1993); Ilana Shamir, Hantzahah ve-zikaron (Commemoration and Memory) (Tel Aviv, 1997); idem (ed.), Galed: Andartot le-noflim be-ma'arakhot Yisrael (Galed: Memorials to the Fallen Soldiers in Israel's Military Campaigns) (Tel Aviv, 1989).

7   I wish to thank the Division for Soldier Commemoration and the Statistical Department at the Israeli Ministry of Defense for providing me with the relevant statistical data. Emanuel Sivan claims that 108 women in uniform were killed during the 1948 war and that the total number of female casualties, civilian and military, was 469. Emanuel Sivan, Dor tashah: Mitos, dyokan ve-zikaron (The 1948 Generation: Myth, Profiles and Memory) (Tel Aviv, 1991), pp. 35–39.

8   The term "statist" (mamlakhti) is used in Zionist history to denote the principle of the primacy of the nation and supremacy of the state over civil society, of political power over social action and voluntary bodies. See Zeev Sternhell, The Founding Myths of Israel: Nationalism, Socialism, and the Making of the Jewish State (Princeton, 1998), p. 35; also Eliezer Don-Yehiya, "Memory and Political Culture: Israeli Society and the Holocaust," Studies in Contemporary Jewry, Vol. 9 (1993), p. 144.

9   Chava Ironi-Avrahami, Almoniyot be-haki: Sipuran shel haverot ha-Haganah be-Tel Aviv (The Unknown in Khaki: The Story of the Women Members of the Haganah in Tel Aviv) (Tel Aviv, 1989). To compare with the number of women in the Red Army during the Second World War see Kate Muir, Arms and the Woman (London, 1992), pp. 69–73.

10 Regarding this mission and its historical and gendered interpretations, see my articles "The Heroism of Hannah Senesz: An Exercise in Creating Collective National Memory in the State of Israel," Journal of Contemporary History, Vol. 31 (1996), pp. 521–46; "Akh nizkor et kulam: Hantzahat ha-tzanhanim-shlihim mi-milhemet ha-olam ha-shniyah ba-shanim 1945–1949" (Commemorating the Yishuv's Second World War Parachutist Emissaries to Europe, 1945–1949), Cathedra, Vol. 84 (July 1997), pp. 107–32; "The 'Parachutist's Mission' from a Gender Perspective," in Ruby Rohrlich (ed.), Resisting the Holocaust (Oxford and New York, 1998), pp. 95–113.

11 Pe'ulot ha-haverah ba-Palmah (Activities of the Female Members of the Palmach), proceedings of a seminar held by the Center for the History of the Fighting Forces — the Haganah, at Yad Tabenkin, 22 December 1986 (Tel Aviv, 1988).

12 Nashim ve-sherut be-tzahal: Metzi'ut, ratzon ve-hazon (Women and Israeli Army Service:

Reality, Desire and Vision), proceedings of a symposium held on 21 February 1995 (Jerusalem, 1995).

13 See Zwerman, "Mothering on the Lam," p. 42.

14 See Dowler, "'And They Think I'm Just a Nice Old Lady'," p. 16.

15 Yuval-Davis and Anthias, *Woman-National-State*, p. 7.

16 Netira Ben-Yehuda, *1948: Bein ha-sfirot* (1948: Between Calendars) (Jerusalem, 1981); idem, *Kshe-partzah ha-medinah* (When the State of Israel Broke Out) (Jerusalem, 1991); Tamar Avidar, *Ksheha-kova hayah gerev* (When the Sock Was a Hat) (Tel Aviv, 1988).

17 Levinger, *Andartot le-noflim*, p. 29; Rina Porat's interview with Eliyahu Amitzur, Kfar Yehoshua, 22 March 1998; author's telephone conversation with the archivist of Kibbutz Tel-Yosef, 18 March 1998.

18 Aharon Priver, "Ha-tavlit al kir ha-zikaron leyad 'Beit Trumpeldor'" (The Relief on the Memorial Wall at Trumpeldor House), *Me-Hayenu*, No. 1002, 18 April 1952, p. 1

19 "Hineh hi nitzevet" (Here She Stands), *Kol Negbah*, No. 5 (103), 20 October 1953.

20 Colin McIntyre, *Monuments of War: How to Read a War Memorial* (London, 1990), p. 144.

21 Avraham Harman and Yigael Yadin, *Asor le-Yisrael* (On Israel's Tenth Anniversary) (Tel Aviv and Jerusalem, n.d. [1958?]); Ben-Yehuda, *1948: Bein ha-sfirot*; Avidar, *Ksheha-kova hayah gerev*; Yael Dayan, *New Face in the Mirror* (London, 1967); *Hill 24 Doesn't Answer*, dir. T. Dickenson, Israel 1955. Regarding the image of Israeli women soldiers in popular international culture, see Anne R. Bloom, "Israel: The Longest War," in Nancy L. Goldman (ed.), *Female Soldiers — Combatants or Noncombatants: Historical and Contemporary Perspectives* (Westport, CT, and London, 1982), p. 156.

22 One exception to this trend is Maya Lin's Vietnam memorial erected in Washington, DC in the form of an enormous commemorative stone wall on which the names of the soldiers who lost their lives during the Vietnam War were engraved. In other places, such as France, there is a return to figurative statues which commemorate not only military, but civilian casualties as well. Regarding the history of commemoration in France, see Daniel J. Sherman, "Bodies and Names: The Emergence of Commemoration in Interwar France," *American Historical Review*, Vol. 103, No. 2 (April 1998), pp. 443–66.

23 Pictures of the original models appear in *Yad le-mem daled halilei ha-ma'arakhah al Negbah u-mevo'oteha* (Memory to the 44 Dead from the Defense of Negba and its Surroundings) (Tel Aviv, n.d).; Sivan, *Dor Tashah*, pp. 37–9.

24 Indeed, 40 percent of the war dead in 1948 were Holocaust survivors even though they composed only 20 percent of the general population; author's telephone conversation with Mordechai Cafri, 30 March 1998.

25 See, for example, the weeping figures in the cemetery in Bremen Osterholz who commemorate the victims of concentration camps, the statue of women crying over the graves of Russian soldiers in Bergen-Hoersten, bordering with Bergen Belsen, the statues of two women weeping in the Bad Kreuznach cemetery at the graves of murdered camp prisoners. The older women is pictured with a kerchief on her head and wearing shoes, the younger figure, with clasped hands, is barefoot with her hair in braids.

26 Insa Eschebach, "Geschlechtsspezifische Symbolisierungen im Gedenken: Zur Geschichte der Mahn- und Gedenkstaette Ravensbrück," *Metis: Zeitschrift für historische Frauenforschung und feministische Praxis*, Vol. 8, No. 15 (1999), pp. 12–27.

27 McIntyre, *Monuments of War*, p. 153.

28 From a survey of 50 military memorials in southern and central England which the author conducted during the summer of 1999.

29 Melnikov's statue was the first memorial to list women casualties and whose original cast was of a female form.

30 Priver, "Ha-tavlit al kir ha-zikaron"; "Hineh hi nitzevet."

31 Esther Levinger, "Women and War Memorials in Israel," *Woman's Art Journal*, Vol. 16 (1995), p. 45, n. 1.

32 Author's telephone conversation with Mordechai Cafri, 30 March 1998.

33 Author's interview with Ruth Ayash (mother of fallen soldier Hofit Ayash), Ashdod, 22 June 1999. In order to express Ayash's femininity, her mother had a silk bird and silk flowers placed

in the niches of the memorial stone.

34 Following the kibbutz's evacuation during the 1948 war it was reestablished on a different site, across the coastal road, approximately three kilometers from its former location.

35 Author's telephone interview with Shosh Hefetz, 20 February 2000. The history and development of the Women's Army Corps Memorial is a complex issue and will be dealt with in a separate study.

36 Mayer (ed.), *Women and the Israeli Occupation*, p. 123.

37 Simon Schama, *Landscape and Memory* (New York, 1995), p. 61.

38 Dafna N. Izraeli, "The Women Workers' Movement: First Wave Feminism in Israel," in Deborah S. Bernstein (ed.), *Pioneers and Homemakers: Jewish Women in Pre-State Israel* (Albany, NY, 1992), pp. 183–210; Sylvie Fogiel-Bijaoui, "From Revolution to Motherhood: The Case of Women in the Kibbutz, 1910–1948," in ibid., pp. 211–34.

39 Georgina Waylen, "Analysing Women in the Politics of the Third World," in Haleh Afshar (ed.), *Women and Politics in the Third World* (London and New York, 1996), p. 15. This process is common to many developing nations outside of the Third World, as may be seen by the Australian example of the 1930s. In a poetry contest held on the "white continent" in 1938, women's constant fertility was lauded and encouraged in order to preserve the cultured nation: "Ye girls of British race, Famous for your beauty, / Breed fast in all your grace, For this is your duty. / As Anzac gave in war, So daughters at your call, / Will quick respond the more, To replace those that fall." H. McQueen, *Social Sketches of Australia, 1888–1975* (Harmondsworth, 1978), p. 158.

40 "The National Assembly Sends the Parents of our valiant defenders and particularly their mothers ... special honor," meeting of the National Assembly, Tel Aviv, Keren Kayemet House, 4 May 1948, in David Ben-Gurion, *Be-hilakhem Yisrael* (When Israel Fought) (Tel Aviv, 1957), p. 98; "Far away from a stranger's vision and also possibly hidden, innocence and beauty, courage and love, softness and power were hidden in these cubs of Israel, revealed maybe only to their mothers." David Ben-Gurion, "Al ha-banim she-naflu" (On the Children Who Fell [in Battle]), 25 March 1950, in ibid., p. 357.

41 For expressions of this process in other cultural spheres, see Nurit Gertz, *Sipur meha-sratim: Siporet yisre'elit ve-ibudeha le-kolno'ah* (Motion Fiction: Israeli Fiction in Films) (Tel Aviv, 1993).

42 Ben-Gurion, "Al ha-banim she-naflu," pp. 357–8.

43 Author's interview with one of the initiators of the Nitzanim Women's Army Corps memorial, former army commander Yitzhak Pundak, Kfar Yonah, 9 May 1999.

Do Not Weep Rachel:
Fundamentalism, Commemoration and
Gender in a West Bank Settlement*

Michael Feige

Introduction

On 27 October 1991, Palestinian terrorists opened fire on a bus coming out of the settlement of Shiloh on its way to a large political rally in Tel Aviv. The bus driver, Yitzhak Rofeh and one of the passengers, Rachel Druk, were killed, and several children were injured. In the months following the event, a few dozen national-religious women affiliated with the Gush Emunim (Bloc of the Faithful) settlers' movement took it upon themselves to establish a new settlement at the site of the murder in commemoration of their dead friend, Rachel, mother of seven from Shiloh. The settlement was to be called "Rehelim" (literally: Rachels). This was the first time that a Jewish settlement in the West Bank (or anywhere else, for that matter) had been engineered, conceived and headed solely by women. While they were busy holding the fort at Rehelim, their spouses stayed at home to attend to the household chores and cater to the women.

At face value Rehelim can be seen as a case of feminism within what many scholars regard as a fundamentalist movement.[1] It is feminist in the strict and limited sense that women assumed leadership roles, initiated the establishment of a joint project of national value and proudly displayed their achievements in the public sphere. However, feminism is complex and multifaceted, with various incompatible definitions. One may claim that the acts of conquest by Gush Emunim, the penetration into hostile social environments and erecting settlements, are inherently masculine, and the women of Rehelim suggested no reinterpretation or subversive perspective on the all-important practice of settlement, occupation, let alone the rights of the occupied Palestinian Arabs.

Nevertheless, fundamentalism is usually associated with the reassertion of patriarchy and reestablishment of traditional gender roles. In this case, women engendered role reversal by appropriating the quintessential male role that is synonymous with their movement: settling the land. However, the case of Rehelim can hardly be regarded as a feminist revolution for several reasons, first and foremost because those who took action adamantly insisted that it should not be defined as such. The women of Rehelim never suggested instituting a total or even partial revision of gender roles within their camp and insisted on containing their struggle within the accepted lines of gender. They used the discourse quite common in fundamentalist movements, one that views feminism as a bitter enemy of the true divine order.

Reevaluating this case from a perspective of ten years provokes intriguing questions. National-religious women have indeed initiated, and to a large extent have been successful in bringing about, a totally new way of regarding gender roles within their community. A most impressive feminist revolution is currently under way, focusing mainly on the study of holy texts. The struggle over Rehelim took place on the threshold of a decade of radical change and, in a sense, preempted what was to follow. From a historical perspective, the establishing of Rehelim can be conceived as an embryonic feminist revolt that was suppressed before it had the chance to develop. The historical watershed of its occurrence is what makes the case so stimulating.

In this article I wish to draw on the case of Rehelim to discuss several aspects of the feminist revolution currently taking place in the Israeli national-religious camp. My main objective is to explain why Rehelim, while somewhat successful as a political statement or as a settlement project, failed to create the impression that it was a feminist challenge. In discussing the case I shall focus on two central motifs, which both explain and reflect the aversion of the potential feminist challenge. One is the imposing meanings of the symbol of Rachel, which was the chosen discursive element employed by the agents. I wish to claim that the choice of symbols directed the actions of the settlers towards traditional gender relations. The second is the narrative of commemoration, the overpowering logic of which caused the discourse to veer away from gender issues. The story of the site of Rehelim, by virtue of its being a commemorative site, was locked inside a distinct predetermined web of meanings, that disarmed emergent feminist possibilities. I shall suggest that the negated and averted feminist potential of Rehelim sheds light on the problems encountered by national-religious women today.

Women and Fundamentalism: The Israeli Case in a Comparative Perspective

In her article entitled "Fundamentalism and the Control of Women," Karen McCarthy Brown summarizes what she feels characterizes fundamentalism most of all:

> In conservative religious movements around the world, women are veiled or otherwise covered; confined to the home or in some other way

strictly limited in their access to the public sphere; prohibited from testifying in a court of law, owning property, or initiating divorce; and they are often denied the authority to make their own reproductive choices.[2]

Fundamentalist movements possess an ideal of femininity, which is conceived as part and parcel of the timeless truths represented by their movements' ethos. Fundamentalism can be conceived as a traditionalist response to modern culture, modernist ideas and the rise of science. Feminism, along with the weakening of the traditional family, is one of the most significant "evils" encountered in fundamentalist thought and politics.[3] While recruiting both sexes, religious movements are usually male-led, maintain a strongly gendered division of labor and may even be conceived as patriarchal protest movements. Recently scholars have begun to realize how gender-ridden the rhetoric of fundamentalism is in its aspiration for a separation of the sexes, both physically and conceptually.[4] One may add that the defiant nature of fundamentalism calls for a reassertion of the self, and therefore tends to be strongly affiliated with maleness and masculinity. In the fundamentalist ideal, the role of the woman is confined to the home, and "good mothering" has become the most important standard of evaluation. The restrictions of place and the subservient role of women in the private sphere within a nuclear family, understood by today's scholars as a historical construct, is elevated, in fundamentalist ideology, to mythical and sacred proportions. However, one should consider that in some respects fundamentalism can be empowering to women as well. Helen Hardacre elucidates the persuasive power of the fundamentalist message to women. Fundamentalism thrives where women's labor market situation offers limited possibilities. While it establishes and legitimates women's inferior status, fundamentalism also aids women in their efforts to "domesticate" men, namely, to tie the male breadwinner to home and family.[5] Many women agree enthusiastically with the anti-modernist and pro-family fundamentalist ideology and view themselves as equal partners in furthering the movement's goals.

In national-fundamentalist movements (mainly the Islamic), gendered imagery is transposed on the nation as a whole. William Darrow characterizes the rhetoric of revolutionary Iran: "the nation is like a woman at the mercy of more powerful outside forces."[6] Feminism, in the sense of freeing women from their social and symbolic allotted traditional role, is conceived as morally wrong for both religious and nationalistic reasons, presenting the divine order and national virility with a challenge. Therefore, fundamentalist men active in liberation movements expect the women fighting side-by-side with them to return to the traditional lifestyle after the battle is won, while women find it difficult to retain the achievements of their emancipation.

Many of the motifs discussed above are concordant with the concepts of femininity in the settlers' movement Gush Emunim and the national-religious women's camp in general. Due to the socio-economic affluence of the group and the state, the situation of these women is a far cry from that of Islamic women, and is closer to that of the women of Christian fundamentalist groups in North America. However, there is a crucial difference here as well: while women's issues, abortion in particular, were the most significant in the history of American fundamentalism, in the Israeli case, the struggle over territories and settlements greatly overshadows all other issues.

Research does indicate some significant similarities between the situation of the national-religious women and that of fundamentalist women elsewhere. Institutes of higher religious education, as well as many primary and secondary schools are gender segregated. Studies carried out within Israeli religious educational institutions for girls (ulpanot) have shown that gendered socialization is still the norm, and this is greatly reflected in both the curriculum and accounts given by the girls themselves.[7] The fragile political situation of religious women is demonstrated by the fact that in the course of the last three decades, the NRP (National Religious Party) has not sent a single woman to the Knesset.[8] Within the Gush Emunim camp, political leadership of the early days was uniformly male and the religious authority of rabbis, which is constantly increasing in influence, was an exclusively male prerogative.

The role fulfilled by women in the radical rightist movement is in accordance with the concept of the "republican woman," namely, the woman who through her reproductive role, as educator of children and keeper of the household, constitutes the backbone of the national ethos.[9] It is widely accepted that women's contribution to the national endeavor consists in their wholehearted fulfillment of their female role. But the traditional role of women is given special meaning by the unique characteristics of the settlement project because, in essence, it is a project of private and national home building. The struggle for the national home is conducted through the creation of private homes, and the private homes receive their unique value from their being contributions to the establishment of a national home. As a woman settler told a reporter from *Nekudah*, the settlers' monthly journal:

> ... without the heroism of women to hold on, a family per room in army camps, we would never have reached the caravans, the temporary houses and finally — settled homes. Mothers and children have turned the struggle into something real and serious ... in actuality, we, more than others, determine the nation's policy by giving our support behind the scenes to those around us, to grow, develop, contribute and build.[10]

As in other nationalist and revolutionary movements, women were enthusiastic participants in the Gush Emunim project, impelling their husbands towards greater radicalism. Even before the movement's emergence, religious women had approached the then Prime Minister, Golda Meir, with the suggestion that the national trauma of the 1973 war be remedied through settlement in Shkhem (Nablus). Later they were the first to settle in the densely populated Arab town of Hebron. A few women did reach positions of leadership in Gush Emunim or within certain settlements. On several occasions women's political organizations have emerged, raising political demands and introducing the voice of mothers into the Israeli hawkish discourse.[11] Research by an Israeli political scientist, Yael Yishay, has shown that religious women are among the most extreme elements in the various right-wing political groups in Israeli society today, even more than their spouses.[12]

In the course of the last decade, feminism has become one of the most outstanding issues on the agenda both of the settlers and of the national-religious camp in general. According to researchers of the phenomenon, and Orthodox men and women as well, the most significant change lay in allowing women to study the sacred texts, mainly the Gemara.[13] In a religious community, accessibility to the holy texts is the most esteemed intellectual asset, and hence, it conditions and legitimates social hierarchies. Although the national-religious community was never as gender-segregated as the Ultra-Orthodox community, men have always occupied the most essential religious roles, and women were prohibited from leadership positions in this realm. Allowing formal or informal education for women, therefore, constitutes a direct threat to the established order and is harshly criticized by some rabbis, while halfheartedly endorsed by others. Rabbi Ya'akov Shilat, for example, has pointed out that a woman cannot study the Gemara without encountering contradictions within the text because the Gemara reflects on the pointlessness of teaching women.[14]

Studying the sacred texts is an important example of a more comprehensive transformation in gender relations. As anthropologist Tamar El-Or has noted in her work on religious women's literacy, religious feminism in Israel is a rare non-violent revolution which has so far led to radical change with minimal direct confrontation.[15] Surprisingly, it has not (yet) been accompanied by one of the most noted consequences of feminism around the world, which alarms fundamentalists, namely a decline in fertility. Family values are still highly rated by Israeli religious women, and a newspaper report on the subject titled "Children Are Happiness, but So Is a Career" reflects the persistence of these values in the face of the changes taking place.[16]

The changes are fueled and driven by a growing awareness of feminist issues. A survey has shown that most young Orthodox women either uphold pro-feminist views or take a passive approach, although most of these women also express some concern in regard to the consequences of such changes.[17] However, most salient are the women's anger and anguish at being excluded from direct encounter with the religious texts that determine their sense of self. The title of El-Or's book on this phenomenon, *Next Passover*, is taken from a statement by one of the interviewees who claimed that it was inconceivable for her that by the next Passover she would still know only what she knew at the last Passover. Similarly, Bambi Sheleg, a national-religious journalist, articulates her inner drive to learn, describes her process of revelation and admits regretfully and with apparent anger: "I shall never be able to overcome the huge gap that was created between myself and him who learned the Gemara from the age of 10." And she concludes: "Full partnership in the Torah and in life will transform us all, women and men alike, to be rich in spirit and deeds."[18]

The feminist revolution has institutional articulations as well, mainly the new institutions of higher education for women, which have recently proliferated. A religious-feminist organization, "Kolekh" (Your Voice), has also been established and it organizes popular conferences.[19] An exhibition at the entrance to one of these conferences in 2001 presented the synagogue from the women's viewpoint: all that could be seen was the partitioning wall and some fragments of the rich world perpetually kept screened from the women. The exhibition represents what will most likely be the next stage of the religious-feminist revolution — changing traditions and religious norms that determine the inferior place of women.

Hannah Kehat, a leading figure in the religious-feminist revolution, wrote: "The feminine issue is the national-religious society's current 'hot' story and only the grief for those killed on the roads of Yesha [acronym for Judea, Samaria and Gaza] overshadows it."[20] In what follows, these two issues collide and merge.

Death and Commemoration on the Samarian Hills

The Gush Emunim movement was established in 1974 with a Greater Land of Israel ideology. Its main goal was to settle the territories occupied by Israel in the 1967 war to eliminate the possibility of territory-for-peace negotiations. The movement consisted mainly of national-religious Israeli Jews, adhering to an ideology-theology that viewed Zionism as part of a plan of divine redemption.[21] By the early 1990s, there were 144 settlements in the occupied territories, with some 100,000 residents.[22] Many came because of government subsidies to these settlements and the relative proximity of some of the settlements to the large metropolitan centers, Tel Aviv and Jerusalem. About half of the settlers were national-religious, not all of whom were affiliated with Gush Emunim. Many of the more ideologically minded settlers concentrated in small communities along the hilltops of Judea and Samaria. These ideological settlements, communities of up to a few hundred devoted movement followers, are the moral backbone and political stronghold of Gush Emunim.

The events at Rehelim occurred following three years of Palestinian revolt (the first *Intifada* starting in December 1987). For the Palestinians, the Jewish settlers were the most visible and threatening symbols of Israeli occupation, no less and probably more than the IDF (Israeli Defense Force) soldiers. The settlers were close neighbors who arrived with every intention of remaining indefinitely. Friction between the populations was intense, especially in light of the fact that the settlers used the same roads as the Palestinians, sometimes in an overtly defiant manner. Research has shown that at the early 1990s, among the residents of the "ideological settlements," 73 percent of the men and 53 percent of the children had encountered Palestinian acts of violence at an average rate of once a week or more.[23] In 1991–92 several settlers were killed in such attacks. This escalation of violence occurred at a time when the settlements were attempting to expand, with the support of a rightist government.[24] The routine disturbances of life in the settlements were perceived as a real threat to the future prospects of development. Retaliation, deterrence and confidence boosting became paramount factors in the settler leadership's considerations.

It was in this context that the settlers encountered what was then considered the most severe terrorist attack: the shooting at the bus from Shiloh in which two people were killed, the driver and a settler woman, and many more injured. Rachel Druk's funeral at Shiloh, the first in the young settlement's history, was subdued and well controlled. Immediately afterwards the mourners, accompanied by sympathizers from other nearby settlements, went to the curve in the road where the attack had occurred, demanding what they defined as a "fitting Zionist response," namely, the establishment of a new Jewish settlement on that spot. The settlers tried to establish their presence while the Israeli army surrounded their illegal settlement waiting for the government's decision to evacuate them.[25] The settlers, using their political influence and capitalizing on the popular outrage at the attack, were allowed to stay for the customary week of mourning, and then for the customary month as well. After that month, the government decided to allow the settlers to extend their stay indefinitely. Their intention was to expand the memorial site into a settlement called Rehelim, named after the woman who had been killed, as well as another Rachel, Rachel Weiss, who had perished three years earlier with her three children in a Palestinian terrorist attack near Jericho.

The site was located near the main road of Samaria, 100 meters away from the actual scene of the murder. At first it consisted of mobile homes, and later of two large tents: one served as a kitchen, study room and makeshift synagogue; the other was used for lodging and large events. An overturned army helmet held the perpetual flame burning in memory of the victims. A month after the events, a huge stone monument was erected bearing an inscription with biblical verses about Isaac and Rachel.

While a group was being organized to form the permanent community of the settlement, temporary solutions were found for the time being. Surrounding settlements and educational institutions took turns in sending women by day and men by night to maintain the site. An informal college, named after the bus driver Yitzhak Rofeh, was also established at the site. Neighboring settlements provided food and other supplies for those who stayed there.

For a year, the site constituted a symbolic center of those Jewish settlements in the region that participated in its upkeep. Many of the ceremonial and organizational activities carried out during the year were held there, such as the lighting of candles on Hanukkah, the planting of trees on Tu Bishvat (the New Year for Trees), the annual Samaria march on Lag ba-Omer, and so forth. The most dedicated among the settlers chose to perform their personal rites of passage at Rehelim (such as circumcision for their babies). In short, during that year Rehelim became the social, political and ritualistic center for the West Bank Jewish settlers' community. However, the envisaged settlement, which in the settlers' words was to become "another twinkling star over the hills of Samaria," did not materialize at this time. After the elections of 1992, a new Labor government promised to freeze the development of settlements in the occupied territories. Only in the late 1990s, after another change in government, was the settlement eventually established.

The Women of Rehelim: A Feminist Challenge?

From the outset, women played a dominant role, both in the organization and actual management of the protest and in the occupation of the site. According to the semi-mythic story told by the women settlers, in the first days after the killing the men felt that further protest would be futile and they preferred not to confront the Israeli army troops. It was the women who decided to persevere until a decision regarding a new settlement was reached. Practically and symbolically the women filled the void left by the men.

The organizing group, called "the Women of Rehelim," was comprised mainly of religious women, who were married and had children, from the more established ideological settlements of Gush Emunim. They were veterans of Gush Emunim activities and well connected with the elite group, some through family relations. Most were wage earners, some in the organizations established in the wake of Gush Emunim, such as the settlement organization Amanah.

Due to years of struggling against governments and enduring the rough terrain in the establishment of previous settlements, there was a general feeling of "déjà vu" surrounding the experience of Rehelim. Some of the women who visited Rehelim, either as part of their turn of duty or as passers-by, rejoiced at the opportunity to relive some of their former experiences in earlier Gush Emunim events, including the establishment of their own home settlements. In Rehelim's visitors' book one can find the nostalgic entry: "In the best tradition of Gush Emunim: all serious beginnings are in wintertime. Again it is cold and there is much rain: just like in Sabastia."

However, the leadership group expressed frustration and disappointment given the fact that 18 years after the historic events of the establishment of the settlement at Sabastia, the same tactics had to be used again. Nonetheless, not even the image of Sabastia, the ultimate act of defiance against the government from Gush Emunim's early period, was enough to render meaning to the act of settlement. The settler women did not wish their act to be understood merely as paying homage to past movement heroics. Neither was the act of terrorism in itself sufficient in providing the women with an explanation for their decision to dwell in the barren hills of Samaria in the middle of the winter. To account for their actions, towards themselves and others, the settlers looked elsewhere. To be sure, for the settlers the very act of settling was self-evident and needed no rationalization; however, the meaning of the act, by which women took upon themselves to erect a settlement in response to the killing of a friend, did require explanation.

To onlookers, for example for some journalists who visited the site, Rehelim was regarded as a feminist act *par excellence*, occurring rather surprisingly at the heart of a fundamentalist movement.[26] The women took upon themselves the movement's quintessential practice of settlement, which can be interpreted as the masculine act of erection and penetration. The men were recruited to bring food and take care of the homes and children while the women situated themselves "on the front" or "on the battlefield." In a sense, the women did to the men what the men had been doing in Israeli society at large: they appropriated the key symbol of national settlement and made it theirs.

Two caveats should be borne in mind before we attach a feminist definition to the act of Rehelim. First, this was not the first time that women had found themselves in such a situation; for example, the Jewish settlement in Arab-populated Hebron was initiated and carried out by women. The advantages of employing women in such activities have little to do with feminist sensitivities but can rather be understood as a cynical manipulation of the stereotypical gender images in Israeli society.[27] The settlers assume (rightly) that Israeli soldiers will find it more difficult to evacuate women than to evacuate men. Furthermore, femininity bears images of peaceful existence and established households; the settlers send women with their children to confront soldiers in order to illustrate how rooted they are in their newly established homes. This is not meant to imply that the women of Gush Emunim are not as devoted to the cause as the men are; as noted above, typically they are even more militant. However, there are clear strategic advantages in sending women to carry out settlement duties. Therefore, the act of placing women at front stage in Rehelim may have had little to do with feminist interests and motivations, but precisely the opposite — it may have indicated the desire to capitalize on relative advantages stemming from established gender stereotypes.

A second point is the women's own self-image, as revealed ceaselessly to newspaper reporters and university researchers. The women of Rehelim never defined or regarded themselves as "feminist," and the reason they gave was that feminists "acted negatively" (had negative attitudes and destructive goals) while they were "positive" (had positive attitudes and creative goals). Rather than challenging the national-religious gender regime, they insisted their acts were, in fact, strengthening it. They regarded themselves as Jewish and Zionist women and mothers, fulfilling their maternal role of protecting their children, according to the accepted dominant discourse. They did not formulate a critical perspective on their gender situation either within their community or in their households.

The site itself clearly and proudly displayed traditional feminine motifs. The women took pride in their cleaning and cooking abilities, and in their competence at tending to all the male visitors who came to visit. The older women taught the younger ones how to sew and kept a watchful eye on their "proper" feminine behavior. In a film they made about their enterprise, the women are shown cleaning the caravan and preparing soup for the male visitors. The entries in the visitors' book also shed light on the meaning Rehelim held for the settlers. Thus, one visitor expressed admiration for the women, noting that "the talent to overcome the little everyday troubles, to clean and nurse what tomorrow will again need repairing, and at the same time understand the big account of building the future and to constantly draw power from it, that is the talent of righteous women." The republican Mother could hardly find better advocates than the women of Rehelim and their supporters.

Their anti-feminist stance was further stressed by their construction of their significant "other." The left-wing group Women in Black was chosen by the women of Rehelim to epitomize the feminist and leftist antithesis. This group of women stood every Friday afternoon (when according to traditional conventions they were supposed to be at home preparing for the Sabbath), dressed in black, holding signs bearing a single message: "End the occupation!" Women in Black, though small in numbers, posed a conceptual threat to the Israeli conservative imagery of maternity and nationalism, as was expressed in many chauvinist and sexist remarks of passers-by.[28] Conversely, the act of Rehelim was intended to present maternal values in the public sphere, which, in the eyes of the women of Rehelim, the Women in Black were not doing. When asked about their motivations, the women of Rehelim explained that since a fellow woman and mother had been the victim, they felt that it was their sacred duty to make what they defined as a fitting response. They were, according to their definition, protecting their children, which they regarded as the quintessential role of women.[29]

However, following the logic expressed by the women, it is apparent how maternal thinking can evolve into a multilayered and self-contradictory concept.[30] Looming large before them was the idea of collective national defense. The terrorist act was conceived as a threat to all Israeli children, either directly, by endangering them and their parents, or through threatening their rights to live on the land. Women were therefore called upon to leave their households and rush to the rescue. It was taken for granted that women had a certain intuitive understanding and reaction to the dangers threatening the safety of their families, best expressed by the claim that the women of Rehelim were drawn to the site, arriving spontaneously and unpremeditatedly simply by virtue of their feminine essence. However, collectivizing the grievance meant abandoning their actual homes, thus embracing the metaphorical collective, the national family, at their own expense. As the women of Rehelim expressed the dilemma, a Jewish mother's essence lies in nurturing the community and Jewish continuity and not merely in caring selfishly for her own private family and home.[31]

An additional aspect of constructing "responsible motherhood" is apparent here, even though it was not brought up by the women settlers themselves and was shrugged off as a non-issue when evoked by others. In their moving to reside in a contested area, parents make decisions that affect, and sometimes endanger, the lives of their children. Academic observers as well as those who oppose the settlement project have noted that the settlers pay a heavy price for their ideology, not only with their own lives but also with the lives of those they hold dear and who are dependent on them. The settlers, however, often dismiss this price, claiming that all Jews who choose to live in Israel share this danger. The terrorist act opened an abyss of existential fear that had to be re-closed in order for the settlement project to continue functioning.

The dramatic events of Rehelim can partly be understood as a response to a mortal threat — the threat not only to physical existence, but to the ability to maintain a viable image and identity of responsible parenthood as well. Consequently, the self-definition of the women of Rehelim could only be a conservative one because it was their basic capabilities and roles as "responsible mothers" that were being threatened. They had to overcome and suppress the disturbing allusions that their settlement project might fail and that they were incapable of securing the safety of their loved ones in the place they had come to by choice.

The question of a patriarchal versus a feminist interpretation of the events is complex and cannot be determined by the declarations of the agents alone. Regarding the women of Rehelim as feminists would be in discordance with their self-definition and an imposition from an external perspective. That does not mean that such a definition is not justified, especially as, in retrospect, it can be seen as being linked to the feminist challenge of the following years. The behavior of the women of Rehelim can still be perceived as subversive to the established, taken-for-granted, patriarchal order, even if at the time they were not overtly aware of it and tried relentlessly to convince themselves and others that the opposite was true. However, following the implicit challenge of Rehelim's role reversals, the reestablishment and reproduction of the patriarchal role was put to the test for both genders.

"Rachel" as the Jewish Mater Dolorosa

The name of the settlement itself can illuminate the ways in which gender relations were reinstated and reaffirmed in Rehelim. The memory of Rachel Druk and the tragic circumstances of her death were evidently not sufficient in themselves to bestow profound meaning on the new site. In Israel there is an established tradition of naming villages after fallen soldiers and deceased leaders; therefore, a settlement called, for example, "Kfar Druk" (Druk Village) would have accorded well with the symbolic geography created by Zionism. However, the settlers chose not to commemorate their dead friend in such a direct manner; rather they preferred to give their settlement a name with a more historic and mythical resonance. Rachel Druk and Rachel Weiss, who was killed some years before, were conceived not merely as individual women but also as representing a wider ideal of nationalism and maternity, both strongly associated with the biblical name "Rachel." Significantly, the slogan chosen by the actors was "we are all Rachels (Rehelim)."[32]

Using the meaningful symbol of Rachel, the ultimate mother, placed the events in a traditional, patriarchal and nationalistic narrative. Of all the biblical names, Rachel has the most gendered connotations. Etymologically, the name comes from ewe or sheep, the primal capital of the biblical man (as well as the most common sacrifice). Rachel was the beloved woman for whom Jacob worked for 14 years. She died fulfilling her wish to give her spouse a second son, and her midwife consoled her in words that may sound horrifically insensitive to modern ears: "Fear not; thou shalt have this son also" (Genesis 35:17). She was buried on the road to Bethlehem, the only one of the four matriarchs who, according to tradition, is not buried in the Cave of the Makhpelah in Hebron.

In the context of the Babylonian exile, the prophet Jeremiah related God's promise to Rachel that the people of Israel would return to their homeland. God urged the weeping Rachel to "[r]estrain thy voice from weeping, and thine eyes from tears; for ... thy children shall come again to their own border" (Jeremiah 31:16–17). Not only is her unique status as mother of the nation evoked here, but there is also significance in her place of death, on the road, in a location enabling her to oversee and encounter both exile and return. The fact that the tomb of Rachel is near Bethlehem, in the contested territories, intensifies her importance to the settlers.

The people of Israel significantly refer to themselves as "the Children of Rachel,"[33] a phrase not fully substantiated by the biblical narrative: Judah was the son of Leah, not Rachel, and Sarah and Rebekah are more clearly the mothers of the mytho-nation in a genealogical sense. The story of Rachel, however, touches on a more profound meaning of maternity and its connection to the continuing national existence between homeland and exile. The place traditionally known as Rachel's Tomb has for centuries served as a site of pilgrimage for barren women, and it still serves as a major fertility shrine. Anthropologist Susan Starr Sered examined records left by pilgrims during the 1940s and found several exemplary statements, for example: "Rachel, Rachel, mother of the Israeli Nation, for how much longer will the tears of Israel be shed in vain? Arise, arise from your sleep." Starr concludes:

> The themes that "took-off" at Rachel's Tomb in the 1940s — fertility, nationhood, the return of the exiles, the holocaust — are intrinsically and dramatically linked to Rachel's biography as it is described in the Bible and Midrashic literature. Rachel, in the Jewish tradition, is the *mater dolorosa*.[34]

For the religious settlers, Rachel held special significance, as they continued in the nationalization of the religious biblical figure. They regarded themselves as returning to the actual places where the biblical stories had occurred, feeling that, for them, the prophecy of returning to Rachel's grave had come true. Gush Emunim leader, Hanan Porat, extensively employed the image of Rachel, claiming that the evacuation of Judea and Samaria was tantamount to spitting in her face and telling her that she had waited for two millennia and should wait another two millennia.[35] With the Palestinian revolt, Rachel's Tomb became a fortress, and visiting the site became ever more dangerous. In a poem on the Hebron settlers' website, a poetess writes to Rachel: "It wasn't my way / I was forced to leave you / by those who don't love you / don't speak or pray through you / or pour out their hearts and cry to you / and try to be near you. / But I hear you / calling to your sons / and for me to return."[36]

A report on the settlement published in one of the settlers' periodicals was entitled "Rehelim Sits on the Road," thus drawing an analogy between the mythical Rachel and the new settlement. There are two semiotic meanings linked with the figure of Rachel that bear special importance: her role as mother of the nation, and her death on the road, where she weeps and waits for the people of Israel to return from exile. In the context of the early 1990s, neither constitutes a basis for subversive feminist thought; both, when interconnected, strengthen the link between traditional maternal values and nationalism in the Zionist sense, namely, the return of the people to their homeland, where the mythic Mother was buried.

Apart from Rachel Druk and Rachel Weiss, another "Rachel" readily evoked by the name "Rehelim" was the renowned poet Rachel Bluestein, known simply as Rachel, whose poems are among the most popular in Israel and are often set to music. Rachel lived in one of the celebrated first collective settlements on the bank of the Sea of Galilee and died childless in 1931. Her poems reflected her yearning for a child, relating to the experience of Rachel the Matriarch. The Rehelim settlers cited one such poem in their pamphlet: "Her blood flows in mine / Her voice sings in me / Rachel shepherdess of Laban's herd / Rachel, the mother of mothers." This is the most extreme broadening of the symbol: All the Rachels, and by implication all Jewish women, have the same blood and voice, and hence the same essence: they are all first and foremost, potentially or actually, national mothers.[37]

Nonetheless, the decision to name the settlement "Rehelim" symbolizes a silencing of gender issues. A possible pluralization of "Rachel" in Hebrew would be "Rehelot," with the feminine plural ending; using the masculine plural form, Rehelim, therefore somewhat mitigated the feminine connotations of the name. Gender issues were thus controlled so as not to pose any threat to the basic premises of daily life or to divert attention from the main goal of settlement-building.

The Hegemonic Order Reconstituted

Processes of a social, political and interpretative nature took place at Rehelim. Tamar El-Or and Gideon Aran observed the interactive dynamics that turned Rehelim into a consciousness-raising workshop for women.[38] Due to their partly differential social roles, Gush Emunim women often come together to learn about their common situation as women. Rehelim was, in fact, a result of such a network, and the dramatic events strengthened pre-existing ties and formed new ones. This type of interaction could lead to new insights regarding gender relations. However, in this case the interaction only strengthened existing notions and ensured that the empowerment of the women of Rehelim would occur only under strict established rules. Feminism is linked to a subversive reading of the texts; the women of Rehelim merely performed according to the script they had received, shaped through years in which it was applied in different places of the occupied territories by Gush Emunim settlers.

Throughout the history of Gush Emunim, practices of commemoration have followed a structural pattern, meaning that, whenever possible, the killing of a Jewish settler entails the construction of a new settlement at the spot where the killing took place. Constructing a new settlement in response to terrorism was, by the early 1990s, a standardized and ritualized practice, well integrated in the narrative structure of bereavement. Death was framed within an encompassing plot, which led to a defiant act of settlement supposedly to be followed deterministically by the establishment of a flourishing village. This is an uplifting narrative, which serves as a blueprint for similar events, the "happy end" predetermined by the story's ritualistic nature. In the case of Rehelim, the availability of a former institutionalized form of action was the vehicle that reconstituted the established gendered order.

The narrative of Rehelim, namely the story of death and revival in the Land of Israel, was presented as a metaphor of the entire Gush Emunim settlement project, and of the entire Zionist project as well. The site was established as a showcase, where the well-known components of the Jewish drama were reenacted: great defeat and tragedy, followed by national and religious heroic persistence, culminating in a victorious return to the original site. Rehelim was conceived as a ritual of revitalization.

Only a few weeks after the terrorist attack, the site's spirit changed dramatically, from grief and anger to joy and jubilation. An entry in the visitors' book reflects the transformation explicitly; an adolescent girl from the settlement Ofra contributed a poem, culminating with the famous line from the official *Yizkor* (memorial prayer) for fallen Israeli soldiers:

> and there is much sorrow inside
> and from the great sorrow emerge tears of joy
> yes, of joy
> because there is life in this place …
> and I tell myself
> blessed is the people that knows how to rise
> that out of death awakens to life …
> blessed be the dead who in their death commanded us
> life!

In a dialectical process the meanings of the commemorative site were transformed and assimilated to the narrative structure of other such events. In a pamphlet distributed at one of their meetings, the women of Rehelim told their admirers how their story should be related: "What started as a spontaneous vigil following the murder of Rachel Druk and Yitzhak Rofeh, turned into a fact in the settlement landscape of the Land of Israel." Joy and satisfaction, not shock and bereavement, were the desired and required emotional responses from visitors. When the children of neighboring settlements made pilgrimages to the site, they were greeted with happy music; it was not what one would expect to find at a memorial site. All symbols of solemnity were either subdued or secluded in one of the tents.

The above-mentioned film that the women made about Rehelim relates a similar story. It opens with the noise of gunshots, followed by scenes of the bus and the two victims. From there it moves on to reveal a pastoral landscape and the heroic story of the women of Rehelim. They become the focal point, the reason there is a story to tell at all. The movie ends on an optimistic note, with the women's smiling faces and the promise that another twinkling star will soon shine on the hills of Samaria.

With the change in the solemn atmosphere came a redefinition of the heroes. In place of the slain man and woman came the women of Rehelim who were elevated to a mythical status. They were the ones who took it upon themselves to fulfill the demands of the sacred tradition and create life out of death. They were hailed as heroines, and in public events were invited time and again to retell their story, which became included in the lore of the settlers' community. They became potential political leaders and made (unsuccessful) attempts to create a broad women's movement. Their standing as heroines, however, was dependent on their acting according to the established script, and was therefore inherently temporary, valid only until such a time that "their" story reached a satisfactory end and a new story began. At that point, it was the women who took center stage; at another time, it would be a different social group that would hold the symbolic position of leadership. The position of temporary hero was filled each time anew, in a modular fashion, by different agents from within the settlers' camp. Becoming a hero and leader was, therefore, conditional upon accepting the normative system as a whole.

Once the narrative moved towards what was considered the successful closure, gender issues disappeared from the discourse, and feminism ceased to count as an issue. Tradition safely embraced the potentially subversive events, and the "rightful order" was restored. In actual fact, it was never seriously threatened, though men and women alike caught a glimpse of a potentially different order that was slowly taking the form of a feminist revolution with no violence and little confrontation.

On the Possible Limits of Religious Feminism

The story of Rachel Druk as told by the settlers cannot be understood in isolation. Her life and violent death were appropriated by the movement and the ideology. They were placed within broader schemes of meaning, which concentrated on the connotations of the name "Rachel" and the meaning of maternity, and on the reenactment of a consecrated plot, with a prescribed and uplifting ending. While the concrete image of a woman can serve a feminist cause, the mythical image of Rachel could only support the existing patriarchal order. Rehelim occurred at an early stage in the feminist revolution of Orthodox women in Israel. The patriarchical mechanisms of control were still strong enough to dull its radical edge. Hence, the women of Rehelim found themselves in a golden cage: they were hailed as heroes of the day, but could not — and showed no desire to — use their position to challenge gender relations within their camp.

Research on religious women today concentrates on literacy, how women appropriate the sacred texts and comprehend them in subversive ways. In the case of Rehelim, the women left the interpretation of religious texts to the men; they concentrated on appropriating the all-too-important commemorative text. They did not rewrite the script but were content merely to temporarily play the leading role. Later in the decade, they turned their attention to radical appropriation and alteration of other identity-forming texts.

However, if the case of Rehelim is indicative, Orthodox Judaism includes potent mechanisms that redirect women's energies from feminism to more traditionally accepted venues and averts the subversive potential that looms before women approaching the arena of public action. It remains to be seen whether the radical transformation of gender relations within the national-religious camp will continue to be contained within the normatively accepted boundaries of the believers.

NOTES

* This essay is based on a chapter from my doctoral dissertation, recently published as a book: *Shtei mapot la-gadah: Gush Emunim, Shalom Akhshav ve-itzuv ha-merhav be-Yisrael* (One Space, Two Places: Gush Emunim, Peace Now and the Construction of Israeli Space (Jerusalem, 2002). It is based on qualitative research methods, including observation interview and document analysis. The material was collected in the years 1991–95. I am grateful to the Israel Foundation Trustees, the Bernard Cherrick Center for the Study of Zionism, the Yishuv and the History of Israel, and the Shaine Center for Research in Sciences for their financial support of my research. I wish to thank Pnina Motzafi-Haller and Hannah Naveh for their remarks.

1 Regarding the debated question of whether or not Gush Emunim is a fundamentalist movement, I wish to claim the affirmative. For a strong argumentation of this point, see Gideon Aran, "Jewish Zionist Fundamentalism: The Bloc of the Faithful in Israel," in Martin. E. Marty and R. Scott Appleby (eds.), *Fundamentalisms Observed* (Chicago, 1991), pp. 265–344.
2 Karen McCarthy Brown, "Fundamentalism and the Control of Women," in John Stratton Hawley (ed.), *Fundamentalism and Gender* (New York 1994), p. 175.
3 It should be mentioned that in some religions there are fundamentalist movements led by

women. Nevertheless, these movements propagate strict gender differentiation and the return to a mythical "golden age" in which women fulfilled their "appropriate" roles in society, i.e. in the household. See Helen Hardacre, "Japanese New Religions: Profiles in Gender," in Hawley (ed.), *Fundamentalism and Gender*, pp. 111–34.

4 For a general discussion on the research of gender and fundamentalism, including critical remarks on how little attention was given to the subject until lately, see the introduction to Hawley (ed.), *Fundamentalism and Gender*.

5 Helen Hardacre, "The Impact of Fundamentalism on Women, the Family and Interpersonal Relations," in Martin E. Marty and R. Scott Appleby (eds.), *Fundamentalisms and the State* (Chicago, 1993), pp. 129–50.

6 William R. Darrow, "Woman's Place and the Place of Women in the Iranian Revolution," in Yvonne Haddad and Ellison Banks Findly (eds.), *Women, Religion and Social Change* (Albany, NY, 1985), p. 310.

7 Tamar Rapoport, Anat Penso and Yoni Garb, "Contribution to the Collective by Religious-Zionist Adolescent Girls," *British Journal of Sociology of Education*, Vol. 15, No. 3 (1994), pp. 375–88.

8 Not that other political parties have done much better, though most assure one or more places for women among their candidates. Women political representation in the Knesset has remained relatively stable at about 10 percent. Gideon Doron and Daniella Schoenker-Schreck, *Mehakot le-yitzug* (Waiting for Representation) (Tel Aviv, 1998).

9 See Nira Yuval-Davis, *Gender and Nation* (London, 1997). Lately the Israeli case has received much academic attention. See, for example, Nitza Berkovitz, "Motherhood as a National Mission," *Women Studies International Forum*, Vol. 20 (506) (1977), pp. 605–19, and "Citizenship and Motherhood: The Status of Women in Israel," in Yoav Peled and Adi Ophir (eds.), *Yisrael: Me-hevrah meguyeset le-hevrah ezrahit?* (Israel: From Mobilized to Civil Society?) (Jerusalem, 2001), pp. 206–43.

10 Dvorah Arziel, "Hapes et ha-ishah" (Look for the Woman), *Nekudah*, No. 154 (1987), pp. 24–5.

11 Two noted examples are the Women in Green (*Nashim Be-Yarok*) and Many Women (*Harbeh Nashim*), both advocating hawkish policies in the name of women and motherhood. Interestingly they both emerged as a response to the dovish women's movements, Women in Black, and Four Mothers respectively. The Israeli right and left struggled over the definition of motherhood and its political meaning.

12 Yael Yishai, "Eshet hayil ve-eshet herev: Ha-omnam kvodah shel ha-ishah ha-datiyah be-veitah pnimah?" (Woman of Force and Woman of Sword: Is the Honor of the Religious Woman inside her Home?), in Dana Arieli-Horovitz (ed.), *Dat u-medinah be-Yisrael* (Religion and Society in Israel) (Jerusalem, 1996).

13 The most important research on the subject is Tamar El-Or, *Ba-Pesah ha-ba: Nashim ve-oryanut ba-tziyonut ha-datit* (Next Pesach: Literacy and Identity of Young Religious Zionist Women) (Tel Aviv, 1998).

14 Rabbi Ya'akov Shilat, "Ha-feminizm ha-marir hu oyev ha-halakhah" (Bitter Feminism Is an Enemy of the *Halakhah*), *Panim*, No. 11 (1999), p. 135.

15 El-Or, *Ba-Pesah ha-ba*, p. 317.

16 Bambi Sheleg, "Yeladim zeh simhah, aval gam karyerah," *Kol ha-Ir*, 21 October 1994.

17 Hannah Kehat, "Maamad ha-nashim ve-limud torah be-hevrah ortodoksit" (Women's Status and Torah Study in the Orthodox Society), in Yael Azmon (ed.), *Ha-tishma koli? Yitzugim shel nashim ba-tarbut ha-yisre'elit* (Will You Listen to My Voice? Representations of Women in Israeli Culture) (Jerusalem, 2001), pp. 355–64.

18 Bambi Sheleg, "Neshot ha-torah ha-hadashot"(The New Women of Torah), in Ruvik Rosenthal (ed.), *Kav ha-shesa* (The Inner Split) (Tel Aviv, 2001), pp. 142–53.

19 The organization also published a volume of essays that covers many of the issues discussed in this article: Margalit Shilo (ed.), *Lihiyot ishah yehudiyah* (To Be a Jewish Woman) (Jerusalem, 2001).

20 Hannah Kehat, "Irgun Kolekh" (The Kolech Organization), *Al Nashim ve-karyerah*, No. 1 (July 2001), p. 33.

21 On Gush Emunim, see Aran, "Jewish Zionist Fundamentalism"; David Newman (ed.), *The Impact of Gush Emunim* (London, 1985), Ehud Sprinzak, *The Ascendance of the Israeli Radical Right* (New York, 1991); Ian Lustick, *For the Land and the Lord: Jewish Fundamentalism in Israel* (New York, 1988).

22 These are the figures supplied in a report issued by the Peace Now movement in November 1992 named "The Real Map."

23 Irit Gutman, "Tifkud ve-emdot shel yeladim be-Shomron be-heksher le-ramat ha-hasifah le-alimut" (The Functioning and Attitudes of Children in Samaria in the Context of Their Level of Exposure to Violence) *Mehkarei Yehudah ve-Shomron*, Vol. 2 (1992), pp. 377–87.

24 This was the rightist government under Prime Minister Yitzhak Shamir that emerged after six years of "national unity" coalition government.

25 In view of international law, all settlements are "illegal," being the transfer of population into the occupied territories by the occupying force. In Israeli terms, however, "illegal" means that the establishment of the settlement has not been approved by the government.

26 Tamar El-Or and Gideon Aran have done research on the question of the gender issue of Rehelim. Approaching this issue from a different angle, namely collective memory research, I offer a somewhat different perspective. See Tamar El-Or, "Me-shilo lo ro'im et island" (From Shiloh You Can't See Iceland)," *Alpayim*, Vol. 7 (1993), pp. 59–82. Tamar El-Or and Gideon Aran, "Giving Birth to a Settlement: Maternal Thinking and Political Action of Jewish Women on the West Bank," *Gender and Society*, Vol. 9, No. 1 (February 1995), pp. 60–78.

27 Using women and children as "human shields" is a common practice among political movements. The Palestinians have done the same in face of the Israeli army.

28 On Women in Black, see Sara Helman and Tamar Rapoport, "Women in Black: Changing Israel's Gender and Socio-Political Order," *British Journal of Sociology*, Vol. 48, No. 4 (1997), pp. 682–700.

29 The Women in Black also presented their conception of their role as women and mothers, protecting their own and other children, Israeli and Palestinians. However, with their sole slogan of "End the Occupation," the message was implied rather than expressed openly. Other peace movements accentuated the parental role, most notably Parents against Silence and Four Mothers, both protesting against different stages of the Israeli involvement in Lebanon. On Israeli peace movements and motherhood, see Sara Helman, "From Soldiering and Motherhood to Citizenship: A Study of Four Israeli Peace Protest Movements," *Social Politics* Vol. 6, No. 3 (1999), pp. 291–313.

30 The term "maternal thinking" is taken from Sara Ruddick, *Maternal Thinking* (Boston, 1989).

31 This issue again reflected opposition to the Four Mothers group that struggled for the withdrawal of Israeli troops from Lebanon in the name of maternal feelings. National-religious women were critical of the use of a biblical metaphor by an essentially secular and left-wing group (whose name evokes the four biblical matriarchs), claiming that Four Mothers failed to understand the national responsibilities of motherhood. See Hava Pinhas-Cohen, "Imah, shalom, ha-em ha-hamishit" (Mother Peace, the Fifth Mother), *Panim*, Vol. 17 (2001), pp. 44–50.

32 I have analyzed Rehelim as a site of memory elsewhere. Here, I want to note that the concept of Rehelim as a commemorative settlement is somewhat different from other cities, towns or agriculture settlements that were named after Israeli dead. The difference is in the openness of Rehelim as a symbol. Kibbutz Yad Hannah, for example, commemorates Hannah Senesh, the Jewish paratrooper who, during the Second World War, was sent on a mission to occupied Hungary from Mandatory Palestine and was executed by the Germans. The name of the kibbutz refers to her alone and does not function as a symbol for all brave women in Jewish history. The inclusiveness of Rehelim is a novelty in Israeli commemorative practices. See Michael Feige, "Hanihu la-holkhim? Yahasan shel Gush Emunim ve-Shalom Akhshav le-martirim tnu'atiim" (Let the Dead Go? The Martyrs of Gush Emunim and Peace Now") in David Ohana and Robert S. Wistrich (eds.) *Mitos ve-zikaron* (Myth and Memory) (Jerusalem 1996), pp. 304–20.

33 For one example in scholarly writings, see Debra Renee Kaufman, *Rachel's Daughters: Newly Orthodox Jewish Women* (New Brunswick, 1991).

34   Susan Starr Sered, "Rachel's Tomb: Societal Liminality and the Revitalization of a Shrine," *Religion*, Vol. 19, No. 1 (1989), pp. 33, 37.

35   For one such statement, see Arie Naor, *Eretz Yisrael ha-shlemah* (Greater Israel) (Haifa, 2001), p. 351.

36   Written by Rachel P. Klein (see: www.hebron.org.il/liter/racheltomb.htm.

37   The title of a volume of feminist articles analyzing the representation of women in Israeli culture, "Will You Listen to My Voice?" (see note 17 above) is also taken from a poem by Rachel.

38   El-Or and Aran. "Giving Birth to a Settlement."

Discourses of Negotiation:
The Writings of Orthodox Women in Israel

Tsila (Abramovitz) Ratner

Veils and Visibility

At a time of escalating social and political divide between the secular and the Orthodox communities in Israel, the surge of writing by women of Orthodox background is intriguing.[1] It is difficult to ignore its political meaning since it takes place in the secular community: it is published there and is aimed at secular readers. For the majority of secular Israelis the Orthodox world is closed and exclusive, as much as it is excluded and inaccessible. Alongside the rejection of Orthodoxy on political grounds, an impending sense of curiosity is fed by this inaccessibility, especially about Orthodox women, whose political and "sexual" invisibility nurtures the mystification of their otherness. This is a desire to unveil whatever is concealed behind doors and "modest" clothing for whatever reason: proving political wrongs and rights, prurience, voyeurism or genuine interest. No wonder then that the publication of prose writing by Orthodox women draws so much attention, as it breaks the silence surrounding Orthodox women through a detailed portrayal of the social context its women protagonists inhabit. The particularity of this social context, whether overtly relating to the Orthodox background or not, distinguishes this prose writing from others such as the "poetry of religiosity" (*shirah emunit*), which transfers itself to a "universal" frame of reference by highlighting its apolitical aspect.[2]

Being Orthodox and women automatically categorizes these writers as twice marked: female as opposed to male writers, the bearers of the hegemonic national discourse, and Orthodox as deviants from the hegemony of secular discourse. Thus attention focuses on their political agenda, blurring the diversity and particularities of their writing, laying upon them the burden of representing their twice-marked social category. This tendency became more apparent between 1966 and 1998 with the increasing number of publications by Yehudit Rotem, Hannah Bat-Shahar, Mira Magen, Yochi Brandes and Yocheved Reisman. It reached a peak in October 1997, when the novels of four Orthodox women writers, Magen, Bat-Shahar, Brandes and Naomi Ragen, were among the top ten bestsellers in Israel. Subsequent newspaper interviews with the four reflect the fascination, or perhaps the sensationalist interest, of the public with the phenomenon.[3] When interviewed by Yaron London, the four writers expressed a variety of perceptions regarding their position as writers, ranging from a didactic stand as educators of secular readers (Ragen) and bearers of political messages (Brandes), to a protest against being categorized as "Orthodox women writers" (Magen and Bat-Shahar).[4] While the first two views are transparent enough, in the sense that they correspond to the expectation that these works should either endorse or criticize the religious way of life, the protestation raises a complex of issues regarding the motivation of the secular readership as well as of the writers themselves.[5] Demarcating the writers indicates the secular world's need to appropriate these works, to mark their difference and at the same time to recruit them to the "cultural war" between the two communities, using them to attest to the superiority, or the advantage, of the secular.[6] Yehuda Friedlander has stated that secular readers might now claim that the Haredic (Ultra-Orthodox) world suffers the same social ills as those attributed to the secular, thus warding off the Haredic self-righteous position.[7] Categorizing these women writers focuses attention on sensationalism, eliminating or at least marginalizing other issues in their writing, thus reinforcing Bat-Shahar's protest.[8]

However, the implication that secular readers are only interested in prurience, preoccupied with the excitement of peeping into a world of prohibitions, is not as straightforward either. It is rather naive to ignore the political significance of these publications, significance of which the writers are aware, regardless of the position they claim to take.[9] One might assume that the different stands these writers take depend on their proximity to Orthodoxy: Hannah Bat-Shahar and Yocheved Reisman live in Orthodox communities and share similar cultures, Yochi Brandes and Mira Magen now live in the secular community. Bat-Shahar and Reisman describe their affinity born of being "truly" religious women thus disassociating themselves from the others.[10] Though Magen's and Brandes's works differ greatly from each other, they share a less defensive and more critical view of Orthodoxy and its relation to the secular world.[11] Ambiguity underlies the relationship between the writers, their designated readers and the world depicted in the works. Whatever interpretation is given to this complexity, publishing the works in the secular world obviously invites readers to visit, observe and interpret. One of my aims in this article is to point out the diversity of the works, their dialogue with their secular counterparts, rather than drawing a picture of a homogenous and sensational group of veiled and veil-liberated women writers. There is little doubt that the recent dominance of women's writing in Israel has played a major role in the emergence of Orthodox women's writing. It has empowered women, raised feminist awareness and provided literary models.

The dominance of women's writing paved the way for Orthodox women to cross the traditional boundaries set by the public/private dichotomy that lies at the core of all women's writing, Orthodox and secular alike. Although secular women's writing does not necessarily address issues that specifically concern the Orthodox way of life, it is similar in its fight against exclusion and taboo-ridden sites and thus it serves as a precedent. The success of Israeli women writers who not only dared to confront the stronghold of male dominance and ethos, but also became the forefront of Israeli literature, most probably enabled Orthodox women writers to voice their own agenda. By publishing in the secular world for secular readers, Orthodox writers are closely allying themselves with the main body of women's writing in Israel, thus benefiting from its approved status.[12]

Bat-Shahar's writing, in particular *Likro la-atalefim* (Calling the Bats) (1990) and *Rikud ha-parpar* (The Dancing Butterfly) (1993), illustrates clearly the empowering impact of secular women's writing. Both books bear a strong resemblance to Amalia Kahana-Carmon's fiction in style as well as the characterization of their women protagonists. Furthermore, I would suggest that Kahana-Carmon's model offered Bat-Shahar a modus of negotiation between her apprehension of breaking Haredic norms and her need for self-expression. Bat-Shahar's hazy narrative in these two collections avoids direct references to the Orthodox community and taboo issues in it, such as women's sexuality and patriarchy, which are her major themes. By using lyrical styles, which lend themselves to introverted and sometimes obscure and fragmentary narratives, she manages to bypass these obstacles. Her model was already at hand, in the well-established, accepted and acclaimed writing of Kahana-Carmon, thus facilitating a literary and thematic model that enabled the telling of that which should not be told in public.

However, on their own, models of women's writing from the "outside world" would not have been sufficient, unless they coincided with internal changes regarding women's roles in the Orthodox communities. As Tamar El-Or's research has shown, before Orthodox women are willing to embrace any novelty they check its sources and authority.[13] Quite a number of research works point to two inter-linked areas of change in the world and life of orthodox women: going out to work to support their families and their consequent exposure to the outside world. The establishment of the "society of learners" kept Orthodox men in the yeshivas while women had to assume the role of providers, brought up to believe that by doing so they are sharing the holy duty of Torah study from which they are excluded.[14] However, going out to work exposed women to the secular world, which led to inevitable changes in family life and the way women perceived their social roles and status. Working outside the family meant acquiring new skills, in other words, widening the scope of secular, though pragmatic, education allocated to

Orthodox girls/women that consequently led to women's demands to expand their religious education as well. The subversive potential of this latter demand is quite clear, as it involves the infiltration of women into the exclusively male domain of Torah study. This development is well documented in Tamar El-Or's books. Of special interest is the shift from El-Or's early book *Educated and Ignorant* to her second one *Next Pesach*. While the first book describes the mechanism that limits women's education under the pretense of educating them, the second book attests to an almost revolutionary pressure coming from young women to expand their education. The narrow and pragmatic syllabus set to perpetuate a state of ignorance and thus of subjugation, can no longer satisfy these young women. Their demands to be allowed access to Torah study correspond to their defiance of authority.[15] Hannah Kehat's research supports El-Or's findings as 80 percent of the religious women taking part in her survey expressed their support and identification with current feminist thinking.[16] Although focusing on religious Zionist women, El-Or's arguments are equally valid in the context of Ultra-Orthodox communities.[17] Young Orthodox women are far more exposed to and familiar with the secular world than the secular world seems to acknowledge. They are certainly more knowledgeably acquainted with it than the men locked away in their yeshivas.[18]

The impact of widening the accessibility of linguistic and literacy skills nowadays prompts an analogy with Jewish women's education in the nineteenth century. Iris Parush argues that while traditional education prevented women from acquiring literacy skills in Hebrew and thus access to the canonized texts, it had paradoxically liberated women by allowing them unsupervised space, learning languages and reading whatever caught their fancy. In other words, they could take the advantage of their marginalized position and become the carriers of subversive ideas. Parush points out the different "reading biographies" of women and men: unsupervised reading led women not only to different texts but also eased the move from traditional to secular reading, which was dramatic and sometimes traumatic for men. Therefore, women's exposure to the ideas and influence of enlightenment and modernization was unique, especially since their agency as carriers of subversive ideas was not limited only to the elite.[19] Learning from those "mistakes," Haredic communities were careful to seal possible cracks in the control mechanisms, using Beit Yaakov seminars to perpetuate the desired educational outcome.[20] The religious Zionist stream has reacted similarly through the *ulpanot* (boarding secondary schools for girls). Though the *ulpanot* are Zionist and endorse involvement in Israeli society, unlike the seminars of the Haredic communities, the overall concept of girls' education and its objectives are the same, i.e. compliance with traditional values regarding women.[21] Nevertheless, women's recent exposure to the secular world has introduced inevitable changes into the Haredic as well as the religious Zionist communities, just as it did in the nineteenth century. Moreover, their published works prove that they took things a step further.

Yocheved Reisman, author of *Tzipor yeshenah* (Sleeping Bird) (1998), is an example of this process of change. She lives in a Haredic community, is married to a Gur Hassid, has four children and works as an accountant in the family business. Unlike Bat-Shahar, she does not hide her artistic creativity, to the contrary, her family is familiar with her work, her paintings were exhibited in a gallery in Tel Aviv and her book was published under her own name. She describes herself as a devout reader of literature; she openly discusses her political views, among them her attitude towards feminism, which do not necessarily follow the mainstream Orthodox stance. Unlike Bat-Shahar who claims that she feels alienated in Israeli society, Reisman is fully involved, familiar with newspapers and current affairs.[22]

A testament to the threat these changes are posing to the Orthodox order is the intensified stringency in recent years of *halakhot* (rules) concerning *tzni'ut* (modesty). The close link between this process and the increasing pressure to obey the authority of religious leadership (*Da'at Torah*, Torah knowledge, and *Emunat hakhamim*, faith of the wise) leaves no doubt as to its use as a political mechanism to ensure the subordination of women.[23] It seems that this process, combined with the separatism of the Orthodox community, has contributed greatly to the stereotypes of Orthodox women among secular Israelis. From a secular perspective, Orthodox women epitomize the subjugation of women by a fundamentalist patriarchy. Women are controlled by strict codes of behavior to perpetuate their exclusion from the male public space. For the secular, "free and liberal" eye, the codes of modesty are symbols of oppressive inequality, stifled individuality and exclusion. Writing and publishing are therefore immediately interpreted as explicit acts of defiance, breaking the boundaries of the traditional divide between private/invisible (modest woman) and public/visible (man).

Coming-of-Age Narratives

Reading the works of a "marked" community of writers such as Orthodox (or of Orthodox background) women requires a balance between an anthropological approach that might blur their diversity and a literary study that will enhance heterogeneity. Therefore, I propose to look at the works as coming-of-age narratives (*Bildungsroman*). In the context of such reading, the political meaning of the works will be shown to be grounded in processes of feminist/female consciousness raising, concerning issues of subject autonomy and identity constitution and not only as statements concerning the "cultural war" between the secular and the Orthodox worlds. Models of coming-of-age narratives, as Pnina Shirav has shown in her research, will enable tracing patterns of development and change in individual works (even those in which these processes are incomplete) as well as in the overall writing of an author.[24] Thus, changes of attitudes and their representations could be followed and they in turn could open the dialogue between the writers of Orthodox background and secular women's writers. The study of the works against the background of coming-of-age narratives enhances the heterogeneous nature of the works and at the same time points out similarities that illuminate their specific social context.

Female narratives of coming-of-age follow the protagonist's struggle to realize her right to express her autonomy.[25] They evolve around the conflicting questions of sexual differences, the site of individual aspirations, and social propositions, the site of compliance. In Orthodoxy the gender divide is non-negotiable and conformity is elevated as the path to spiritual, communal and national fulfillment. Thus the space for negotiations, which is necessary for a process of identity constitution, is narrowed down. The rules of *nidah* (impurity) are instrumental in perpetuating compliance by regulating women's sexuality, thus controlling individual expressions of sexual identity. Furthermore, delegating their implementation to women (the *mikveh*, the ritual bath, and self-examination) turns women into the enforcers of the law, thus intensifying their mediating role and reducing their options for autonomy.[26] When the narrative focuses on a daughter's coming-of-age, this implication of *nidah* rules is far-reaching, as it denies her possible access to the pre-symbolic relation with her mother who is perceived mainly as patriarchal. Mothers on the other hand are caught in the tangle too, since *nidah* rules channel sexuality into motherhood and at the same time separate the two. Paradoxically, the rules set to ensure pro-creation restrict motherhood by limiting mothers' authority, as Julia Kristeva and Mary Douglas have argued.[27] In the context of this discussion this restriction is of special interest because in Orthodox society motherhood is the main path for women's participation in the public space.[28] When narratives focus on mothers, this ambiguous status determines the nature of their coming-of-age process. Motherhood is pressurized even further when the rules of "purity of the family" expand and are applied to the national space.[29] It is presented as the fulfillment any woman should aspire to as well as an imperative condition for the survival of the nation and the redemption of *Eretz Yisrael*.[30] Subsequently, protagonists of daughters' coming-of-age narratives are either unable to separate from their mothers or else they choose to move away from the Orthodox way of life altogether.

The way women protagonists negotiate the inevitable conflict between these constraints and the determination of their sexual identity and subject autonomy varies greatly in the works discussed here. It ranges from submission to defiant manipulation within the terms of the law and from reconciliation to opting out of it altogether.[31] Naomi Ragen's novel *Sotah* (1995) and Yehudit Rotem's *Kri'ah* (Mourning) (1996) illustrate the wide span of these negotiations. The two novels share a similar point of departure, as their women protagonists are assertive women/girls striving for knowledge and fulfilling love whose married life fails to meet their expectations. The choices made by the protagonists, the processes that determine them and their subsequent description as coming-of-age narratives differ greatly.

In the beginning of the novel Ragen's protagonist is a "dutiful" daughter whose frustrating married life leads her astray from her marriage vows. After a long saga of persecution by the "mishmarot tzni'ut" (modesty vigilance), fleeing from the country and illness, she returns to her husband and child, reconciled. The decision made by the protagonist signifies her successful reintegration into society. She learns to accept the superiority of devotion over desire and care over intellectual aspirations, or in other words, she reaffirms the social/cultural values. Ragen's novel carefully portrays the parents who initiated the arranged marriage and the husband who could not fulfill the protagonist's needs as equally victimized by the system, thus avoiding any conflict that might jeopardize the probability of the reconciliation. The initial defiance aims at the system implementing the law rather than at the law itself. What seemed to be a quest for autonomy and self-determination of sexual identity at the onset of the novel ends with the acceptance of social norms that constrain this quest. The protagonist's flight to New York, which might be taken for a daring move, maintains her powerless position. Not only that it is initiated by the threats of "modesty" vigilantes, but staying away from home depends on a charitable family that cares for her during her illness, substituting parental care. In this sense the novel may be read as a classic male coming-of-age narrative. Its successful completion relies on the ability to integrate in society by means of adjusting individual aspirations to the social order and not on inner growth and awareness, which characterizes female coming-of-age. In turn, this outcome corresponds with Naomi Ragen's own decision to lead her life as an Orthodox activist, critical of the social system while endorsing Orthodox values.[32]

The victimization of women in the name of purity is the subject of Yehudit Rotem's novel *Kri'ah*. The novel follows the protagonist's way from a free-spirited and assertive girl to a woman whose zealous husband oppresses her sexuality and intellectual pursuits in the name of Torah law. Rotem's protagonist is too powerless to act upon the failure of her marriage; nevertheless, her realization of the failure, its reasoning and implications, completes her coming-of-age process. Unlike Ragen's, Rotem's criticism of the system is not contained within its official representatives but goes deeper to include Oedipal motivations, whereby the protagonist's choice of husband is an attempt to break away from the pattern of her mother's marriage. The futility of the attempt, manifested by the replication of this pattern, leads to a wider feminist awareness of women's position within the Orthodox hierarchy, as it portrays the manipulation of rules for the sake of control by both father and husband. The blatant protest against Orthodox patriarchy categorizes women as powerless victims and men as the oppressors whose religiousness shields them from inner weakness, a somewhat grotesque realization of Daniel Boyarin's view of Jewish male identity.[33] This does not mean to say that women's coming-of-age narratives are evaluated by the ferocity of the criticism of men they unleash. Mourning opens other options as it includes male characters that do not fall within the category of insensitive and domineering oppressors and thereby it calls for women's awareness of their choices' determinants.

This reading is strengthened in Rotem's second novel Ahavti kol kakh (I Loved So Much) (2000) which is structured around a plot of initiation. The protagonist of the novel is called to her elderly aunt's deathbed to listen and record the aunt's life story. The aunt, the older mentor/initiator, tells a life story of powerlessness and abuse which is rooted in the Orthodox code of social propriety. The imminent death lends a sense of urgency to the initiation plot, but the protagonist's role as a younger apprentice is not straightforward. As the aunt's story unfolds it constructs a dialectic process of reflections. The stories of both mentor and apprentice seem to correspond and differ from each other. Like the aunt, the protagonist has chosen to break away from repression: she divorced her husband and moved out of her Orthodox community. Like the aunt, the protagonist seems to have chosen individual pursuits over social and maternal obligations as defined by her former Orthodox community. Unlike the aunt, she has chosen to break away. While the aunt's story accentuates powerlessness as the underlying theme of women's narratives, the niece's highlights empowerment at the most vulnerable site of women's autonomy, that of motherhood. At the same time, a new intimacy established between her and the daughter she has left repudiates the "bad mother" label and reaffirms her decision to break away.

In a way, I Loved So Much carries out the realization reached by the protagonist of "Mourning." Trends that were introduced in the first novel are elaborated upon as the feminist awareness strengthens. Though both aunt and niece could trace back their misery to Orthodox social decrees, the novel suggests that Orthodoxy is only one form of intolerance shared by other ideologies that men misuse. Rotem's two novels may be read as a developmental narrative of female coming-of-age, which follows a process of consciousness raising to its completion. In turn, both novels correspond with Rotem's own biography and political stance. She divorced her husband and moved out of her Orthodox community. Her writing, especially her nonfiction book *Ahot rehokah* (Oh, My Sister) (1992) describes compassionately the struggles and resolutions of Orthodox women.

Within the range of the various negotiations, which construct the protagonists' coming-of-age, Ragen's and Rotem's novels stand wide apart. Ragen's novel assumes that the Law and the social mechanism assigned to implement it are two separate issues. The protagonist struggles with this mechanism rather than with the Law, thus she is able to reconcile the rift between her individual aspirations and the social order in a way similar to that of a classic male coming-of-age narrative. Rotem's novels on the other hand are feminist coming-of-age narratives, addressing issues of women's position in patriarchy as manifested in the Orthodox social order. Thereby the novels construct the move of their women protagonists towards a consolidated identity, which involves negotiating their family history as well as the wider social context. The novels reflect quite clearly a correlation between the writing and the political stance of the writers: Ragen takes the stance of a religious political activist while Rotem has opted out altogether.

The following sections will discuss coming-of-age narratives in the works of three writers: Mira Magen, Yocheved Reisman and Hannah Bat-Shahar. The three were chosen to present different thematic focuses of such narratives as well as for the complexity of their writing. The following discussions will use women's sexuality and motherhood as paradigms although each section will focus on a different aspect.

Mira Magen: From Oppositions to Inclusion

Magen's novels *Al takeh ba-kir* (Don't Knock against the Wall) (1997), *and Be-shokhvi uve-kumi ishah* (Love After All) (2000) represent the quest for consolidating sexual and maternal narratives. The first one tells the story of Yiska who moves from her religious village to the secular town. The second novel follows Zohara as she reconciles motherhood and sexuality in the secular town. Both novels construct female coming-of-age narratives based on the move from an initial binary position to inclusiveness that encompasses questions of individual identity constitution and links them to the wider context of Israeli society.

Magen's first novel, *Don't Knock against the Wall*, is constructed around the protagonist's move from the village, a religious *moshav*, which appears at first to be a site of innocence, to the secular town, initially preconceived as a site of materialistic promiscuity. Yiska, the protagonist, is in love with Elisha, her widower neighbor, whose wife died in labor. Haunted by Alma, the dead wife, she is trying to find out all she can about her, to exorcize her memory, so that Elisha will be free to return her love. The journey from village to town is a journey into the mystery of the dead wife that ends with Yiska's decision to leave the village, to refuse Elisha's longed-for proposal of marriage and live her own independent life in the town. The novel seems to follow the conventional progress of a male *Bildungsroman* plot: Yiska is set on her journey, pursuing her quest from which she emerges a mature adult, able to adjust and situate herself in society. However, Yiska's professed quest, the unraveling of the mysterious Alma in order to gain Elisha's heart, turns into another one, namely, the constitution of her own identity, encompassing former social codes and preconceptions but not solely determined by them. In this sense *Don't Knock against the Wall* might be defined as a *Bildungsroman* with a twist. The conventional pattern is overturned when the initial quest is replaced by the quest for Yiska's own identity. Knowing about Alma is a way of assuming the dead woman's identity in order to replace her in Elisha's life. Refusing Elisha's proposal in the end marks Yiska's discovery of her own identity, independent of Alma and Elisha. The narrative thus diverges from the course of the classic male *Bildungsroman* and that of a classic female one (that usually ends in marriage) and turns into a modern feminist narrative that ends with the decision to lead an independent life.

Yiska's move to town means moving away from the Orthodox way of life which had shaped her world, her sexual identity in particular, and against this background her actions regain their meaning.[34] Rather than elaborating on the conventions of Orthodox village life, the novel implies them through contrasting stereotypical representations of secular and Orthodox life. In turn, these stereotypes (mainly those of secular sexuality) and their deconstruction, impel Yiska's coming-of-age process. She constructs her sexual identity by negotiating the rift between the propriety and repressed sexuality of married village women and the overt, sometimes ridiculed, sexuality of single non-Orthodox women, such as her aunt and the owner of a café in town. Both women are middle aged, single, and looking for partners. While the aunt is pathetic and ridiculed for her desperate attempts to find a husband, the café owner is resourceful, independent and open about her somehow vulgar sexuality. Although both women live in town, the aunt shares the village's perception of women's status while the other one represents a "true urban" woman. Being urban women not only plays into the binary relation between village and town but also reinforces the contrast between options of sexuality derived from the initial Orthodox/secular dichotomy.

Moving to the town means breaking Orthodox rules regarding women's modesty. Furthermore, the town is characterized by what she fantasizes are "free" sexual relationships and tries to realize when she initiates a series of sexual encounters with a gynaecologist. This sexual affair stereotypes urban secular life as devoid of any spiritual or emotional dimension, a blatant "way of the flesh." Promiscuity in the secular world stands in contrast to Elisha's apparent ascetic and virtuous stand when he does not respond to Yiska's attempts to seduce him. Whether because of his religious convictions or a family pathology (Elisha duplicates his father in many ways), Elisha is initially set in the novel against the category of the secular world.

Binary structures collapse as the process of Yiska's coming-of-age reaches its completion. The novel moves from sharp categorizations at its beginning, towards tolerant inclusiveness, as Yiska learns to accept and live with ambiguity. She does not separate sex from emotion any more. She refuses Elisha's proposal and is drawn even further to the café owner, to Margit's warmth and compassion. She learns to negotiate opposing outlooks: she lives at Margit's flat, eating only dairy food off glass plates, but reassures her mother that Margit's cakes are kosher. Her old self-absorbed concerns are replaced by compassion towards Elisha's daughter that is no longer utilitarian. Yiska moves to town, but her ties with the village seem to strengthen, as illustrated by the wild growth of the geranium plant, Elisha's gift, in the town. Yiska acquires an ability to observe differences and determine her own scale of preferences, contrary to her perception of her Orthodox mother who: "was not taught to differentiate between desecration of the Sabbath, trousers, baring of one's head and incest, everything was a one-piece sin and punishment was scaled by the same yardstick" (p.131).[35] She subverts the initial structure of her narrative when she moves from dichotomy to diffusion as the underlying principle. Consequently, the expected outcome of a conventional female *Bildungsroman* plot, such as marriage to Elisha, is turned round when she chooses uncertainty which characterizes her life in the secular town over predictable regulation which characterizes the Orthodox village.[36]

Magen's later novel, *Love, After All,* uses the same developmental structure. Similarities between the two novels expand beyond the overall pattern and embrace so many details that *Love, After All* might be seen as a sequel to the first novel, beginning where the latter had ended. While *Don't Knock against the Wall* had left Yiska as she was about to begin her independent life in the secular town, Zohara, the protagonist of *Love After All*, is a single mother and a nurse, who has moved to the secular world of the town from a religious kibbutz where she was brought up. Both women face similar dilemmas as they try to negotiate between conflicting sets of norms and preconceptions. Characters in both novels are set in oppositional analogies, thus representing the initial stereotypes that are to be deconstructed at the end.

Love, After All posits the traditional separation between sexuality and motherhood at the core of its initial binary structure and the *Bildungsroman* narrative evolves as the protagonist negotiates this separation. Zohara's son was conceived in a most unorthodox manner: she paid a young doctor at the hospital she works in for his sperm, after hearing him talking about his "sperm trade." Sexual intercourse with the doctor had one purpose only: conception, and was devoid of any emotional or erotic meaning. It was, rather, a business transaction stipulated by a legal document signed in a lawyer's office. Detached and calculated, Zohara acts defiantly against her religious upbringing (single, unmarried mother), against what she interprets as secular urban life (sex rather than engaging in emotional/marital relationship) and conventions (by taking the initiative). Her challenge of patriarchal order is magnified if we take her action to be an extreme execution of the separation between sexuality and motherhood, both of which hardly need the participation of men.

Separating motherhood from sexuality determines other binary relations in the novel, most notably: the contrast between ideal motherhood, which is Orthodox and is linked to harmonious family life as represented by Zohara's sister, and failing parenthood which is secular and linked to dysfunctional families, as represented by the family of Mishael, her future partner. Other stereotypes, which are added to this set of oppositions, such as urban and materialistic secular life against rural and idealistic Orthodox life, are similar to those of the earlier novel. As the narrative evolves, the imposed distance between motherhood and sexuality decreases gradually until the process of coming-of-age is completed with Zohara's decision to share her life with Mishael, the father of her future second child. This second pregnancy is not deliberately planned but is the consequence of a passionate affair. Choosing Mishael as a partner and father expands the implications of the changes she has gone through. Mishael is as far removed from her Ashkenazi religious background as possible and in the beginning of the novel he represents the maladies of the stereotyped secular world. He is "rescued" from categorization alongside his parents, as Zohara learns to see through preconceptions. While regulated and prescribed motherhood reinforces differences in the beginning of the novel, it becomes instrumental to the move towards inclusiveness in the end as it breaks away from those constraints.[37] By shifting the focus from the narrative of the daughter (Yiska) to that of the mother (Zohara), *Love After All* diverts the narrative away from the stereotypical inevitability of the rift embedded in mother/daughter discourse to female solidarity.[38] When Yiska leaves the village she is also "liberating" herself from her patriarchal mother. Zohara on the other hand, although breaking traditional norms even further, maintains close relationships with both her mother and her Orthodox sister despite the fundamentally different life each one of them has chosen.

Furthermore, by embracing the Sephardic, urban and secular family of Mishael as her own, Zohara bridges wider cultural and social differences which are at the heart of Israeli society. She goes through a process of inner growth that allows her to situate herself differently in the world whereby she is able to accept ambiguity and pluralism. *Love, After All* moves a step further than *Don't Knock against the Wall*. Its exceptional political agenda opens up to address wider issues at the center of Israeli society, including questions of ethnicity, cultural divides and political affiliation.

Yocheved Reisman: The Mother/Daughter Plot

Mira Magen's protagonists of *Love, After All* and of the stories "Half-Priced Gerberas" and "Petro" (in *Kaftorim rekhusim heitev* [Well Buttoned Up], 1994) are mothers of young boys. Yocheved Reisman's novel, *Sleeping Bird*, and Hannah Bat-Shahar's writings both center on mother/daughter relationships. These distinctively different choices are significant. By focusing on mothers of boys, Magen lets her protagonists negotiate between sexuality and motherhood without having to resolve questions of subordination and autonomy inherent to mother/daughter relationships in patriarchal orders. The boys' young age neutralizes to some extent the confrontation between mothers and their sons' masculinity. Gender segregation in Orthodox society enhances the differences between these two types of maternal narratives, since boys are physically removed from their mothers at the age of 12, when they enter the yeshiva. Daughters on the other hand stay at home (those girls educated in the *ulpanot* become boarders at the age of 14 or 15), thus further increasing the complexity of negotiations between mothers as enforcers of the "Law of the Father," their daughters' autonomy and their own sexual identity.[39]

Symbiotic relations between mother and daughter are the focus of Yocheved Reisman's novel *Sleeping Bird*, which tells the story of Faigie (bird in Yiddish) and her mother Miriam. For over 20 years Faigie pretends to be in a coma after her intended husband deserted her on her wedding night apparently without any warning or explanation. Faigie chooses illness as a means of punishing her mother whom she accuses of sabotaging her wedding, although the real culprit is Faigie's half-brother. Throughout these years she leads a double life: during the day she is in a coma, while at night she comes to life, reading, listening to music, working as a translator and managing her affairs with the help of various women she has recruited through her nocturnal activities. Miriam, a Holocaust survivor and the adoptive mother of her late husband's four children, cares for Faigie, her own child, bound by maternal devotion and duty. Miriam and Faigie are locked in their relationship, mirroring each other and unable to break away. Their relationship is best described by what Luce Irigaray refers to as the ongoing game of mutual reflections which binds the daughter as much as it binds the mother: "In our patriarchal society the daughter is unable to control her relation to her mother. Nor can the woman control her relation to maternity, unless she reduces herself to that role alone." Symbiotic relationships, she argues, stress the need for a "new syntax" that will enable daughters and mothers to relate to each other outside the context of the patriarchal family, into which

Freudian prepositions are written, such as that a daughter must turn away from or "hate" her mother.[40] Faigie's narrative is an exaggerated tale of a bound daughter subverting the meaning of coming-of-age to imply liberation from her mother's hold. Following conventional preconceptions, Faigie comes of age when she causes her mother's death, taking the psychoanalytical concept of the removal of the mother to its extreme. Her rebellion binds her mother to her maternal role, while she deludes herself that she is free to determine when and if she is to be liberated. The novel's alternating perspectives do not resolve this entanglement though they provide different readings of events and their interpretations by numerous characters. They rather reinforce and expand the "mutual reflections" beyond the daughter/mother plot to encompass all the elements of the narrative. Thus, the subversive potential inherent to the ambiguity that underlines symbiotic relationships is applied to the wider social context and destabilizes it.

Matchmaking and marriage are the pivotal centers of the narrative. Around them Faigie's and Miriam's plots evolve. They magnify the destabilizing effect of the symbiotic relationship and its consequences. Success or failure of arranged marriages reflects on the mother's competence, the daughter's worth and the future marriages of family members. Thus it puts mother and daughter under intense pressure exacerbated by the father's absence. Although Faigie's rage is directed at her mother, it is her father's death that looms over the canceled marriage, the immediate cause of her "illness." Her engagement is arranged hastily because of his failing health and is entered into by his deathbed. Although he is portrayed as a gentle and loving father, his death during the engagement ceremony transforms him into a foreboding authority in whose name the ill match is carried out. Bound by loyalty to her father's sanctified memory, Faigie cannot fully articulate her resentment of his illness and death, which were instrumental to her "misfortune." She cannot rebel against him neither can she turn to her mother. Miriam, in turn, is equally trapped by her husband's memory, unable to express her own resentment at her loveless marriage as well as the need to care for her "disabled" daughter.

The context of matchmaking sharply raises inevitable tensions between subject autonomy and contrived social constructions, which are inherent to the construction of motherhood. Women in the novel struggle to fulfill their prescribed roles as mothers. "Failing" mothers inhabit it almost compulsively: mothers who die too young; mothers whose children are deformed physically or mentally; women who cannot have children and mothers who lost their children. The genuine and its dissembling constantly mirror each other, implying that their ambivalent relationship is inherent to them, as Miriam's narrative reveals. Miriam is a stepmother of her husband's four children (dissembled motherhood), as well as the natural mother of Faigie (genuine motherhood). All four stepchildren are caught in the stereotypical representations of stepmothers.[41] Miriam herself is trapped in the ambiguity and fluidity of adoptive motherhood and tries to stabilize her position by formally adopting the stepchildren. The futility of her attempts lies in the inevitable ambiguity of her step-motherhood, which cannot be sorted out by the law. Natural motherhood does not offer any clarity either. Miriam's fragile sense of motherhood is rooted in her traumatic youth in the Holocaust: "She tried to produce motherhood out of the emptiness in her and had no one to learn from" (p. 86). Not knowing how to mother leads to Miriam's attempts to do what mothers should do, thus deepening the emotional want of her stepchildren and the inseparable ties with her natural daughter.

Throughout the novel different perspectives juxtapose to construct and deconstruct perceptions and preconceptions around the center of the narrative, namely Faigie's canceled wedding and subsequently faked coma. Pretense, dissembling and substituting overwhelmingly dominate the narrative. In fact, they are introduced already in the book's cover: a painting of a framed suit by Yocheved Reisman herself, entitled "This is my substitute, my vicarious offering," taken from the Propitiatory Rite (*Seder Kaparot*) for Yom Kippur, which goes on to say: "my atonement, this cockerel shall meet death but I shall find a long and pleasant life of peace."[42] The novel subverts the expiation narrative of Yom Kippur in every possible way. Thus, for example, the symbolic sacrifice of the cockerel becomes the real sacrifice of both mother (physical) and daughter (mental); the atonement which is based on self-searching and truth is swapped for deceit and suspicions and the substitutes lose their ceremonial function as they become central to the plot of mistakes and dissemblance. The stability implied by the clear propriety of the repenting discourse of Yom Kippur is swapped for instability and fragmentation: characters pretend, invent and conceal their stories and their rationale. Thus the novel presents a fragmented world that only looks composed and united. Faigie's half sister sums up the situation: "her family is glued like a collage, or like a puzzle which was assembled and framed into a boring picture, its joints invisible unless you look closely" (p. 153). Orthodox life, supposedly stable and ordered, is revealed to be as fragmented and as disjointed as the stereotypical representations of the secular world in the novel.

The novel introduces a great many characters. It portrays an extended social context, allowing space for diverging into expositional material, drawing deterministic links between characters' histories and their present selves. By accumulating personal histories it constructs a social and genealogical profile of an Orthodox Ashkenazi family where parents and their contemporaries are Holocaust survivors who came to Israel in the early fifties. Their children, who were either born in Israel or came there at a young age, bear the marks of their parents' past.[43] The older generation is bound by past experiences, and their friendships and relationships originate there, hence the inclusion of non-Orthodox characters in the close circle of the family. The younger generation, that of Faigie and her half-sisters and -brothers, does not seem to have any relationships outside the Orthodox community, even when traveling as far as America. Contacts with the secular world are therefore limited and described as venturing into foreign lands, that is, either prohibited (Faigie's hidden nocturnal activities revolve around consuming secular culture) or else totally different and unworthy (Miriam's excursion to Tel-Aviv, for example). This tightly closed existence engenders grotesque stereotypes of the outside world whereby the "other" characters, are either connected to secular art and culture (valued and consumed by Faigie at night) or else vulgar non-European.

The separatism of the community does not lead to communal support as might have been expected. Its parochial nature imposes isolation and despair, as apprehension of social shame overrides any other consideration. Faigie's condition is considered so shameful that for the first time stepchildren and stepmother collaborate to hide it. They invent a successful marriage in America; they even produce contrived photographs of her supposed children. The need to hide the truth is so great because of its severe implications for the family as it will tarnish reputations and jeopardize the chances of good matches. Faigie's own match, which led to catastrophe, originated in such considerations. Her past "instability" and her family's finances were the motivation behind the choice of the intended bridegroom who in turn was a "bad match" himself.

The novel does not offer its women protagonists any option other than identifying with the roles they are allocated in the Orthodox family/community. Yocheved Reisman interpreted Faigie's rebellion in this context: "Faigie's morbid passivity is a terrible kind of rebellion against the Haredic society she lives in."[44] Faigie's rebellion is "morbid" because she cannot opt out completely. The only woman who does so successfully in the novel did not choose to leave the Orthodox community but was rather kicked out of it. Women are categorized as either "good mothers" or "smart women." The only woman in the novel who escapes this categorization is Colette, Miriam's friend, who does not belong to the community. Therefore, women's (or for that matter men's) sexuality as instrumental to the constitution of their identity is absent from the narrative. All the Orthodox characters in the novel are busy maintaining or establishing their family life within the terms of the law, and even Faigie's rebellion, which is obviously Oedipal in its nature, does not step beyond its metaphorical/emotional representation.[45]

The subversive nature of the symbiotic relationship in Sleeping Bird stands out when compared to conventional mother/daughter narratives, such as Yochi Brandes's novel Gemar Tov (Getting out for Good) (1997). Brandes's novel focuses on a daughter who rebels against her mother when she insists on marrying her cousin. Choosing the cousin is a clear act of defiance that signifies the daughter's preference of her aunt over her mother. The aunt represents an alternative to the mother's pious and self-righteous values and therefore is accused by the mother of transgression and immorality. On the surface, the assertive daughter achieves a successful separation from her mother. However, the marriage is soon over, and the daughter returns to reaffirm her mother's set of values. Although both protagonists fail to achieve their liberation, the two novels portray this failure very differently. Brandes's novel might be read as a classic female *Bildungsroman* that ends with suitable marriage whereby the daughter's rebellion is an adolescent phase that is eventually overcome. The patriarchal system, endorsed by the mother, remains intact and the novel indicates it from its onset, as it opens with the failure of the first marriage. Brandes's novel resolves the Oedipal tangle in a similar way to Ragen's *Sotah* even though the latter does not address it. These similar resolutions testify to the threatening subversiveness of Oedipal issues in narratives that resolve to reaffirm Orthodox patriarchy. Like these two novels, *Sleeping Bird* bypasses the father's role in the conflict, but it argues that mother/daughter relationships cannot be reconciled within the patriarchal order by definition, and that extends the subversive potential even further.

Hannah Bat-Shahar:
The Subversive Ambiguity of Maternal Narratives

Most mother/daughter narratives are presented from the daughter's perspective. Thus the emergence of mothers' narratives marks an important shift in Israeli women's writing.[46] Central to the conceptualization of sexual difference and consequently the constitution of subject identity, they are a threat to any narrative based on women's compliance and conformity.[47] Silencing the maternal voice is not an exclusively Orthodox strategy. Secular Israeli literature has taken maternal narratives and assimilated them into the Zionist narrative of liberation, thus silencing their subversive potential, as Yael Feldman has argued.[48] Hannah Naveh's analysis of the deconstruction of this narrative's symbolic language by the maternal voice conceptualizes its far-reaching political implications. The maternal narrative in the context of the national discourse has shifted the boundaries between the private and the public, diffusing and showing them to be categories of perspectives not of essence.[49] Similarly, the categorization of motherhood becomes fluid and inclusive once it is voiced through the maternal language. The precedent of secular narratives of motherhood enabled Orthodox women writers to address these multifaceted narratives, which threaten to destabilize Orthodox patriarchy, based on an unequivocal gender divide.

Unlike Mira Magen and Yocheved Reisman, Bat-Shahar's writing avoided exposing Orthodox values and their critique for sometime. Most of the stories and novellas in her first two collections *Calling the Bats* and *The Dancing Butterfly* do not refer directly to the Orthodox world, which their protagonists inhabit. The universal patriarchal order is blamed for the powerlessness and the subsequent atmosphere of oppressive suffocation prevalent in these narratives. Only in the later collection *Sham sirot ha-dayig* (Look, the Fishing Boats) (1997) do all three novellas explicitly relate the mental and emotional state of the protagonists to the Orthodox context, attesting to Bat-Shahar's high profile and exposure on the one hand and the impact of secular women's writing on the other hand. This move towards exposure also attests to the increasing volume of writing from the Orthodox world concerning gender issues.

Whether overt or masked, Bat-Shahar's women protagonists subvert the hegemonic discourse by their ambivalence and the constantly shifting boundaries expressed by their elusive narratives. This nature of the texts reflects Bat-Shahar's anxiety of authorship, as expressed in her interviews, but is also a mimetic expression of the discursive fluidity referred to as markers of female language. Collision between this unstructured, symbiotic language and the highly structured language of the "law" is inevitable, especially in her maternal narratives.

Bat-Shahar's mothers-protagonists are introverted women living on the edge, drifting in and out of reality and their fantasies, dangerously close to losing hold of reality and opting out altogether. These women appear passive and submissive, sometimes disorientated. They provide the focus of the texts, following their emotions and thoughts through associative narrative, reminiscent of the interior monologue. The narratives progress through half-articulated thoughts, using psychoanalytic symbols and metaphors that appear to be evasive and sometimes obscure. Critical readings of *Calling the Bats* pointed out an awareness of patriarchy as the inhibiting force that drives these women protagonists to this state.[50] In the first two collections this awareness is not fully articulated, following the overall pattern of hovering around the edges of disruption, avoiding the foreboding "unhomely moment."[51] Whether fully articulated or not, the maternal narratives reflect a complex of symbiotic relationships with daughters (e.g., Felina in "Among the Geranium Pots"; Gitzi, in "Wintry Journey"; Sara in "Look, the Fishing Boats" and Trudy in "Sweet Honey-Birds" [in the 2000 collection by that name]). The most prevailing feeling in these mothers' narratives is that of guilt and powerlessness.

The elusive nature of these narratives in itself carries a subversive potential by hinting at and alluding to a destructive power that lies beneath the apparently subdued and submissive women protagonists. This potential is usually realized towards the end of the stories in an act of explicit defiance such as when Felina smashes the pots Dafna has put in the garden, symbolically smashing motherhood itself. Similarly, Gitzi stops her daughter's medical treatment and rushes her back home. Sara encourages her younger daughter's attraction to her brother in-law, jeopardizing her chances of marriage, and Trudy is physically attracted to another woman whom she encourages to take her daughter's place and flirt with her husband at the same time.

All these stories of mothers are tales of ambiguity underlined by a deep sense of failure, which is presented as the inevitable consequence of the patriarchal construction of motherhood. The suffering of Felina, Gitzi, Sara and Trudy is traced back to their husbands and fathers who undermined them, and in some cases abused them, accusing them of being bad mothers. In the early collections this accusation is concealed behind the elusive narrative, but later collections articulate it unequivocally: Sara, in "Look, The Fishing Boats" is told by her furious husband: "You knew and kept silent. You didn't tell anyone. How could you? You are not a mother" (p. 66). The husband accuses Sara of her failure to collaborate with the scheme to marry off the younger daughter to a man whose prospects as a future husband are highly valued. While the husband emphasizes the man's future fortune, Sara thinks of his late wife who had committed suicide. Whether she is a "bad mother" for jeopardizing the match or for her silence over the suicide, Sara's sense of failure is inevitable. Matchmaking as the background for the accusation intensifies the conventional role of fathers in a patriarchal order. However, the novella goes beyond stereotypes as it juxtaposes patriarchal blaming with maternal guilt at the most vulnerable (or "contaminated") point in mother/daughter narratives, that of mothers' silence. A conventional reading of this silence interprets it as epitomizing mothers' mediation or patriarchal motherhood. Yet the novella turns it around: silence here means transgression, breaking the terms of the law from a patriarchal perspective. Sara observes her elder daughter's distress without breaking her compliant silence and maintains her silence as she observes the younger one's infatuation, sharing her daughter's excitement, valuing it against the silent suffocation of her own marriage and of her elder daughter's despair. Silence then is both powerless and subversive when it is part of maternal narratives.[52]

Furthermore, when the perspective of mothers is juxtaposed with that of daughters, as in "Sweet Honey Birds" and "Osnat" (1999), conventional reading of both narratives is deconstructed. "Sweet Honey Birds" is based on the assumption that Trudy's daughter left home out of rage and a sense of betrayal after finding that her mother is attracted to a Japanese student. She turns her back on her mother, allying herself with her father by choosing an Ultra-Orthodox boarding school. The school is a clear statement, a preference of the father's law, indicating the clear boundaries and propriety that Trudy has allegedly broken. The novella "Osnat" alludes to the biblical story of

Joseph and Potipher's wife, thus seeming to reinforce the blame of the mother. However, the daughter's version of the event offers an alternative interpretation. The daughter's account oscillates between conflicting emotions and loyalties, portraying adolescent confusion over one's sexual identity. It expresses a childish disappointment at the failure of the assumedly omnipotent mother to carry out the seduction; an Oedipal rivalry, sexual insecurity and sexual desire that turn into brotherly love. The overriding feeling is not that of rage and blame, quite the opposite. Infatuation empowers the world around the mother (the garden bursts into bloom) and makes her a better mother (she radiates generous love onto her daughter). The novella balances these emotions against the alliance that the daughter forms with her father, while offering, if only temporarily, a very different reading of the mother/daughter discourse. Juxtaposing the two novellas outlines a new discourse, based not on the patriarchal narrative of separation, suspicion and silence, but on the fluidity of options which Irigaray refers to as "new syntax."

By articulating both mother's and daughter's narratives, the dichotomy between motherhood and sexuality is destabilized. The daughter in "Osnat" projects onto her mother her own sexual desires, turning the mother into a sexual woman whose actions take her outside of the family realm and rules. This in turn improves mothering, contrary to the binary assumption. In contrast, the inability to see the mother outside the familial context, as in "Sweet Honey Birds," leads the daughter to reject her and to side unequivocally with patriarchy. Stepping outside the larger family context is not an option for Orthodox mothers, a notion that might explain Bat-Shahar's choice of different settings for the two novellas. "Sweet Honey Birds" takes place within a tightly knit Orthodox family, while "Osnat" takes place in an undefined setting, hovering between reality and biblical allusions, as if only by removing the narrative from its specific setting can a new daughter/mother discourse be allowed to surface. In the larger family circle, which mirrors patriarchal Orthodoxy, as in "Sweet Honey Birds" and "Look, the Fishing Boats," relationships between women are guarded; they lack solidarity and therefore cannot allow intimate openness. Regulating sexual and family life positions the family within the public space, thus isolating women rather than supporting them. The family, with which an Orthodox woman is called to identify herself, becomes, to quote Bat-Shahar, "the outside"; she defines self-expression as the "inside" that must not be exposed for fear it might hurt and damage the family/outside.[53] Equating the maternal with the familial silences women even further, since they cannot express their marital complaints for fear of condemnation equal to that of betraying their maternal duties. Thus, when Trudy tries to justify to herself her infatuation she recalls Jacob Steinberg's story "Daughter of Israel," which ends with the protagonist's desperate letter to her mother, a letter that the mother cannot respond to.

Trudy loses her daughter because she cannot disclose her husband's sexual violence. Sara in "Look, the Fishing Boats" is accused of bad mothering when she is actually trying to save her daughter from replicating her own marriage or even worse.

Exposing the symbiosis of mother/daughter relationships and the ambiguity of mothers inherent to them leaves Bat-Shahar's mothers detached and disassociated from their surroundings, including their daughters. Once they travel into their inner worlds they enter a fluid space of ambivalent emotions and become disorientated, as they lose the clearly mapped world they are supposed to inhabit.[54] They become what Judith Butler has termed "subversive within the terms of law."[55] The extent of their subversion becomes clear when set against the background of mothers complying with the "terms of law," as observed by Yehudit Rotem: "It seems to me that mother/daughter relationships in the Orthodox sector are free, to some extent, of the very familiar emotional, symbiotic and heavy dimension of mother/daughter relationships. Haredic mothers cannot allow themselves the openness necessary for deep relations with their daughters."[56] They therefore relate to their daughters on a more pragmatic level, or in other words, as "good patriarchal mothers."[57]

Bat-Shahar's women protagonists are placed in an unchangeable reality predetermined by their gender, dominated by fathers, husbands and ex-husbands. This basic view of reality does not undergo many changes. But a chronological reading of the works draws a progressive line of increasing feminist awareness and direct reference to the Orthodox social order. Questioning and pondering that were interwoven in the lyrical style of narrating are placed at the front of the narratives in later works. The subversiveness of the later maternal narratives manifests this tendency clearly, enabling them to be read as a modern female *bildungsroman*.

Conclusions

Coming-of-age narratives were used in this study as paradigms of the ways women protagonists negotiate the conflicts between Orthodox/social dicta and subject autonomy. The patterns that have emerged point out a diversity of the types of coming-of-age processes and their outcomes. The different types clearly correspond with the writers' own resolutions regarding their position within (or outside) their religious/Orthodox communities. Thus, the works of Mira Magen who leads a religious life in a secular community are notably different from those of Reisman and Bat-Shahar, who live in Orthodox communities. Magen's two novels construct complete coming-of-age processes. Her women protagonists fulfill their aspirations for self-determination and independence, or are on their way to doing so. In

Reisman's and Bat-Shahar's works, women protagonists are not free to establish the separation needed for an independent constitution of their autonomy. Their coming-of-age has to stay within the terms of the law and is therefore manifested either as a process of consciousness raising that is not fully acted upon (Bat-Shahar) or a contrived and dissembled independence of detrimental consequences (Reisman). Other options, such as reaffirmation of the law (Brandes and Ragen) and the move from consciousness raising to opting out (Rotem), strengthen the links between writers' biographies and their protagonists. Using coming-of-age as a paradigm points out unexpected similarities between writers. In Brandes's later novel *Lekhabot et ha-ahavah* (Quench Love) (2001) for example, the safe outcome of the protagonist's rebellion is achieved only when her mother disappears. In this respect Brandes and Reisman have chosen similar strategies to resolve the mother/daughter conflict, which forms the coming-of-age processes of their protagonists. Although the two novels as well as the biographies of the writers are very different, this choice indicates that Brandes's critique of Orthodoxy is not necessarily a sign of a significant move away from it. Magen's narratives of coming-of-age strengthen this assumption. Her protagonists' move towards a consolidated identity reflects the overall progress towards tolerant inclusiveness in the novels, which allows an alternative view of female relationships and which is rooted in the acceptance of both secular and Orthodox ways of life.

This paradigm draws attention to the diverse positioning of protagonists in relation to the Orthodox/secular divide. Bat-Shahar's protagonists, wrapped in their personal struggle, do not venture out of their social context. Her works hardly touch upon the Orthodox/secular divide reflecting thus her underlying ambiguity concerning Israeli society. On the one hand, her professed feeling of alienation is apparent in the foreign names and locations of her protagonists and some of the plots.[58] On the other hand, Israeli landscape is precisely drawn through detailed imagery of its fauna. Reisman claims the opposite, yet her work situates her closer to Bat-Shahar than to Magen. For all her obvious acquaintance with secular culture, her protagonists can venture into the secular world only under cover and the majority of her secular characters exhibit a very grim and stereotypical picture of moral deficiency. Although the novel encompasses a wider social context than that in Bat-Shahar's works, Reisman's characters move within a tightly closed circle. The contrived nature of the narrative and its extraordinary coincidences contribute to a claustrophobic atmosphere not dissimilar to that in Bat-Shahar's works.

Magen, Reisman and Bat-Shahar share a dissident stand with their women protagonists. Their writing and publishing in the secular world is an act of disclosure opposed by the Orthodox community. All three writers (as well as

Brandes) have stated, albeit to different degrees, their apprehension of criticism and therefore of what they expose, out of consideration for their families and loyalty to their communities. As the study of the works has shown, the narratives manifest apprehension in a variety of strategies designed to resolve these issues of authorship. Publishing in the secular world raises issues of readership as well. Secular reading of the works tends to interpret them as secular texts, thus bringing to light questions of cultural differences. Bat-Shahar's style for example, is usually attributed to secular aesthetic models (such as Kahana-Carmon's works), but it might equally be a mimetic representation of Orthodox sexual and emotional discourse.[59] Reisman's novel — a tale of intriguing schemes and unusual coincidences evolving around matchmaking — is reminiscent of nineteenth-century Yiddish popular stories. From a contemporary perspective the improbable twists of the plot might be interpreted highly critically. However these might appeal differently to Orthodox women readers who are able to identify in them an intimately known reality.[60] Consequently the notion of "subversiveness" in the works alters considerably.

A diachronic study of coming-of-age narratives reveals their use as paradigms of shifts (or immobility) in the overall body of works by a specific writer. Such shifts, when they are present, testify to wider political changes (as in Brandes's works), the increasing volume of writing coming from the Orthodox world and the dialogue with secular writing. Bat-Shahar's works clearly illustrate this tendency. Her individual works do not construct a whole process of coming-of-age and they might be referred to as developmental plots, since they follow women protagonists on their way to articulation. In the wider context of Bat-Shahar's works, they indicate a process of change. The representations of women in the works hardly vary, but the portrayal of their social surroundings becomes more detailed and particular, reflecting a clearer notion and articulation of women's position in their society. This shift heightens the political critique in the later works, although, true to the works' ambiguous nature, women protagonists do not fully disclose their dissent. Her women protagonists subvert the Orthodox discourse through their awareness of their sexuality and that determines their defiance as wives, daughters and mothers. Yet, they disguise the effect of their subversiveness on the world around them, thus stripping it of overt political significance. This representation of womanhood allows Bat-Shahar to claim that her works are "feminine" rather than "feminist" and enables her to avoid taking sides politically. The narratives imply inwardly expressed defiance that might or might not be understood by other characters within the fictional world, but is certainly interpreted as such by the secular reader outside it.

The use of coming-of-age models indicates the extent of the dialogue of Orthodox women writers with their secular counterparts and against this background their difference is marked, most significantly in their approach to the Oedipal tangle.[61] Quite naturally, models of female coming-of-age narratives place Oedipal conflicts at their onset as daughters negotiate their sexual identity and autonomy. In the secular female narratives of coming-of-age, as Pnina Shirav has shown, the protagonists have to choose between the heritage of the father and that of the mother. The prevailing tendency is to acknowledge the need for separation from the father and for a revision of the presumed need of the daughter to remove the mother in order to establish autonomic identity.[62] Within the Orthodox context, which does not tolerate any shift of its abiding codex, these options and choices are denied. Daughters cannot choose to turn away from their fathers and their access to the presymbolic connection with the mother is blocked by her patriarchal role. Mothers' position is equally precarious, since motherhood, which binds them and stifles their autonomy, is their only path to visibility and acknowledged social position, thereby leading to deepened fragmentation. Subsequently, male characters, the immediate symbols of the law, are portrayed differently in narratives that take place within the Orthodox community from those whose protagonists opted out. Men in Bat-Shahar's and Reisman's works (as well as in Yehudit Rotem's *Mourning* and Yochi Brandes's *Getting out for Good*) are abusive, domineering and untrustworthy or else weak and absent. Reisman's novel illustrates this tendency quite clearly. The narrative evolves around the Oedipal tangle, placing the mother/daughter relationship under extreme pressure that results in matricide, the ultimate removal of the mother. Yet, the father remains intact, not only because he is already dead at the onset of events but also because retrospectively his memory is untouchable. What seems to be the redundancy of men is not the result of empowered women as in current secular Israeli women's writing, but rather a strategy to express criticism within the terms of principles that cannot be altered. In a similar way Bat-Shahar uses tactics of disguising and masking defiance through metaphors and fragmented monologues.[63]

Rejecting powerless mothers pushes daughters who do not opt out to side with their fathers. Consequently, disassociated mothers such as Bat-Shahar's protagonists and failing mothers such as Reisman's inhabit maternal narratives. The works of writers who live in the Orthodox world cannot therefore share the current inclination of secular Israeli narratives to turn to mothers "in order to decipher a forgotten code."[64] In contrast, Mira Magen's novels open up other alternatives for male characters and consequently for women and mothers. The move towards inclusiveness in her works allows the presence of ambivalent and multifaceted male characters, as women characters manifest their empowered state of mind by the use of androgynous characteristics (such as determining terms and rules in *Love, After All*, and using sex in a stereotypical male fashion in *Don't Knock against the Wall*, etc.).

When I embarked on this study I was struck by the similarities between the writing of Orthodox women and that of women travelers to the Orient in the nineteenth century.[65] Both share the alluring attraction of unveiling the mystified invisibility of women for the reader, yet they appear incompatible as one observes veiled women, whereas the other is the voice of the so-called veiled women themselves. However, this same incompatibility reflects the complex position of Orthodox women writers, who observe women yet are bound like them, who travel in their own land, crossing into secular countries as they negotiate their right to travel in the first place. The writing of Orthodox women allows the readers into their private rooms, providing insights into the veiled (or supposedly veiled) life from which secular readers are excluded. Traveling in those rooms exposes their diversity and demystifies the women who inhabit them. It draws a picture of heterogeneity of responses and negotiations similar to that which has surfaced in secular women's writing and remains at the same time particular and different.

NOTES

1 Throughout the article I use "Orthodox" as a generic term because differentiating the various communities has little or no bearing on the themes discussed.

2 Admiel Kostman and Miron Issacson edited an anthology entitled *Shirah hadashah* (New Poetry) (Tel Aviv, 1997). It is a collection of poems by religious and secular poets, attempting to reconstruct a non-secular tradition in Israeli poetry. The title "poetry of religiosity" points to a universal essence shared by all the contributors, blurring the distinctions between the political inclinations of secular and religious writers. The distinction between writers of prose and of poetry is significant in the context of gender politics. Poetry, especially lyrical poetry, was accepted as "suitable" for women alongside other "subordinate" genres such as diaries and the epistolary novel as Tova Cohen has shown in "Betokh ha-tarbut u-mihutzah lah: Al nikus 'sfat ha-av' ke-derekh le-itzuv intelektuali shel dmut ha-ani ha-nashi" (Inside and Outside Culture: On the Appropriation of "the Father's Language" as a Method of Intellectual Representation of the Female Subject), *Sadan: Mehkarim ba-sifrut ha-ivrit*, Vol. 2, *Prakim nivharim be-shirat nashim ivrit* (Poetry of Hebrew Women) (Tel Aviv, 1996). Even though poetesses were accepted into the canon, this was done only conditionally. See Dan Miron, *Imahot meyasdot, ahayot horgot* (Founding Mothers, Stepsisters) (Tel Aviv, 1991). However, their inclusion was not as problematic as that of women authors. See Hannah Naveh, "Leket, pe'ah ve-shikhehah: Ha-hayim mihutz la-kanon" (Gleaning, the Forgotten Sheaf and the Poor Man's Tithe: Life outside the Canon), in Dafna N. Izraeli et al., *Min, Migdar, Politikah* (Sex, Gender, Politics: Women in Israel) (Tel Aviv, 1999), pp. 49–106.

3 Such as: Dana Gilerman, "Tzohar mishelahen" (A Window of Their Own), *Ha'aretz*, "Galeriyah" section, 28 July 1997; Yehudah Koren, "Metzitzim le-olam shel isurim" (Peeping into a World of Prohibitions), *Yediot Aharonot*, culture section, 8 August 1997; Yael Israel, "Kol be-ishah ergah" (A Woman's Voice Is Yearning), *Maariv, Zman Tel Aviv*, 9 January 1998.

4 Yaron London, "Ve-el sifrekh tshukatekh" (And You Shall Desire Your Book), *Yediot Aharonot*, Supplement, 15 October 1997, pp. 48–50.

5 Consequently one might find a clear correlation between the didactic stand and the transparency of the texts in Ragen's and Brandes's writing. Ragen, whose inclusion might be taken as a testament to postmodern Israel since she writes in English, declares herself *metakenet olam* (a reformer). Her writing is blatantly simplistic. Brandes's novels are equally

transparent in their use of allegorical devices (*Hagar*, 1999) and language. When interviewed she talked about using different registers in her books, unaware of the transparency of this technique when combined with overt use of symbols and metaphors.

6 Hannah Bat-Shahar is the wife of a Haredic rabbi living in a Haredic community and writing under a pseudonym to conceal her identity. She was "interrogated" by Yaron London. Rather than accepting her view that her writing and the conflicts she has to resolve are no different from those of any writer, the interviewer persistently pursued an "admission" of unbridgeable rift between her life in a Haredic community and her writing, insisting on interpreting her writing as a political act by a tormented activist.

7 Gilerman, "Tzohar mishelahen."

8 Koren quotes her as saying: "I don't like it when they group several women who don't have other common interests, treat us as if we were some literary club and label us 'religious writers.' Did anyone call Agnon a religious writer?" ("Metzitzim le-olam shel isurim").

9 Interviews with Hannah Bat-Shahar from the publication of *Likro la-atalefim* (Calling the Bats) in 1990 until the recent publication *Yonkei ha-dvash ha-metukim* (Sweet Honey Birds) in 2000, portray an interesting correlation between writing and awareness of her position in her own community as well as among her secular readers. In the first interviews she talked about her fear of exposure and the need to conceal her writing from her family and community: if the truth comes out her daughter would not be able to find the right match and would be ostracized at school as would all members of her family; she would be branded crazy; her family would find the content of her work shocking. Billie Moskuna-Lerman, "Erotikah me'ahorei ha-shavis" (Erotics behind the Head-Scarf), *Maariv*, 5 January 1990. *Sham sirot ha-dayig* (Look, the Fishing Boats) was published in 1997 and subsequent interviews are more ambiguous: protesting against categorization on the one hand and talking about providing the secular reader with a window onto the Orthodox world on the other hand. Furthermore, she defends the Orthodox dismissal of artistic writing as unnecessary (London, "Ve-el sifrekh"). The tone of the last two arguments is quite defensive, testifying to the pressure to negotiate between the two worlds.

10 Dalia Karpel, "Hayeha ha-kfulim" (Her Double Life), *Ha'aretz*, Supplement, 9 July 1999, pp. 56–8; David Shalit, "Me-ahorei ha-shavis" (Behind the Head-Scarf), *Maariv*, 6 August 1999, pp. 78–80.

11 Mira Magen stated that writing for the secular world allows freedom of thought and creativity while the Orthodox world does not value artistic expression unless it is instrumental. She believes that there is a wish to be more integrated in Israeli society and that the writing coming from the Orthodox world reflects an attempt to have a dialogue with the secular world (Gilerman, "Tzohar mishelahen"). However, in another interview she expressed the view that the divide between the two communities has deepened (London, "Ve-el sifrekh"). Brandes's criticism of Orthodoxy, especially of the national religious sections, is clearly stated in her recent book *Lekhabot et ha-ahavah* (Quench Love), 2001. In an interview following its publication she describes her "crossing" to the secular left as a gradual process. Both Brandes and Magen express ambivalent relations with Orthodoxy: loyalty to its traditions and their families on the one hand combined with criticism, especially of its intolerance regarding change, on the other hand.

12 When asked: "Are your books a feminist protest?", Bat-Shahar answered: "And what is new here? It is not uniquely religious. Isn't the book 'Love Life' by Tzruya Shalev a feminine protest?" And later on: "what is important is not the social frame but the feminine essence. No male writer could have portrayed Shalev's protagonist the way she did it" (London, "Ve-el sifrekh"). Bat-Shahar's answers indicate the extent of her reliance on other women's writing when called to address "difficult" issues such as sexuality. Shalev's novel is explicitly and aggressively erotic. Bat-Shahar is careful not to relate to it as "feminist" but rather as "feminine," avoiding a direct statement. Her stand is very different from that of Yocheved Reisman with whom she associates herself quite readily. Reisman talks freely about feminism and feminist activists, approving of their struggle. See Karpel, "Hayeha ha-kfulim."

13 Tamar El-Or, *Ba-pesah ha-ba: Nashim ve-oryanut ba-tziyonut ha-datit* (Next Pesach: Literacy and Identity of Young Religious Zionist Women) (Tel Aviv, 1998), pp. 298–303.

14 Amnon Levy, *Ha-haredim* (The Haredim) (Jerusalem, 1989); Menachem Friedman, "Ha-ishah ha-haredit" (The Haredic Woman), in Yael Azmon (ed.), *Eshnav le-hayehen shel nashim* (A View into the Lives of Women in Jewish Societies) (Jerusalem, 1995), pp. 273–90; Yair Sheleg, *Ha-datiim ha-hadashim: Mabat akhshavi al ha-hevrah ha-datit be-Yisrael* (The New Religious Jews: Recent Developments among Observant Jews in Israel) (Jerusalem, 2000); Tamar El-Or, *Maskilot u-vurot: Mi-olaman shel nashim harediyot* (Educated and Ignorant: On Ultra-Orthodox Women and Their World) (Tel Aviv, 1992); and *Ba-pesah ha-ba*.

15 El-Or, *Ba-pesah ha-ba*, pp. 311–8, 297–307.

16 Hannah Kehat, "Maamad ha-nashim ve-limud Torah ba-hevrah ha-ortodoksit" (Women's Status and Torah Study in the Orthodox Society), in Yael Azmon (ed.), *Ha-tishma koli? Yitzugim shel nashim ba-tarbut ha-yisre'elit* (Will You Listen to My Voice? Representations of Women in Israeli Culture) (Jerusalem, 2001), pp. 355–64.

17 Tzvia Greenfield quotes a letter from a woman published in the popular Haredic magazine *Mishpahah* (Family). The writer of the letter is responding to an article about women's status arguing against the exclusion of women from the world of *Halakhah* and Torah study. Her letter echoes the arguments of the young religious Zionist women in El-Or's book. Furthermore, the writer of the letter discloses her full name, willing to subject herself to disapproval and gossip, which in itself is evidence of major change. See Tzvia Greenfield, *Hem mefahedim: Eikh hafakh ha-yamin ha-dati veha-haredi le-ko'ah movil be-Yisrael* (Cosmic Fear: The Rise of the Religious Right in Israel) (Tel Aviv, 2001), pp. 170–2.

18 Life enclosed in the yeshiva determines the vocabulary available to men. Yehuda Friedlander argues that the language of Orthodox men is too poor for literary writing (cited in Koren, "Metzitzim le-olam shel isurim").

19 Iris Parush, *Nashim korot: Yitronah shel ha-shuliyut ba-hevrah ha-yehudit be-mizrah eiropah ba-me'ah ha-tsha-esrei* (Reading Women: The Benefit of Marginality in Nineteenth Century Eastern European Jewish Society) (Tel Aviv, 2001), pp. 135, 172.

20 El-Or, *Maskilot u-vurot*, pp. 83–107

21 Cf. Tamar Rapoport et al., "'Zeh davar hashuv be-Eretz Yisrael latet la-tzibur'": Ne'arot tziyiniyot tormot la-le'om" ("It's an Important Thing in Eretz-Israel, Giving to the Public": Religious-Zionist Girls Contribute to the Nation), *Teoriyah u-Vikoret*, No. 7 (Winter 1995), pp. 223–34. Rapoport's research shows clear similarities with traditional concepts of women's education. Her research is of special interest to this article because it discusses various practices used to resolve the divide between the traditional roles of women and their involvement in the Zionist project, in other words, seeking a way to channel the public profile of Zionist women's involvement into the traditional confinement of women to the home/family. The private/public or visibility/invisibility divides that challenge the religious Zionist movement are similar to those confronted by Orthodox women writers; although they appear to be different.

22 See interview with Bat-Shahar in Shalit, "Me-ahorei ha-shavis." In her interview with Dalia Karpel, "Hayeha ha-kfulim," Reisman talked openly and critically about the relationship between Haredic and secular communities, pointing out stereotypical views in both.

23 See Orah Cohen, *Tzn'iut ha-ishah ba-idan ha-moderni* (Women's Modesty in Modern Time) (Beit-El, 2000), pp. 92–3. Cohen traces rules of modesty concerning women throughout history. Her book clearly shows an overwhelming tendency to tighten these rules which she links to the increase in the quantity of written works on *Halakhic* practices. Those written works have taken the place of passing on family traditions and values through personal models, eliminating the immediacy and flexibility that enabled adjustments to actual life experiences in the past. Thus, school rather than home became the major vehicle for shaping Jewish identity. Rabbi Dessler's concept of *Emunat hakhamim*, according to which the *Halakhah* is a system of instructions passed on through speakers whose authority cannot be challenged, had intensified this process. The role of women, especially of mothers, as educators, was therefore considerably reduced, reinforcing the exclusion of women beyond the obligatory *Halakhic* rules.

24 Pnina Shirav, *Ktivah lo tamah: Emdat si'ah ve-yitzugei nashiyut be-yetziroteihen shel Yehudit Hendel, Amalia Kahana-Carmon ve-Ruth Almog* (Non-Innocent Writing: Discourse Position

and Female Representations in Works by Yehudit Hendel, Amalia Kahana-Carmon and Ruth Almog) (Tel Aviv, 1998), pp. 22–3.

25 See Elizabeth Abel, Marianne Hirsch and Elizabeth Langland (eds.), *The Voyage In* (New England, 1983).

26 Yehudit Rotem, *Ahot rehokah*, (Oh, My Sister) (Tel Aviv, 1992), pp. 68–73, records women's attitudes towards the *mikveh* and they range from accepting and reiterating the ideological reasoning, especially those endorsing impurity rules as a recipe for happy marital relationships, to dismay. Most women interviewees confessed to a feeling of extreme discomfort as they are being watched on their way back and forth to the *mikveh*. Their evidence echoes Devora Baron's story "Fradel," where going to the *mikveh* is a public act of oppression.

27 Following Mary Douglas, Elizabeth Grosz, *Volatile Bodies: Towards a Corporeal Feminism* (Bloomington, 1994), concludes that rituals designed to cleanse and purify are metaphors for cultural homogeneity. This homogeneity is challenged by the diversity of women's writing, hence its subversive nature is enhanced.

28 El-Or, *Ba-pesah ha-ba*, pp. 185–8.

29 Nitza Yanay and Tamar Rapoport, "Ritual Impurity and Religious Discourse," *Women's Studies International Forum*, No. 20 (1997), pp. 651–66.

30 Tzvia Greenfield takes this matter even further when she claims that motherhood is manipulated for financial gains (*Hem mefahedim*, pp. 163–5)

31 The two women in Mira Magen's "Kishu'im" (Courgettes) in *Kaftorim rekhusim heitev* (Well Buttoned Up) (Jerusalem, 1994), pp. 165–83, subvert codes of *tzni'ut* to serve their own ends either as an expression of defiance or as a way to run away from "bad" sexuality. A similar strategy is recorded in David Greenberg and Eliezer Witztum, *Sanity and Sanctity: Mental Health Work among the Ultra-Orthodox in Jerusalem* (New Haven, 2001), which discusses therapeutic attitudes towards obsessive behavior among ultra-Orthodox communities in Jerusalem. They record a case of a woman who became obsessive about her practice of impurity rules after her marriage. She was so anxious to ensure that she was cleansed of any traces of menstrual blood that she could hardly stop her self-examination. By doing so she prolonged the "impure" period so that whatever time was left before her next menstrual period did not coincide with ovulation, thus avoiding conception (pp. 117–20). The woman in this case was using the mechanism set to regulate sexuality and maternity to beat this regulation. She broke the traditional concept of sexuality for the sake of procreation. She had subverted the authoritative discipline in the same way as the two women in Mira Magen's writing. The protagonist of Haya Ester's story "Nechama-Gittel" uses another strategy, which is not dissimilar. While she immerses herself in the *mikveh* she lets her thoughts wander into "prohibited sites," as she recalls her love for the man she was not allowed to marry. By doing so she reclaims her right for private intimacy (thoughts), subverting the controlling role of the *mikveh* as a site designated for the public gaze. See Risa Domb (ed.), *New Women's Writing from Israel* (London, 1996), pp. 58–65.

32 Ragen expresses her political views in newspaper columns and on her website. Her column in *The Jerusalem Post* is used quite frequently to resist rabbinical ruling concerning women's issues such as in the case of *agunot*, 9 March 2001.

33 Daniel Boyarin, *Unheroic Conduct: The Rise of Heterosexuality and the Invention of the Jewish Man* (Berkeley, 1997).

34 Here I disagree with Tamar El-Or, "Nahalal, im rak nirtzeh" (Nahalal, If Only We Want), *Ha'aretz*, book section, 24 December 1997, who argues that the novel does not provide insights into the Haredic world and that its characters' religiousness is hardly discussed. El-Or defines the novel as "Israeli," and protests against the categorization of both the novel and its writer as "religious." However, removing the religious frame of reference would mean that vital elements would be left unanswered for. These include Elisha's abstaining from sexual relationships, his obsession with his daughter's hair which he cuts every month, Alma's puzzling choice of the village, the dramatic change in Yiska's life once she has moved to the town, her view of her mother and others.

35 All translations from the Hebrew texts are my own.

36 Predictability and religious practice are linked to fatalistic views of detrimental consequences in the village. Such is the case of Alma's hair, which is linked to the biblical story of Absalom. Elisha's subsequent treatment of his daughter's hair raises questions about the nature of his devoutness and its connection to superstitious beliefs.

37 The turning point of the novel centers on motherhood, when Zohara's son falls ill. The crisis heightens and resolves many issues: Mishael expresses his commitment and care, and his parents care for Zohara and her son the way real grandparents do, thus easing Zohara's way into a formal familial bond. The son's natural father comes to the child's bed and thereafter visits him at home, thus ending Zohara's attempt to separate motherhood from sexuality.

38 Marianne Hirsch, *The Mother/Daughter Plot* (Bloomington, 1989), pp. 12–14, 167–76.

39 Yehudit Rotem suggests that gender segregation has a deep impact on Haredic mothers. Her discussion (*Ahot rehokah*, pp. 177–94) implies that mothers "give up" on their sons, not knowing how to relate to their needs, solving their problems as if they were girls. Rotem holds a critical view of Haredic mothers, suggesting that: "any woman educating her daughter traditionally, epitomizes the image of matriarchal woman and enables society to perpetuate fixed models passed on from one generation to another" (p.191).

40 Luce Irigaray, *This Sex Which Is Not One* (New York, 1985), p. 143.

41 Their aunt reads them fairytales about wicked stepmothers, blatantly delivering their message by her faulty Hebrew pronunciation that changes "stepmother" into "killing mother."

42 The Hebrew for "my substitute" is "halifati" which can also mean "my suit." This second meaning is used for the painting on the cover and alludes to several main junctions in the narrative: a suit as a formal and social "face" one puts on, corresponding to the theme of pretense and compliance; literal suits, that of Faigie's brother and her intended husband, are instrumental to the plot as they impelled the cancellation of the wedding. Disclosure of the brother's betrayal is delayed until almost the end of the novel (chapter 23, pp. 213–8) and is revealed only to the reader, ironically illuminating Faigie's and Miriam's story as pathetic rather than heroically tragic.

43 The Holocaust and its subsequent uprootedness affect most layers of the novel: it leads to desperate pairing, determines familial relationships and intensifies the fragmentation of the social fabric. Brandes's and Rotem's works use the Holocaust in a similar way.

44 Karpel, "Hayeha ha-kfulim," pp. 56–8.

45 The closest Faigie comes to discussing the meaning of married life is via an old Venetian *Ketubah* (marriage contract) her half-brother Gabriel had sent her. She constructs the fictional married life of the woman mentioned in it, but does not discuss its sexual aspect. Faigie's projects on her ancestral counterpart her feelings of suffocation and frustration, describing married life as "caged life." Naturally, this perspective enhances her rebellion and expands its object to include the overall social system. Yet by avoiding the sexual side of married life, Faigie's denies the Oedipal meaning of her acts.

46 Secular writers, such as Yehudit Hendel, Orly Castel-Blum, Eleonora Lev and Lily Perry, voiced mothers. Their subversion of conventional representations of motherhood questions the basic assumptions of the Israeli narrative.

47 Tamar El-Or analyzes the ways in which Orthodox women are educated to view motherhood as the peak of self-fulfillment (*Ba-pesah ha-ba*, pp. 183–215). The women studied in her research are young, religious-Zionists, taking part in higher education programs. That sets them apart from women in more traditional, Haredic communities. The education program exposes the attempt to adapt, portraying motherhood as either a source of ultimate happiness or a laborious job.

48 Yael Feldman, *No Room of Their Own: Gender and Nation in Israeli Women's Fiction* (New York, 1999), pp.108–9.

49 Hannah Naveh, "Al ha-ovdan, al ha-shkhol ve-al ha-evel ba-havayah ha-Yisre'elit" (On Loss, Bereavement and Mourning in Israel), *Alpayim*, No. 16 (1998), pp. 85–120.

50 Tamar Hess, "Kfar ein lah ikuvim: Kriyah feministit be-'Likro la-atalefim' le-Hannah Bat-Shahar uve-'Heikhan ani nimtzet' le-Orly Castel-Blum" (She No Longer Has Scruples: A Feminist Reading of Hannah Bat-Shahar's "Calling the Bats" and Orly Castel-Blum's "Where Am I?") in Azmon (ed.), *Eshnav le-hayehen shel nashim*, pp. 375–94; Ariel Hirshfeld, "Be-

mehozoteiha shel Titania" (The Lands of Titania), *Ha'aretz*, 23 February 1990.

51 I use the term following Homi K. Bhabha, in *The Location of Culture* (London, 1994), pp. 10–11.

52 In this respect "Look, the Fishing Boats" differs from earlier works such as "Among the Geranium Pots," "Wintry Journey" and "The Dancing Butterfly" which contain a clearer distinction between husbands' accusations and mothers' guilt. Mothers perceive their "failure" on a different, almost existential level, as they watch their daughters powerlessly, unable to free themselves from the social construction of good motherhood. The accusations of husbands and fathers are more concrete and always abusive, as is Oded's in "The Dancing Butterfly."

53 London, "Ve-el sifrekh."

54 "Disassociated mothers" is a term used by Elaine Tuttle Hansen in *Mother without Child* (Berkeley, 1997). Hanson discusses mothers whose subversion is taken to the extreme, abandoning their children, giving them up for adoption or even killing them like Seth in Tony Morrison's *Beloved*. Their disassociation is the consequence of the traumas they had suffered. Bat-Shahar's mothers bear a strong resemblance to the mothers discussed by Hanson, although it seems that their "childlessness" is not as severe. However, the strict codes they live by brand their activities criminal and the protagonists accept them as such. For example, Trudy's affair in "Sweet Honey Birds" is justifiable in light of her husband's sexual aggression and his ruthless handling of her money, yet she behaves like a sinner when she sets out on a pilgrimage to purify herself.

55 Judith Butler, *Gender Trouble: Feminism and the Subversion of Identity* (New York, 1990), p. 93.

56 Rotem, *Ahot rehokah*, p. 143.

57 The mother in Rotem's *Mourning* fits this definition. She follows her husband's rules even though she is very different by nature. Her silence is the conventional silence of mothers' mediation within patriarchy. Tili's mother in the novel takes her silence even further, as she does not protect her daughter from being abused by a family member. Only in *Ahavti kol kakh* (I Loved So Much) (2000) does Rotem portray other options of motherhood.

58 See Shalit, "Me'ahorei ha-shavis."

59 Mimy Fegelson, "Zo'akot lihiyot et hayeihen ke-nashim" (Screaming to Live Their Lives as Women), *Ha'aretz*, book section, 7 January 1998.

60 Parush, *Nashim korot*, pp. 148–62.

61 In 1999 Yocheved Reisman shared the Bernstein Prize with Alona Kimchi. Kimchi's novel *Weeping Susannah* portrays the relationships between a daughter declared mentally disabled and the mother who cares for her at home. The obvious difference between the two novels, which share common themes, is the treatment of sexual/Oedipal issues.

62 Shirav, *Ktivah lo tamah*, pp. 266–9.

63 See Shalit, "Me'ahorei ha-shavis" and Karpel, "Hayeha ha-kfulim."

64 Shirav, *Ktivah lo tamah*, p. 267.

65 Sara Mills's *Discourses of Difference: An Analysis of Women's Travel Writing and Colonialism* (London, 1991), and Billie Melman's "Hofesh me'ahorei ha-ra'alah — Hitbonenut ba'aher' be-me'ot ha-18 veha-19: Nashim ma'araviyot al nashim yam tikhoniyot" (Freedom behind the Veil — Viewing the "Other" in the Eigtheenth and Nineteenth Centuries: Western Women Look at Mediterranean Women), in Azmon (ed.), *Eshnav le-hayehen shel nashim*, pp. 225–44, discuss the differences between nineteenth-century male and female writing about the Orient. They are relevant to this article because in many ways the perception of the "veiled" body/life of Orthodox women is similar to that of Oriental women. Sensationalizing the writing of Orthodox women derives from similar motivations. The fundamental difference is the fact that Orthodox women are exposed through their own writing. Nevertheless, Mills's and Melman's analysis of female travel writing about the Orient is useful, providing a model for this discussion by highlighting the access of women travelers to Oriental women's life and hence the particularity of their accounts and the diversity of their perceptions and the women they observed.

"Information about women is necessarily information about men": On Iris Parush's *Reading Women*

Tova Cohen

In the 1920s, when Virginia Woolf browsed the British Museum's shelves of history books, she was struck by the number of biased descriptions of women written by men, naming the authors "angry professors."[1] As a matter of fact, feminine history was already beginning to be written, with considerable achievements, precisely in her time and place.[2] It was then that the discovery of women as a distinct group, possessing a shared identity and a history of their own, led to an unprecedented exposure of new information and a reconceptualization of the historical processes of change.

The new feminist historiography of the 1970s, which emerged after 30 years of regression in the field, stressed the need for a "history of women" that would be studied and taught separately. The theoretical justification for this approach was based on two considerations. One was the need to compensate for the absence of women from classic historiography by providing a balanced historical account. The other was the assumption that men and women do not share the same historical experience. Since the mid-1980s, however, the notion of feminist history has changed significantly, with the concept of gender being introduced as the major paradigm of historical descriptions. In the words of the feminist historian, Joan Scott:

> "Gender" as a substitute for "women" is used to suggest that information about women is necessarily information about men, that one implies the study of the other. ... The world of women is part of the world of men. ... To study women in isolation perpetuates the fiction that one sphere, the experience of one sex, has little or nothing to do with the other.[3]

Iris Parush's *Reading Women: The Benefit of Marginality in Nineteenth Century Eastern European Jewish Society* perfectly fits this definition.[4] By retrieving forgotten female figures and unfamiliar stories from the diverse texts that she has investigated, Parush has indeed written a "history of women." Yet, at the core of her study lies the attempt to provide a new description of the entire *Haskalah* (Hebrew Enlightenment) revolution, by viewing it from the perspective of a new argument about the role played by women in its process of development.

Even without reconceptualizing the development of the *Haskalah*, Parush's book makes a very meaningful contribution to the historiography of the Jewish woman, which has hitherto lagged behind the achievements of feminist historiography in Europe and America. Although the history of Jewish women has recently begun to be written, it confronts especially difficult problems as a result of the dearth of sources.[5] Traditional Jewish culture, which concentrated on the spiritual and public life of men, marginalized the social and spiritual world of women. Consequently, the uncovering of Jewish feminine history — far more than its European counterpart — involves intensive "resistant" reading of the canonical sources, aimed at extracting as much information as possible about the history of women.[6]

As far as the nineteenth century is concerned, the absence of historical accounts of Jewish women in Eastern Europe is especially striking — given the important connection between the story of the Jewish women in the new *Yishuv* (pre-state Jewish community in Palestine) and in twentieth-century Israel, on the one hand, and that of their Eastern European spiritual mothers of the nineteenth century, on the other. Thus, for instance, there exists an important connection between Jewish feminism (under the influence of Russian Socialism) at the end of the nineteenth century and the first female pioneers in the land of Israel;[7] and, similarly, between the first women to write in Hebrew during the *Haskalah* period and the first Hebrew women writers in the land of Israel.[8] A different sort of connection, crucial for the understanding of contemporary Ultra-Orthodox women, is that which Jewish religious Orthodox society establishes between the current Ultra-Orthodox feminine ideal and that of these women's great grandmothers, who lived in East European towns.[9]

Most of the few studies hitherto devoted to the relatively recent history of women in the nineteenth century have focused on the figure of the traditional woman in the East European *shtetl*. Some such studies address this subject with reference to the issue of family (as do the books written by Zborowski and Herzog, Knaani, and Biale, as well as Etkes's discussion of the family life of the "lomdim" (learning) circles in Lithuania).[10] For others (such as Stahl-Weinberg and Hyman) the study of traditional Jewish society serves as a background for the history of those women who emigrated from Eastern Europe at the beginning of the twentieth century.[11] Very few studies specifically discuss the traditional women in nineteenth-century Eastern

Europe. Those that do, focus on such aspects as women's education and their age of marriage (as particularly exemplified in Stampfer's articles), or their spiritual life (Rappoport-Albert's article on women in Hasidism and some chapters in Weissler's book on women's prayers [tehinot]).[12]

Until recently, nothing had been said about the place of women in the major cultural revolution generated by the Haskalah — the movement that impacted the life of East European Jewry in the nineteenth century. This absolute silence was broken in 1993 by Feiner's important pioneering article on modern Jewish women and the Haskalah movement.[13] In analyzing the Haskalah attitude towards women, Feiner became the first scholar to present the reality of maskilot — women devotees of the Haskalah. In this respect, his article may be ascribed to the first category of historical writing indicated above. Rather than attempting to transform the historiography of the entire Haskalah, its aim was to fill the gaps in our knowledge about certain aspects related to the position of women. This is also true of Balin's more recently published work, in which she uncovers the existence of maskilot who wrote in Hebrew and Russian.[14]

Parush's book adds a great deal of information to this almost neglected field and herein lies her most important accomplishment. Displaying considerable industry, talent and fluency, Parush pieces together the details she gleans from autobiographical and literary texts written mainly by men, and out of the reflections produced through the masculine prism she manages to draw captivating portraits of women. The forgotten figures of maskilot from various circles and different periods of time in the nineteenth century vividly emerge from her book. Amongst the characters we meet are: "Grandma Lea" (who is depicted in the memoirs of Yehiel Isaiah Tronk, Poland) and her daughter Itka: the grandmother who found "hours of comfort … thanks to the Yiddish books of tales" and the daughter "who found interest in [Hebrew] grammar and the rationalist satire of the maskilim [male devotees of the Haskalah]" (p. 158). No less fascinating is "Ettil, the Rabbi's daughter," namely Esther Aaronsohn-Hurgin, who ran a sort of a transit hostel for girls who had left home to pursue their studies, as described by Citron in his Anashim ve-sofrim (People and Writers):

> In her day, she was the first, and possibly the only woman, among the intelligent maidens of Minsk who made a decent living from her labor without being dependent on her parents' support. In particular, she was interested in the plight of suffering girls who resented the restrictions imposed by their "narrow-minded, bourgeois" parents and longed for freedom, light, and the wide world. She was touched by the fate of her

wretched friends and this is what urged her to take the treatment of run-
aways under her wings. (p. 182)

Page after page of Parush's book is peopled with nineteenth-century female
characters, each of whom inspires admiration for her strength and courage, her
intelligence and the education she acquired. The abstract concepts of
"traditional women" and "*maskilot*" assume faces and bodies, souls and a story;
in this gallery, women readers can even find Jewish feminine figures — the
counterparts of their own great-grandmothers — with whom they can identify.[15]

Furthermore, Parush's book dispels the great void in our knowledge of
nineteenth-century women; the entire field now becomes mapped with details
and processes. We learn about the exclusion of the Jewish woman from the
traditional world of learning, the development of girls' schools, and above all
about women who read texts in Yiddish, German, French and Hebrew. The
majority of the facts are known to experts in the period, but the thickness of
the details, together with their rich illustration by excerpts from memoiristic
literature, creates a rich and novel totality.

The descriptive passages that Parush anthologizes from personal memoirs
are particularly vivid and appealing. They depict the groups of women who,
together, read Yiddish literature, ranging from *Tzeinah u-re'einah* (a collection
of weekly biblical readings in Yiddish, for women) to translated novels. What
is important is not just this habit itself but also its influence on, for instance,
the young boys who were to become writers, such as Scharfstein (p. 140) and
Sheikevitz. The latter not only recollected how avidly his mother read the
Yiddish rendition of *Arabian Nights* but also how she shared her reading
experiences with other members of the family (p. 143).

Similarly, while there is no novelty in Parush's account of the girls' school
experiences, the historical facts assume a face and vitality through the
descriptions written by the girls themselves, which Parush collects and cites.
Thus, for instance, the graceful depiction of the girls' school in Kishinev,
which appeared in *Ha-Melitz* in 1863, juxtaposes this pleasant institution with
the unpleasant *heder* attended by the boys:

> In spacious rooms that were clean and pure, far away from human noise
> and the bustle of cities, the girls are sitting comfortably, dressed in
> European attire, ready to attend to their studies, which are presented in
> a correct and proper order. The voice of the cruel *belfer* is not heard....
> No girl is crying because the teacher, who is incapable of discerning
> between his right and left hands, is cursing her for not being able to
> follow his words.... What is heard is the voice of a cultured and

understanding teacher, who speaks straightforward, honest words, and the voice of a girl that tells her instructive teacher and tutor what she has learned and understood! (p. 89)

The major historiographic importance of Parush's book lies in its principal purpose: a description of the gender history of literacy during the *Haskalah* period. Hitherto, and with a large measure of justice, the Hebrew *Haskalah* has been considered a masculine movement: it was thought to have produced texts written strictly by men and for men, within a framework of masculine fraternity.[16] Feiner was the first to show that some women tried to participate in the Hebrew *Haskalah* by acquiring reading and writing skills in Hebrew and even publishing their own writings in that language. Parush, however, goes even further. In her opinion, it was the cultural "marginality" of women — namely their double exclusion: from the study of Torah and of Hebrew, and from the *Haskalah* movement — that proved to be their greatest advantage. Because they did not study Torah, they became the family breadwinners and a knowledge of foreign languages was considered an asset to their education. Moreover, since girls were not obliged to study Torah (indeed, were forbidden to do so) their schooling was much more lenient than that of boys. Free from the constraints of *heder* studies, they enjoyed the opportunity to acquire what schooling was offered to them (reading and writing in Yiddish) in the relaxed atmosphere of the home. Most salient of all, they were allowed to study foreign languages, a practice that was considered superfluous and harmful for the boys. It is true that most of the women did not know Hebrew and were hence relegated to the periphery of the Hebrew literary *Haskalah*. Nonetheless, they became educated and their knowledge expanded to reading Yiddish and modern European languages.

Parush argues that, as a rule and as far as European culture was concerned, women were more educated than men. They read considerably more modern European literature and were more familiar with the European way of life than were men. In fact, the very existence of women readers "suggested a constant presence of a subversive element in Jewish society" (p. 189). Moreover, in many cases the women were the active "agents of change and modernization."[17] They set an example to their brothers and sons in the formation of new reading habits. They also exerted an initial, important influence on the men in their milieu by pointing in the direction of European education. From the socio-literary point of view, contends Parush, it is erroneous to restrict our investigations to the impact of the Hebrew canonical literature on its exclusively male readership. All readings, in all languages, "contributed to the processes of modernization and secularization within

Jewish society" (p. 25). Even though women's reading lay at the "margins" of the system, and was thus far-removed from the prestigious *Haskalah* center, women still played an important role in the processes of Enlightenment, modernization, and secularization.

This description of women's role in the *Haskalah* alters both our knowledge about women and our perception of the way the entire Enlightenment process unfolded. We can now appreciate how intricate this process was. Contrary to the impression that the *Haskalah* was a purely "masculine" movement, both sexes in fact operated and exerted a reciprocal influence on each other. The exclusion of women from the dominant culture (by the masculine hegemonic center) led to their cultural marginality and this is precisely what facilitated their European acculturation. Once acculturated, these women, in turn, exerted an important influence on the Jewish world at large and on men in particular, thereby taking advantage of their marginality. They specifically impacted men by acquainting them with the world of the European Enlightenment. They also established new social patterns of behavior, such as rejecting arranged marriages and running away from home to pursue their studies. Nevertheless, women's marginality was to their advantage only as far as their reading in Yiddish and foreign languages was concerned. Hebrew education, according to Parush, remained the protected sphere of men.

In Parush's study, the detailed portrait of nineteenth-century "reading women" becomes a tool for a renewed understanding of gender roles in the history of the Enlightenment and, by extension, of the contemporary socio-historical processes. Hence her book amounts to more than "a history of women." It involves the writing of gender history based on an interpretation of the sources that seeks to bring women from the periphery to the center, thus creating a new balance in historical depictions.

The interpretation of pertinent sources plays a major role in a historiography of this kind, which is entirely based on written sources. Since they are autobiographic descriptions, these sources (mostly produced by men) are almost professedly subjective, and on the whole they reflect a masculine point of view.[18] Hence Parush has had to engage in an interpretive effort designed to "extract" knowledge about women from male-oriented texts (see her remarks on p. 56), in addition to cross-collating a great deal of information from varied sources so as to arrive at "facts" that are as solid as possible. She accomplishes all of this. Nonetheless, I would like to suggest that her interpretation of sources is not the only one possible; a different interpretation may somewhat change the nuances of the picture she portrays. It is not my intention to challenge Parush's main conclusions as to the "contribution" of women's marginality to their education and European acculturation and the impact of this process on the development of the *Haskalah* as a whole. Yet it seems to me that Parush has failed to substantiate some of her views about the details of the processes. In the pages that follow I will focus on three issues: first, the policy of literacy and rabbinical control; second, whether the woman who served as the family breadwinner was indeed also a "reading woman"; third, the Hebrew *maskilot* and the "principle of marginality."

The Policy of Literacy and Rabbinical Control over Society and Culture

One of Parush's basic assumptions is the existence of a deliberate rabbinical policy designed to control the level of literacy within traditional Jewish society. In her view, this control possessed two goals. The first was to reinforce "the position and prestige of a restricted scholarly elite" (p. 31). The second was to bar the access of those trained within the system to "dangerous corpuses of knowledge" (p. 32), such as the Hebrew language, the Scriptures, *Haskalah* literature, and, naturally, modern European languages.

The elite attained its first goal by excluding most of the population from educational frameworks that provided higher learning. While all men in Jewish society did indeed attend a *heder*, where they studied the rudiments of Hebrew reading and writing, only a gifted minority went on to *yeshivot* (Talmudic academies) and attained the rank of scholars capable, among other things, of fully understanding a Hebrew canonical text. The girls received no formal education in Hebrew and the reading of canonical texts, though a considerable portion of them learned how to read and write in Yiddish (in Hebrew characters) in various private, voluntary frameworks. It is no wonder, then, that only a small minority among the men (and almost none of the women) took part in the traditional canonical activity of studying Talmud and *Halakhah* (Jewish law) while at the same time participating in the Hebrew *Haskalah* movement. It follows that this was not an egalitarian literate society, but rather a society in which literacy was limited to a restricted elite that consciously tried to keep knowledge — a source of power — to itself.

As suggested by all the accounts available to us, the Talmudic scholars undoubtedly constituted a restricted and elitist group. Indeed, for most of the Jewish public, men and women alike, Talmudic texts, as well as the canonical texts of the *Haskalah*, were simply inaccessible. But these facts in themselves do not indicate a deliberate policy on the part of the elite to maintain its power by exclusion. Nor does Parush provide any proof that any such conscious or unconscious "policy" did indeed exist.

In my opinion, it is possible to posit an almost contrary argument, at least as far as the education of men is concerned: opening the portals of study in the *heder* to all boys made the study of Torah accessible to them all. Guided by the rabbinic saying, "Take heed of the poor, for Torah emerges from them" (Babylonian Talmud, Tractate *Nedarim* 81a), the community leaders ensured that a low socio-economic status would not disadvantage the gifted student, and that *yeshivah* (talmudic reading) students were maintained and fed by the community members and organizations.[19] The rich certainly studied under more comfortable conditions and were taught by better teachers, but their relatively high economic and even social status (affiliation with the scholarly elite) did not of itself guarantee scholastic success. Moreover, success in the study of Torah was the poor boy's route to economic progress, for in a society in which Torah study reigned supreme, scholarship was the highest asset for a boy who desired an arranged marriage with a rich daughter. The *"lomdim* circles,"* to borrow Etkes's categorization, were restricted and elitist, but this state of affairs derived from the difficulties presented by total dedication to intellectual and abstract studies, for which only a handful of students are suited. Of itself, this circumstance does not constitute proof that the gates of the house of study were deliberately closed by the elite.

Parush's argument that women were deliberately excluded from Torah study in order to deny them access to the centers of power also seems to me exaggerated. Women certainly were excluded from Torah study, but not necessarily as part of a conscious attempt to keep them away from the communal centers of power. Intentional exclusion must be grounded in the assumption that the excluded individual is likely to get "dangerously" close to the center of power. In the consciousness of the rabbinical elite, however, women could not be considered to represent such a threat. The longstanding *halakhic* and social exclusion of women from Torah study was based on an ancient saying attributed to R. Eliezer: "If a man gives his daughter knowledge of Torah, it is as though he taught her lechery" (*Mishnah, Sotah* 3:4).[20] The basic notion was that women were *incapable of studying Torah*. As the Maharil (R. Jacob Halevi Moellin, of the fifteenth century) generalized, following Maimonides: "The sages commanded that a man shall not instruct his daughter in the Torah, because most women have no mind to be instructed therein" (*Mishneh Torah, Hilkhot Talmud Torah* 1:13).[21] If anything, the assumption that women were excluded from the study of Torah to avert the "danger" of their access to the source of power has an anachronistic ring: it is more in line with the apprehensions voiced by the male-dominated rabbinical establishment in the late twentieth century, at a time when women were showing proficiency in Torah studies.[22]

Similarly anachronistic, in my opinion, is Parush's statement that "the traditional educational system devoted itself to reinforcing the "patriarchal gender hierarchy" (p. 63). According to her account, Jewish society violated the contemporary accepted gender division, which assigned the public sphere to men and the private sphere to women. Once married, women became the main breadwinners for their family, they were placed in the public sphere, whereas the men were restricted to "the closed domestic space of the house of study." According to her hypothesis, the educational system strove to restore the old balance by maintaining the conventional patriarchal division, at least as far as Torah study and the intellectual life of the community were concerned. In this area, the woman was confined to the home while the man was active in the public sphere: the house of study.

This explanation seems to me problematic. Partly this is because, in the same paragraph, Parush defines the house of study both as a "closed domestic space" and as a "public sphere." Besides reflecting some logical fallacy, this confusion seems to me to result from the fact that the process is viewed from the outside rather than from within. From the non-Jewish European perspective, the fact that the woman rather than the man constituted the family breadwinner did indeed violate the conventional, patriarchal division of spheres, which in nineteenth-century Europe was considered a socio-familial ideal. In fact, the *maskilim* who adopted this European ethos strongly criticized the inverted norm of their own society.[23] Yet we have no basis for assuming that the *lomdim* themselves considered this situation to be an aberration, requiring some "balancing" in order to restore social equilibrium.

I suggest that the opposite is true. The fact that the Jewish male scholar seemed to the *maskilim* (as he does, perhaps, to us) to be "suffering" from the given socio-economic imbalance does not justify an inference that traditional Jewish society considered it anomalous for the wife to maintain her scholarly husband. Nor does Parush provide any proof to substantiate such an inference. Citing Margaret Mead's conclusions, anthropologist Zimbalist Rosaldo makes the point that in a patriarchal society "the prestige values always attach to the activities of men."[24] Since traditional Jewish society regarded Torah study as the most important of all activities, Torah scholars necessarily occupied the apex of the social hierarchy. That being the case, there existed no need to "balance" anything. Far from being a "closed domestic space," the house of study served as the most important male-oriented public sphere.

Consequently, the education of girls to restrict their spiritual lives to the home was a direct extension of their exclusion from Torah study and not an expression of an attempt to "balance" their dominance as breadwinners.

Let us now turn to the second goal Parush attributes to the scholarly rabbinical elite: forbidding the systematic study of Hebrew grammar and foreign languages. This prohibition might indeed have been motivated by opposition to the *Haskalah*, which the Orthodox community increasingly perceived as posing a real danger. Yet, Parush's statement that "the traditional educational system sought to produce *deliberate ignorance of the Hebrew language*" (p. 63, my emphasis) seems to me too far-fetched and does not do justice to the motivations of the system. Hebrew was certainly considered a "holy language" and did function as what Parush calls "linguistic capital" (ibid.); however, the restrictions imposed on its use were the consequence of the fact that it was not a spoken language; they did not reflect an intent to restrict the number of Hebrew readers. The rabbis must have objected to the study of Hebrew because on the whole they dismissed (and even despised)[25] any study that was not explicitly "Torah"; only much later did the study of Hebrew grammar became associated with the threat of the *Haskalah*. Moreover, the rabbis must have understood that a prohibition against the study of Hebrew grammar could only restrict *Haskalah*-oriented *writing*, it could not possibly prevent the *reading* of such texts. The level of Hebrew that every yeshivah student mastered during the course of his studies (not of the Talmud, which is mostly written in Aramaic, but certainly of its commentaries, which are partly written in Hebrew, as well as of the *Mishnah* and the halakhic literature) was certainly sufficient to allow for an understanding of the texts written by the *maskilim*. This point emerges from contemporary autobiographic accounts that describe how *Haskalah* literature was read without special linguistic preparation.[26] Moreover, the avoidance of Bible study was also not absolute. I find it hard to concur with Parush's assertion that "the practice of skipping [Scriptural] passages, prevented *heder* students from being familiar with the whole narrative context" (p. 69).[27] If anything, *heder* students, as well as most adult Jews, and certainly yeshivah students, regularly used to read the weekly portion of the Torah several times ("shnayim mikra ve-ehad targum": twice in Hebrew and once in the translated version). In addition, they read the *haftarot* (the weekly portions from the Books of Prophets), the *megilot* (the five biblical scrolls recited on the festivals), and — naturally — the Psalms. Thus, even though the Bible was not studied in the yeshivah methodically, mainly because of the supreme importance attached to the study of the Talmud, large portions of it were read on a regular basis. As a result, the potential readership of Haskalah literature must have included all those who studied in yeshivot and who therefore understood a Hebrew text. This state of affairs was beyond the control of any rabbinical policy with respect to literacy.

The objection to the study of foreign languages certainly was intentional, but one must bear in mind that foreign languages (like secular studies in general, including Hebrew grammar) were never included in the traditional religious curriculum. This restrictive practice was undoubtedly rooted in the notion that the main obligation of all Jewish males was Torah study — to the exclusion of almost everything else, as Parush indicates elsewhere.[28] Therefore we would not expect foreign languages to have been *introduced* into the curriculum — least of all during the nineteenth century, when the combined effect of secularization, the Haskalah and European culture was perceived by the religious establishment as a major threat to the community.

In sum, Parush's description of the state of affairs at that time is correct: there certainly did exist an exclusive, male-dominated and scholarly-oriented elite, whose literacy was limited to religious texts. What remains unsubstantiated, however, is her claim that this situation resulted from a deliberate restrictive policy initiated by this elite.

Was the Female Breadwinner a "Reading Woman" Too?

As noted, the central thesis of Parush's book focuses on the "benefit" of female marginality. This thesis is grounded on a fact well known to students of the Haskalah, namely that in the nineteenth century (and, in fact, up to the Second World War) the Jewish woman was the major reader of non-Hebrew literature; it was she who read Yiddish and European languages.[29] Parush provides two explanations for the foreign-language literacy of the Jewish women. The first (especially typical of the traditional family) is instrumental: a knowledge of foreign languages was considered advantageous to women because it enabled them to conduct a greater range of commercial dealings and thereby to fulfill their role as the family's principal breadwinners (pp. 44–61). The second reason for allowing girls to study foreign languages is linked to the fact that traditional society did not consider them duty-bound to study Torah. Hence "the girls' opportunities to acquire modern education were much greater than those of the boys" (p. 79).

Here, too, Parush's account of women's literacy in Yiddish and foreign languages is acceptable. What is open to question, however, is her description of the process. In fact, two questions require more specific answers. One

concerns the precise identity of the "female breadwinner"; the second relates
to the identity of the woman who reads books in foreign languages.

Who was the "female breadwinner"?
According to Parush, the phenomenon of "the wife who maintains the family
and makes it possible for her husband to devote all his time to the study of
Torah and the fulfillment of his religious vocation" (p. 44) was rather
widespread, and originated in the ideal of Torah study as the man's primary
concern. This ideal dictated the behavioral norms of Jewish society:

> Even though in practice not all men were scholars.... Even though most
> men earned a living … the societal effort to fulfill the ideal vision was
> sufficient … to create norms of behavior that charged women with the
> responsibility of making a living. (p. 45)

Citing Jacob Katz as her source, Parush claims that in the nineteenth century
"this phenomenon was the rule."

Parush's description of this social *ideal* is correct and there certainly did
exist cases where the wife supported her husband so that he could devote
himself to Torah study. Yet, was this phenomenon really as prevalent as she
claims? In my opinion, it was in fact quite limited and in the main
characteristic of the "*lomdim* circles," initially in Lithuania and then elsewhere
in Eastern Europe. I base my contention first of all on a different reading of
the same source on which Parush bases her argument. What Katz in fact says
is that in the seventeenth and eighteenth centuries the figure of the *eshet hayil*,
the "woman of valor," was not as prevalent "as in Eastern Europe of the
nineteenth century."[30] It is surely far-fetched to invoke this statement as
support for the contention that "this phenomenon" had by the latter date
become "the rule."

Still more crucial is my different reading of the very texts cited by Parush.
True, all the texts that describe the businesswoman who supports her husband
(such as those written by Mendele, Kotik, Sheikevitz, Gottlober, and many
others) do indeed describe this state of affairs as if it were the rule. In my
opinion, however, these are biased descriptions, which — consciously or
unconsciously — excessively magnify the pervasiveness of this situation. As
far as we know, the phenomenon of the working wife who constituted the sole
provider for the family's material needs was restricted to the narrow, elitist
social stratum of the *lomdim* circles.[31] As I have demonstrated elsewhere, the
generalized descriptions of the *maskilim* must be attributed to the fact that
they themselves originated in these circles.[32] This was the kind of family with

which they were familiar and when writing about it they transformed the familiar into a sweeping generalization, as if it were the governing norm of Jewish society at large. To this must be added a point already made: only Talmudic scholars were capable of understanding and writing Hebrew *Haskalah* literature. This, in my opinion, is true of most of the authors of those testimonies on which Zborowski and Herzog, Knaani, and Stahl-Weinberg based their accounts. Those who wrote memoirs came from relatively enlightened circles which, in turn, were associated with the families of the *lomdim*.

Moreover, as Parush herself describes in detail, the *maskilim* were hostile to the division of roles that established the wife as the family provider. In waging an all-out war against the female breadwinner and her "idle husband," they must have intentionally exaggerated the prevalence of the phenomenon (see for instance Abraham Ber Gottlober's descriptions as cited by Parush on p. 46). They used the same approach in satirizing the businesswoman.[33]

The division of labor within Jewish families must have been more complex than is suggested by the *maskilim*'s own descriptions, and was largely determined by the socio-economic status of each specific family. In *lomdim* families, the wife did indeed maintain her husband; in middle- and upper-class families, the husband, usually a businessman, provided for the family while his wife was the homemaker; in lower-class families, which were the vast majority in the East European Jewish community, everyone worked: the husband, the wife, and — once they were old enough to do so — the children too.[34] Incidentally, a class-dependent division of labor along gender lines is also typical of the non-Jewish family in nineteenth-century Europe.[35]

Therefore it seems to me that *Haskalah* descriptions of the female breadwinner and her scholarly husband are misleading. They exaggerate the true extent of this phenomenon and cannot be adduced as a generally valid explanation for the Jewish woman's status in the family and in society at large.

Who Was the Woman Who Read Books in Foreign Languages?
Parush is correct to distinguish between women who read Yiddish and those who read modern European languages. In her opinion, both groups turned the marginality of their literacy into a social asset.

What emerges from Parush's presentation is that the daughters of the *maskilim* and those who belonged to the middle class were not the only women to read foreign languages. This phenomenon was also apparent in wider circles. Foreign languages were taught in the schools sponsored by the

Haskalah and these schools were attended by poor girls too (p. 90), since the knowledge of a foreign language was considered an asset to those who would need to make a living. (This is an extension of her earlier argument that during this period women were the breadwinners and therefore needed to know foreign languages [p. 45]). She then goes on to make the following generalization: "The female readers of foreign languages emerged from various circles of Jewish society, each with its own motive for teaching girls foreign languages" (p. 174). I consider this conclusion insufficiently substantiated. In fact, it can be refuted by a number of counter-arguments:

First of all, as I have already pointed out, women providers were not the norm in Jewish society as a whole. But even in cases where the woman was responsible for the family livelihood, and for this purpose needed to communicate in the local language, her knowledge of that language was merely superficial. It was limited to dealing with non-Jewish customers, or, in wealthier families, to commercial correspondence. Even if they could chat in the vernacular of their surrounding — or (had they attended school in their youth) even read and write other European languages — it is hard to believe that these women were readers of literature. The latter pastime would have required both a superior knowledge of a modern foreign language and considerable leisure time — neither of which most of them possessed.

Secondly, and more critically, all the sources about women who read European fiction, which Parush cites at length (e.g. on pp. 79, 176, 177, 179, 181, 184), portray girls of the Orthodox or *maskil* middle class — and this makes sense. These girls did indeed study foreign languages at home or at school and also had the time to read and "a room of their own" in which they could do so. Also relevant in this context is the rise in the age of marriage during the nineteenth century,[36] a trend whose result was that girls stayed in their parental home during some of their adult years too. In the wealthy families this was the time when most of them read foreign literature, and when those who were exceptional and courageous favored Hebrew literature. *Haskalah* writers themselves often point out that these young girls came from wealthy families and spent their leisure time reading "Schiller and Mickiewicz" with their teachers and "roaming the fields with them" (p. 76). Presumably, the married women who found time for reading were also members of the middle class. This is suggested by a description of a woman who used to read "novels in Yiddish and the *Voskhod* monthly in Russian" and was otherwise much involved in philanthropic activities: she was "a member of the committee for nursing poor parturient women and giving interest-free loans to shopkeepers." Hence women's reading of literature was not a phenomenon that emerged in "various circles." Rather, it was associated with the well-to-do middle class, in its various guises: assimilationists, *maskilim*, and Orthodox too.

It seems to me that Parush has exaggerated the scope of this phenomenon, though she herself observes that there were many women who read no literature, in any language whatsoever. Though apparently restrictive, the concept of "a Jewish woman in nineteenth-century Europe" is a problematic generalization. In depicting the important phenomenon that lies at the center of her study, Parush occasionally fails to do justice to differentiations between women who belonged to different circles and social classes — factors that are no less important than their shared feminine identity. After all, not all women were cast in the same mold. There were traditional women and assimilationist women. Moreover, women belonged to various classes,[37] with each class characterized by its own way of life and hence exposed to different levels of foreign acculturation. Neither was their standing in the family uniform. Even within the same social circle, women assumed a variety of roles during various stretches of time in the nineteenth century, and Parush does not seem to make sufficient distinctions between various time periods within the nineteenth century. The attitude of the establishment to women's reading must have changed with time. In this respect, surely there is a difference (as Parush herself stresses) between the climate of opinion in the first and last decades of the century.

In sum, it is difficult to speak of a uniform identity of "a Jewish woman versed in foreign languages." This makes problematic the entire equation: a female breadwinner equals a woman who knows foreign languages, equals a woman who reads European literature. Instead, we are left with an alternative and more specific equation: a nineteenth-century middle-class woman who has learned foreign languages equals a woman who reads foreign literature, equals a woman who is aware of the *Haskalah* and exerts an impact on her surrounding.

The Hebrew Maskilot *and the* "Principle of Marginality"

Chapter 8 of Parush's book focuses on the relatively small group of Hebrew women readers and in its first part describes the spread of this phenomenon during the *Haskalah* period. As in her previous chapters, Parush cites fascinating materials that depict the "biographies of reading." But in this part of the book she in addition cites texts written by those women readers who also became Hebrew writers. These texts illustrate the phenomenon — thereto granted little attention in Parush's book — of the Hebrew *maskilot*, which is described in detail on the basis of the same selection of texts adduced in Feiner's pioneering article.[38]

From the point of view of the history of Hebrew literature, the phenomenon of Hebrew *maskilot* (which encompasses over 25 women whose Hebrew writings are accessible to us, as well as an unknown number of Hebrew readers) is most important, as it challenges two widely accepted views. One is that *Haskalah* literature was *predominantly* masculine. The other is that women did not begin writing in Hebrew until the early twentieth century.[39] Against that background, I think it is highly important to explore this issue by gathering and discussing the relevant texts.[40]

As Parush herself correctly points out (p. 225), however, this discussion is hardly relevant in a book that deals with "the benefit of marginality." Parush argues that, in the case of the *maskilot*, women's marginality conferred no benefit, since "women's entry into the spheres of the Hebrew language was subject to constant supervision" (ibid.). In my opinion, the gulf between Hebrew-reading women and those who read Yiddish and foreign languages was much deeper, going beyond the issue of "supervision." There was a difference in principle between the two groups of women. Those versed in Yiddish and European culture took advantage of their marginal place in traditional Jewish culture to advance their intellectual development (which is the subject matter of Parush's study). But another group consisted of women who struggled *against* their cultural marginality and tried to carve out their own position within the hegemonic center — at the heart of the Hebrew *Haskalah* writing.

Describing the apologetic position of the women who wrote in Hebrew, Parush states that "they felt as if they were trespassers." Indeed, the "anxiety of authorship"[41] haunts the Hebrew writing of many of these women. Yet, despite the anxious and apologetic nature of their behavior, they used their knowledge of Hebrew not only to read texts written by others but also to write their own. Several corresponded with the most prominent *Haskalah* writers (Devora ha-Ephrati corresponded with Abraham Mapu; several young women wrote to Y. L. Gordon; Miriam Markel Mosessohn corresponded regularly with some important contemporary *maskilim*), and some (for instance Bertha Rabinowitz and Sara Navinski) published their personal Hebrew letters in the Hebrew journals of the time. Women in this group also wrote essays in which they expressed their views on, among others matters, "Haskalah" issues (as did Merka Altschuler) and on topics of women's emancipation (Sara Navinski,

Toybe Segal). A few even authored literary texts (Rachel Morpurgo and Sara Shapira wrote poetry, while Sara Foner Menkin wrote prose works).

Parush claims that women's entry into the spheres of the Hebrew language "took place under circumstances in which the Hebrew language lost its appeal ... and its value in terms of cultural capital declined" (p. 210). She finds proof for this evaluation in Gottlober's editorial footnote to Sara Navinski's published letter (p. 209), in which he writes: "And the young men of Israel, who turn their backs on the language of their ancestors, shall see and be ashamed of themselves and the *maskilim* of our people ... will praise her deeds at the [city] gates." During that period (circa 1877), some contemporary *maskilim* did indeed sense this rejection of the modern Hebrew *Haskalah* (a sense that finds expression in, for instance, Gordon's poem "Le-mi ani amel" [For Whom Do I Toil?], which is cited by Parush at the beginning of Chapter 8.) Nevertheless, at that time the *Haskalah* was still far from constituting "a forsaken stronghold." The hegemonic center — of writers and readers alike — was still an exclusively male territory, and women writers treated it as such. (Gottlober himself mentions, alongside those who "turn their back" on *Haskalah* literature, the *maskilim*, the enlightened male readers, whom he addresses as the audience of his writing.) Moreover, the penetration of women into Hebrew commenced not in the 1880s but rather in the 1860s, when the Hebrew *Haskalah* reached its peak. It was then that the writings of Devora ha-Ephrati, Miriam Markel Mosessohn, and Rachel Morpurgo made their appearance on the *Haskalah* literary stage.

These women, together with later Hebrew *maskilot* who engaged in writing, had to overcome three hurdles. The first was universal, and one that confronted all women who attempted to engage in literary pursuits within their androcentric society: the widespread notion that literary writing was a masculine activity, totally inappropriate for women.[42] The two other hurdles were unique to Jewish society. One was the linguistic obstacle imposed by the perception of Hebrew as a "holy language" meant to be studied exclusively by men. The other was the notion of *tzni'ut* (chastity), which especially in traditional Jewish society reinforced the segregation between the sexes and turned the silencing of women's voices in the public sphere into a religious prohibition. Most Hebrew *maskilot* were aware of the giant stride they had taken by moving from the "legitimate" margins allotted to them into the very male center of the *Haskalah*. This is precisely what generated their anxiety. As Miriam Markel Mosessohn put it: "[The very thought] that a woman dares put her head between these mountains — why, I am soon to be stoned."[43]

Notwithstanding her explicit statement to the contrary, Parush does nevertheless attempt to establish a link between the Haskalah-oriented activity of the Hebrew-reading women and their marginality in traditional society. But her efforts are unsuccessful. Let us examine the evidence. Parush quotes a passage from the memoirs of Mordechai ben Hillel Ha-Cohen, in which a maskil Hebrew teacher describes how he made use of the "women's territory, which was open to foreign influences and safe from social supervision" (p. 215). In my reading, this quotation only proves that the teacher took advantage of the privacy of the "girls' room" in order to write on the Sabbath (an activity strictly forbidden by Jewish law). But there exists not the slightest intimation that the teaching of the Hebrew language, which is described in the next excerpt ("In addition to writing, I taught the young girl Hebrew as well, which she learned successfully"), took place — as Parush suggests it did — "behind the parents' back."

Parush's second proof of a link between women's territory and Hebrew Haskalah (p. 225) is likewise problematic: the fact that the Hovevei Sefat Ever (Lovers of Hebrew) in Saratov "used to convene in the women's gallery of the synagogue" does not prove any particular link between their activities and the "feminine space" as such. All it indicates is that the women's gallery was perceived as a less holy place and therefore was found to be more suitable for meetings that did not belong in the synagogue.[44]

The principle of "the benefit of marginality" thus indeed had no bearing whatsoever on the Hebrew maskilot. But this was not the outcome of "close supervision," as suggested by Parush. Rather, what made that principle inoperative as far as this group was concerned, was the fact that the very nature of their preoccupation with Hebrew was subversive, as it challenged the exclusion of women from the maskil-oriented cultural center. Not incidentally, the existence of such "close supervision" over Hebrew maskilot is not proven. In fact, the opposite is true: their texts demonstrate the large measure of freedom they possessed, and dared to exploit.[45] The very texts that Parush herself cites demonstrate that they articulated their opinions on Haskalah literature as well as their own feminist views, preaching for women's education and professionalization. This measure of self-confidence, which existed in spite of the understandable anxiety they felt upon courageously invading the male-dominated and maskil-oriented hegemonic center, can easily be explained. I would suggest that it resulted from the fact (also mentioned by Parush) that these women did not have to rebel against their families. As some of them state explicitly, their knowledge of Hebrew was in fact initiated and cultivated by their maskil fathers.[46]

Hence, while it is true that the Hebrew *maskilot* were "reading women," the phenomenon they represent does not indicate the *benefit* of marginality but rather a *rebellion* against it.

* * *

Thus to debate with Parush about the nuances of the processes she describes is not to undermine the solid and impressive basis of her study. She is to be warmly commended for managing to fill the gaps in our knowledge about women's education in the nineteenth century and for her achievement in writing a gender history of the literacy that served as the sociocultural basis of the *Haskalah* movement. This is a fine book, whose importance extends beyond its value to the expert reader who is interested in the history of the *Haskalah* period or in gender history in general. Its appeal to a much broader readership lies in its rich tableau of fascinating excerpts from hundreds of texts that bring to life East European Jewish women of the *Haskalah* period.

NOTES

1   Virginia Woolf, *A Room of One's Own* (1929; London, 1967), pp. 39–49.

2   "Classic" feminist historiography developed, mainly in England, in the period 1870–1940. Billie Melman, "Le-malakh ha-historiyah yesh min: Historiyah shel nashim, historiyah ve-politikah, 1880–1993" (Angelus Novus: Women's History, History and Politics, 1880–1993), *Zmanim*, No. 46–47 (1993), pp. 18–33, notes 34 women historians who made important contributions during this period.

3   Joan W. Scott, "Gender: A Useful Category of Historical Analysis," *The American Historical Review*, Vol. 91, No. 5 (1986), p. 1056.

4   *Nashim korot: Yitronah shel ha-shuliyut ba-hevrah ha-yehudit be-mizrah eiropah ba-me'ah ha-tsha-esrei* (Tel Aviv, 2001). (Page references to this book will be given within the text; translations from Hebrew are my own.)

5   For a survey of Jewish feminist historiography see Paula E. Hyman, "Feminist Studies and Modern Jewish History," in Lynn Davidman and Shelly Tenenbaum (eds.), *Feminist Perspectives on Jewish Studies* (New Haven, 1994), pp. 120–39.

6   For an instructive example of how feminine history is "extracted" from the canonical sources, see Avraham Grossman, *Hasidot u-mordot: Nashim yehudiyot be-Eiropah be-yemei ha-beinayim* (Pious and Rebellious: Jewish Women in Europe in the Middle Ages) (Jerusalem, 2001).

7   The impact of Russian feminism on the pioneer women of the first *aliyot*, the first waves of "immigration to Israel," is manifested, for example, in the figure of Olga Belkind, who began her career by promoting women's professional education in the spirit of contemporary Russian feminism. (See her letter of thanks to the rich family of Peterburg that financed her obstectrics studies; in this letter, which she published in *Ha-Shahar*, a *Haskalah* periodical, in 1876, she also suggests the importance of women's work.) Belkind was to become the wife of Joshua Hankin, of the first *Aliyah*, who was highly involved in land redemption. See Shmuel Feiner, "Ha-ishah ha-yehudit ha-modernit: mikreh mivhan be-yahasei ha-haskalah veha-modernah" (The Modern Jewish Woman: A Test-Case in the Relationship between *Haskalah* and Modernity), in Israel Bartal and Yeshayahu Gafni (eds.), *Eros eirosin ve-isorim: Miniyut u-*

mishpahah be-historiyah (Sexuality and the Family in History) (Jerusalem, 1998), p. 298.

8   This connection finds a personal-biographic expression in the biography of Nehama Feinstein, who as a devotee of Hebrew literature used to correspond in Hebrew with Y. L. Gordon. (See the Gordon Archives, the National and University Library in Jerusalem, Manuscripts). Later she became a Hebrew writer and a fighter for women's rights in Rishon Le-Zion, the first town in the new *Yishuv*. On Puchatschevski, see the chapter "Nefesh me-Rishon le-Zion homiyah: Nehamah Puchatschevski" (A Soul Yearning from Rishon Le-Zion), in Nurit Govrin, *Dvash mi-sela: Mehkarim be-sifrut eretz-yisrael* (Honey From the Rock: Studies in Eretz-Israel Literature) (Tel Aviv, 1989), pp. 114–71.

9   See, for instance, the following statement voiced in the convention of Agudat Yisrael Women (1954): "Back to the grandmother. We must follow in the footsteps of our grandmothers. Our mothers, in as much as we love and cherish them, have absorbed too much of the fragrance of European culture.... Hence we cannot accept our mothers as models of perfect spiritual education. Therefore our motto must be: Back to the grandmother. We must walk in her ways and she shall serve as an illuminating example for us." Cited in Menahem Friedman, "Ha-ishah ha-haredit" (The Ultra-Orthodox Women), in Yael Azmon (ed.), *Eshnav le-hayeihen shel nashim be-hevrot yehudiyot* (A View into the Lives of Women in Jewish Societies) (Jerusalem, 1995), pp. 273–90.

10 Mark Zborowski and Elizabeth Herzog, *Life Is with People: The Jewish Little-Town of Eastern Europe* (New York, 1972); David Knaani, *Ha-batim she-hayu: Prakim be-havayat ha-mishpahah ha-yehudit ba-dorot ha-aharonim ba-sifrut ha-ivrit veha-yidit* (Studies in the History of the Jewish Family) (Tel Aviv, 1986); David Biale, *Eros and the Jews* (New York, 1992); Immanuel Etkes, "Marriage and Torah Study among *Lomdim* in Lithuania in the Nineteenth Century," in David Kraemer (ed.), *The Jewish Family: Metaphor and Memory* (New York and Oxford, 1989), pp. 153–78.

11 Sydney Stahl Weinberg, *The World of Our Mothers: The Lives of Jewish Immigrant Women* (Chapel Hill, NC, 1988); Paula E. Hyman, *Gender and Assimilation in Modern Jewish History* (Seattle, 1995).

12 Shaul Stampfer, "Gender Differentiation and Education of the Jewish Women in Nineteenth Century Eastern Europe," *Polin*, Vol. 7 (1992), pp. 63–87; idem, "The Social Meaning of Premature Marriages in Eastern Europe in the Nineteenth Century," in Alan Mendelson and Chone Shmeruk (eds.), *P. Glickson Memorial Volume: A Collection of Studies on the Jews of Poland* (Jerusalem, 1987); A. Rappoport-Albert, "On Women in Hassidism: S. A Horodezky and the Maid of Ludmir Tradition," in Ada Rappoport-Albert and Steven J. Zipperstein (eds.), *Jewish History* (London, 1988), pp. 495–525; Chava Wiessler, *Voices of the Matriarchs: Listening to the Prayers of Early Modern Jewish Women* (Boston, 1998).

13 Feiner, "Ha-ishah ha-yehudit ha-modernit," first published in *Zion*, Vol. 58, No. 4 (1993), pp. 453–99. Biale's *Eros and the Jews* contains a description of the *maskil*'s attitude towards women but refers only sparingly to the women themselves.

14 Carole Balin, *To Reveal Our Hearts: Jewish Women Writers in Tsarist Russia* (Cincinnati, 2000).

15 See for instance the opening of Judith Baumel's review of this book: "It was said of Dvorah, my grandmother's mother, who was born in Bucovina in the 1870s, that she could read in four languages; she was the progenitor of a dynasty of women that extends to this day, and all of them have been afflicted with the disease of reading" (*Ha'aretz*, Books Section, 15 August 2001).

16 Biale suggests that the masculine fraternity of the *maskilim* was also motivated by biographic-psychological causes related to failure and frustration in their relations with women. See Biale, *Eros and the Jews*, p. 158.

17 In her *Gender and Assimilation in Modern Jewish History*, Hyman describes a similar process involving the Americanization of the Jews who immigrated to the United States early in the twentieth century.

18 On the problematics of knowledge about women that is "filtered to us through masculine autobiographies" see Biale, *Eros and the Jews*, p. 156.

19 "The poor ... whose parents cannot afford to provide for them — are to be maintained by the townsmen ... and the poor student need not maintain himself — all Israel must provide for him." Zvi Scharfstein, *Toldot ha-hinukh be-Yisrael ba-dorot ha-aharonim* (The History of Jewish Education in Recent Generations), Vol. 1 (New York, 1945), p. 10. Already in the seventeenth and eighteenth centuries, yeshivah students used to receive their meals in the homes of various community members on fixed, alternate days of the week; see Jacob Katz, *Masoret u-mashber* (Tradition and Crisis) (Jerusalem, 1986), p. 225. This common practice continued in the nineteenth century (See Scharfstein, *Toldot ha-hinukh ha-yehudi*, p. 12). For a vivid description of the hardships that this arrangement inflicted on the yeshivah students, see Peretz Smolenskin, *Ha-to'eh be-darkhei he-hayim* (The Wanderer in the Ways of Life), Vol. 2 (Warsaw, 1901) ch. 3, pp. 23–6.

20 For details of the *halakhic* rulings that forbid women to study Torah, see Eliyahu. G. Ellinson, *Bein ha-ishah le-yotzrah* (Between Woman and Her Creator) (Jerusalem, 1984), pp. 143–57. Naturally, this prohibition is not exclusive to the nineteenth century, as implied perhaps in Parush's statement on p. 75: "Many of the Ultra-Orthodox in the nineteenth century interpreted this as an explicit prohibition against teaching girls the Torah."

21 Amnon Shapira and Yehezkel Cohen, *Ha-ishah be-tmurot ha-zman* (Woman in Changing Times) (Tel Aviv, 1984), p. 41.

22 On present-day women who study Torah and on the Israeli educational institutions designed to engage women in the study of Torah, see Tamar El-Or, *Ba-pesah ha-ba: Nashim ve-oryanut ba-tziyonut ha-datit* (Next Pesach: Literacy and Identity of Young Religious Zionist Women) (Tel Aviv, 1992).

23 On the influence of the European ideal of the "division of the spheres" on the *maskilim* see Israel Bartal, "'Potency' and 'Impotence': Between Tradition and *Haskalah*," in Bartal and Gafni, *Eros eirosin ve-isurim*, pp. 227–9; Tova Cohen, *Ha-ahat ahuvah veha-ahat snu'ah: Bein metzi'ut le-vidyon be-ti'urei ha-ishah be-sifrut ha-haskalah ha-ivrit* (One Beloved and the Other One Hated: Between Reality and Fiction in *Haskalah* Depictions of Women) (Jerusalem, 2002).

24 Michelle Zimbalist Rosaldo, "Woman, Culture and Society: A Theoretical Overview," in Michelle Zimbalist Rosaldo and Louise Lamphere (eds.), *Woman, Culture and Society* (Stanford, 1974), p. 19

25 See for instance Moshe Leib Lilienblum's description: "My father thought it was crazy to bring his son ... to the high school so that he would learn there things that any scholar could easily study in the toilet." *Hata'ot ne'urim* (Youthful Sins) in *Ktavim otobiografiim* (Autobiographical Works), Vol. 1 (Jerusalem, 1970), p. 85.

26 See, for instance how Lilienblum (ibid., pp. 85–6) describes the ease with which he absorbed the Hebrew language as a by-product of his religious studies. Subsequently, Lilienblum describes his biography of reading, which initially consisted of religious books in Hebrew. The transition to *Haskalah* works is described as an ideological move that posed no linguistic problems (ibid., pp. 121ff.). A scanning of the texts describing the transition to the *Haskalah*, which appear in Joseph Klausner's *Historiyah shel ha-sifrut ha-ivrit he-hadashah* (History of Modern Hebrew Literature) (Tel Aviv, 1952), proves that none of the *maskilim* mentioned in his book encountered any linguistic problems in reading modern Hebrew texts.

27 The first chapters of Bialik's *Safi'ah* are often quoted in reference to studies in the *heder*. Chapters 9 and 10 describe the imaginary world the child constructs on the basis of the weekly portions of the Torah he has learnt in the *heder*. It turns out that the Torah stories, in conjunction with Rashi's commentary, were well imprinted on his consciousness; see H. N. Bialik, *Sipurim* (Stories) (Tel Aviv, 1963), pp. 204–7. For more descriptions of how the children in the *heder* absorbed the biblical stories during the same period see Zvi Scharfstein, *Ha-heder be-hayei ameinu* (The Heder in the Life of the Jewish People) (New York, 1943).

28 In discussing the parents' consent to provide their daughters with European education, Parush insists that the objection to providing sons with the same kind of education was grounded in the obligation to study Torah (see, e.g. pp. 78–80).

29 See Gershon Bacon, "The Missing 52 Percent: Research on Jewish Women in Interwar Poland and Its Implications for Holocaust Studies," in Dalia Ofer and Lenore J. Weitzman (eds.), Women in the Holocaust (New Haven and London, 1998), pp. 55–67.

30 Katz, Tradition and Crisis, p. 164n. I have found no reference by Katz to this issue on p. 136, which Parush indicates as an additional source.

31 Etkes, "Marriage and Torah Study among Lomdim."

32 See my article, "The Maskil as Lamdan: The Influence of Jewish Education on Haskalah Writing Techniques," in Glenda Abramson and Tudor Parfitt (eds.), Jewish Education and Learning (London, 1994), pp. 61–73.

33 On the satirical descriptions of the Jewish businesswoman, see Tova Cohen, "Reality and Its Refraction in Descriptions of Women in Haskalah Fiction," in Shmuel Feiner and David Sorkin (eds.), New Perspectives on the Haskalah (London, 2001).

34 Knaani, Ha-batim she-hayu, pp. 80, 86. The connection between socio-economic status and the division of labor in the family clearly emerges in the realistic fiction that was written during the revival of Hebrew literature. This fiction makes a clear distinction between the bourgeois families, in which the husband was the provider and the wife served as the homemaker, and low class families, in which both spouses worked outside the house. In the former, the wife became the sole provider only upon the death of her husband or when he was too sick to work. See for instance the stories written by Ben-Avigdor, Yaakov Steinberg, and Dvorah Baron.

35 See Joan W. Scott and Louise A. Tilly, "Women's Work and the Family in Nineteenth Century Europe," Comparative Studies in Society and History, Vol. 17, No. 1 (1975), pp. 36–64.

36 Beginning in the mid-nineteenth century, with the rise of the new elite of the rich and well educated, there was a marked trend to adopt western patterns of marrying at a more mature age, as compared to the early marriages hitherto normative among European Jews. See Stampfer, "Gender Differentiation and Education," p. 77; idem, "The Social Meaning of Premature Marriage," p. 68n.

37 The emphasis on differences of race and class, which undermine the uniform identity of "women" as a distinct group, has lain at the core center of feminist discourse ever since the 1980s. See Candace West and Sarah Fenstermaker, "Doing Difference," Gender & Society, Vol. 9, No. 1 (1995), pp. 8–37.

38 Feiner, "Ha-ishah ha-yehudit ha-modernit."

39 See, for example, Dan Miron's basic assumption concerning Hebrew poetry written by women in the 1920s, in his Imahot meyasdot, ahayot horgot: Al shtei hathalot ba-shirah ha-eretzisraelit ha-modernit (Founding Mothers; Step-Sisters: On Two Beginnings of Modern Poetry in the Land of Israel) (Tel Aviv, 1991). On Dvorah Baron's stories as marking the beginning of women's Hebrew prose writing, see Lillie Rattok (ed.), Ha-kol ha-aher: siporet nashim ivrit (The Other Voice: Women's Hebrew-Written Fiction) (Tel Aviv, 1994), p. 272.

40 Shmuel Feiner and I are preparing an anthology of women's writing of the Haskalah period. For a discussion on women's writing during that period see also my article, "Min ha-tehum ha-prati el ha-tehum ha-tzibori: Kitvei maskilot ivriyot ba-me'ah ha-tsha esreh" (From the Private Sphere into the Public Sphere: The Works of Hebrew Maskilot of the Nineteenth Century), in Avner Holtzman and Shmuel Feiner (eds.), Yerushalayim shebe-Lita: Sefer ha-yovel le-Sh. Werses (Jerusalem of Lithuania: Sh. Werses Jubilee Volume) (Jerusalem, 2002), pp. 237–59.

41 This term was coined by Sandra M. Gilbert and Susan Gubar, The Madwoman in the Attic: The Woman Writer and Nineteenth Century Imagination (New Haven, 1979), p. 49.

42 Ibid., pp. 3–16.

43 A letter to Y. L. Gordon dated 1868. The National and University Library in Jerusalem, the Schwadron Collection, Autobiography no. 77455.

44 Cf. the description of the Hevrah Levayah's annual dinner in the women's gallery, in Peretz Smolenskin, Kvurat hamor (Contemptible Burial) (1874; Jerusalem, 1968), pp. 58–64. See also idem, Ha-to'eh be-darkhei he-hayim, Chap. 2, pp. 43–8, where the women's gallery is

described as a place where the yeshivah students sleep, discuss everyday matters and negotiate business deals.

45 Of special interest in this context is editor Baruch Verber's comment on Toybe Segal's poignant feminist article, which he published in the *Ha-Ivri* journal, beginning with issue No. 16 (1879), despite his strong reservations about the contents of this article. "It is an uncommon spectacle these days," says Verber, "to see a maiden writing Hebrew. Hence we shall make room for her words though we do not agree with all of her thoughts" (ibid., p. 69).

46 The father's influence in encouraging his daughter's pursuit of Hebrew culture is acknowledged by Merka Altschuler, Devora Weisman-Hayut, Sara Shapira and Miriam Markel Mosessohn. For details see Cohen, "Min ha-tehum ha-prati," p. 243.

Index

Other Title in the Series

New Women's Writing from Israel

Edited by **Risa Domb**

Choice *Outstanding Academic Book, 1996*

' ... an outstanding anthology of short stories reflecting the wide range of subjects and styles being written by Israeli women today.'

The Midwest Book Review

'This anthology does indeed indicate the breadth of talent in current Israeli fiction, and the change of horizons derived from the major entry of the woman writer.

Risa Domb is to be congratulated on making some of this fiction availableto the Anglophone public in such accessible form.'

Leon Yudkin, Journal of Jewish Studies

This anthology of short stories reflects the wide range of subjects and styles in Israeli women's writing today. The change in the mainstream Israeli experience in the 1970s has brought about a greater openness in literature, and a plurality of voices – including those of women – has emerged.

1996 rep 1999 240 pages
0 85303 307 2 cloth
0 85303 308 0 paper

FRANK CASS PUBLISHERS
Crown House, 47 Chase Side, Southgate, London N14 5BP
Tel: +44 (0)20 8920 2100 Fax: +44 (0)20 8447 8548 E-mail: info@frankcass.com
NORTH AMERICA
920 NE 58th Avenue Suite 300, Portland, OR 97213-3786 USA
Tel: 800 944 6190 Fax: 503 280 8832 E-mail: cass@isbs.com
Website: www.frankcass.com

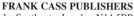